AAA GUIDE TO THE NATIONAL PARKS

D1514828

AAA GUIDE
TO THE
NATIONAL PARKS

AMERICAN AUTOMOBILE ASSOCIATION

COMPILED BY DOREEN RUSSO

COLLIER BOOKS
Macmillan Publishing Company
New York

Maxwell Macmillan Canada
Toronto

Maxwell Macmillan International
New York   Oxford   Singapore   Sydney

Collier Books
Macmillan Publishing
  Company
866 Third Avenue
New York, NY 10022

Maxwell Macmillan Canada, Inc.
1200 Eglinton Avenue East,
  Suite 200
Don Mills, Ontario M3C 3N1

Macmillan Publishing Company is part of the Maxwell Communication Group of Companies.

Library of Congress Cataloging-in-Publication Data
AAA guide to the national parks / American Automobile Association:
compiled by Doreen Russo.—1st Collier Books ed.
          p.   cm.
        Includes index.
      ISBN 0-02-062049-7
1. National parks and reserves—United States—Guidebooks.   I.
Russo, Doreen.   II. American Automobile Association.   III. Title:
American Automobile Association guide to national parks.
        E160.A2   1994
    917.304'928—dc20   92-27001

First Collier Books Edition 1993

10 9 8 7 6 5 4 3 2 1

Printed in the United States of America

Book design by Michael Mendelsohn
Maps by H. L. Saunders

CONTENTS

PREFACE

THE SECRETARY OF THE INTERIOR
WASHINGTON

Dear Friend of the National Parks:

This country's national parks truly represent America's crown jewels. These are the most awe-inspiring natural legacy we can leave to our children and their children.

It is my sense of joy and wonder gained in the spectacular scenery of the American West as a child that most surely charted my path to becoming steward of the nation's resources as Secretary of the Interior. It is my commitment to begin a new era of respect, sensitivity, and focus on the lands, water, and wildlife under my care.

Each of us should view our national parks as responsibly and carefully as we would our finest inheritance. These parks are to be enjoyed, but they are also fragile and to be handled with care.

Take advantage of the lesser-known national parks described in this guide, be an environmentally responsible traveler, and use the recycling containers to leave as little as possible behind.

Please work with me to assure that these scenic wonders will be passed on intact to future generations of Americans.

American Automobile Association

PAUL R. VERKUIL
President and
Chief Executive Officer

1000 AAA Drive
Heathrow, Florida 32746-5063
407/444-7111

FAX/407/444-7120
TELEX 89-9485

Dear National Parks Friend:

Upon viewing the grandeur of the Grand Canyon in 1903, Theodore Roosevelt said, "Keep this great wonder of nature as it is now. You cannot improve on it—not a bit. The ages have been at work on it, and man can only mar it. What you can do is keep it, for your children, for your children's children, and for all who come after you, as one of the great sights that every American . . . should see."

America's national parks truly are a legacy to each American. This country has been blessed with so many natural resources—breathtaking scenery, fascinating wildlife, and cultural history—that we often take for granted the remarkable gifts we have been given.

AAA has published this guide to the national parks to remind Americans of our vast and beautiful heritage and to urge them to visit those resources that have been protected as part of the national park system.

As you browse through the descriptions of the many national parks, notice especially those that may not be so famous. Promise yourself to include those parks in your travel plans to ensure you don't miss out on any of the wonders that America has to offer.

AAA sincerely hopes this information will help you plan many visits to our national parks. As you travel, please keep in mind the information provided in the next few pages to ensure that your visit will be an environmentally responsible one. As Theodore Roosevelt noted, we can keep these magnificent lands for our children, and for their children, to see. But only if we care for them and treat them as the gifts they are.

Sincerely,

Paul M. Verkuil

EDITOR'S NOTE

All operating seasons, hours, entry fees, and camping fees are subject to change—and in fact do change frequently. We suggest you check with the Park Superintendent to get the latest information before arriving.

GENERAL INFORMATION AND ADVICE BEFORE YOUR VISIT

Plan Ahead

Be prepared for the weather by bringing and wearing the correct clothing, including sun protection, such as a hat and sunglasses; extra layers in uncertain weather; waterproof outerwear where warranted; and sturdy footwear for hiking in all climates. Plan for your pets. In general, the national parks require that all pets be physically restrained; pets are not allowed on trails, in the backcountry, or in buildings. Give yourself enough time to get to the campground early. Camping is becoming increasingly popular and most parks have first-come, first-served systems for campsites. If you're visiting a park whose campgrounds are served by MISTIX, a telephone reservation system, try to reserve a spot well in advance. Firearms are generally prohibited in the parks.

A good place to start any visit to a national park is at the visitor center. There you can get advice on planning your visit, see any exhibits explaining park features, and check on road and trail conditions and if there are any closures or warnings you should know about.

Driving in the Parks

Never drive anywhere but on designated roads. Check on road conditions before setting out, especially when you are headed for unpaved routes. Weather conditions occasionally prevent access to some park roads. Summer traffic in many parks is heavy, park roads are narrow, and pedestrians abound: Be careful. Remember that the roads are designed for slow sightseeing. Make sure you pull off at pullouts or designated areas to view scenery; do not stop on the roads.

Wildlife

Remember that all the animals in the parks are wild. They are, therefore, unpredictable and potentially dangerous. Observe and photograph them from a safe distance.

The National Park Service repeatedly warns visitors against feeding wildlife—*any* wildlife. Feeding animals can create serious problems for both the wildlife and park visitors. It can teach them to seek out humans for food; in doing so they may hurt people or damage property. It also causes them to lose their own sense of wildness and may cost them their ability to find food on their own.

Bears

When in a park where bears are present, make every effort to avoid an encounter. Secure food, garbage, and strong-smelling items at least 10 feet above the ground. Some parks have "bear-proof" canisters for this purpose; use them. When you are hiking, make noise—sing, talk loudly, or carry bells—to let bears know you are approaching. They will most likely stay away from you. If you see a bear, make a wide turn to avoid it. If you do encounter one up close, stay calm and it probably will not bother you. Do not make any noise or sudden movement to startle it. If you are going to be doing backcountry hiking or camping in any of the parks where bears are present, write to the park for information on bears. This will give you full instructions on what to do if you encounter a bear.

Hiking

Most parks prefer that you stay on trails wherever possible. Walking off the trails increases erosion and may damage plant life. Know your limits. Don't take a chance on a trail that is too steep, precarious, or long for you. Don't hike or climb alone, as a general rule. If you must, leave your itinerary with a friend and with the rangers and be sure to tell them when you return. If you become lost, stay where you are until help arrives.

Heat exhaustion can be a problem, especially in the hotter, drier climates. No matter what the climate, always take water along, even on short hikes, and hike at a moderate pace. One gallon of water per person per day is generally recommended. Be sure to start your return trip before half your water is gone. The water in many park streams and lakes, although clear and cool, should not be drunk unless properly treated. Untreated water may contain *Giardia, Campylobacter,* and other harmful organisms, which can cause severe gastrointestinal distress. Untreated water must be brought to a boil to kill harmful organisms.

Hypothermia

An ever-present danger in cold climates is hypothermia, a condition created when you lose body heat faster than you create it. This happens when the body's core temperature drops to 94°F or below. If the body's core temperature drops too low, death can occur. Whenever you are overexposed to cold and wet conditions, you are a potential victim of hypothermia.

To prevent hypothermia, plan carefully. Ideally, you need to stay warm and dry, since wet skin will lower body temperature. On extended hikes, take along plenty of dry clothes, bring water-resistant clothing and gear, and avoid risks such as crossing high rivers. Warning signs of hypothermia include uncontrolled shivering, slow or slurred speech, memory lapses, incoherence, fumbling hands, stumbling or lurching, drowsiness, and exhaustion.

To treat a hypothermia victim, seek immediate shelter from any wet weather. Then remove the person's wet clothes and build a fire. If the person is mildly impaired, keep him or her awake, give the person warm drinks, dry clothes, and a warm sleeping bag. If the hypothermia victim is semiconscious or worse, put the person, unclothed, into a warm sleeping bag and get into the sleeping bag as well. Hold the person skin-to-skin against you. Get professional emergency help as soon as possible.

Accommodations

Only lodging and campgrounds located within the boundaries of the parks are listed in the book. Towns nearby may also offer accommodations. Contact the chambers of commerce of nearby towns for listings if those within the park are inadequate for any reason.

Annual Permits

An annual entrance permit, called the Golden Eagle Pass, can be purchased for $25 at any of the national parks. Persons 62 years of age and older are entitled to a free lifetime entrance permit called the Golden Age Passport. Handicapped persons who are eligible for federal benefits as a result of a disability are entitled to a free permit called the Golden Access Passport.

Preserve the Parks

While in the park, do not deface, disturb, destroy, or remove any rocks, animals, plants, fossils, corals, shells, rock art, historical objects, or natural features. In other words, leave the park exactly as you found it. This means you should also carry out *all* your trash.

THE NATIONAL PARKS

Olympic

North Cascades

Mount Rainier

Glacier

WASHINGTON

NORTH DAKO

MONTANA

Theodore Roo

OREGON

Crater Lake

IDAHO

Yellowstone

Grand Teton

SOUTH DAK

Badlands

Wind Cave

Redwood

Lassen Volcanic

WYOMING

NEVADA

NEBRASK

CALIFORNIA

Great Basin

UTAH

Rocky Mountain

Arches

Yosemite

Capitol Reef

Canyonlands

KAN

Zion

Bryce Canyon

Mesa Verde

Sequoia and Kings Canyon

Grand Canyon

OKLA

Channel Islands

Petrified Forest

NEW MEXICO

ARIZONA

Carlsbad Caverns

TEX

Guadalupe Mountains

Gates of the Arctic

Kobuk Valley

Big Bend

ALASKA

Denali

Wrangell –St. Elias

Lake Clark

Katmai

Kenai Fjords

Glacier Bay

American Samoa

Haleakalā

HAWAII

AMERICAN SAMOA

Hawaii Volcanoes

yageurs

Isle Royale

MAINE

Acadia

VT

NH

MA

WISCONSIN

NEW YORK

RHODE ISLAND

CT

MICHIGAN

PENNSYLVANIA

NJ

WA

OHIO

MD

DELAWARE

ILLINOIS

IN

WASHINGTON DC

Shenandoah

MISSOURI

KY

W V

VIRGINIA

Mammoth Cave

NORTH
CAROLINA

Great Smoky
Mountains

ARKANSAS

TN

SOUTH
CAROLINA

Hot Springs

MS

ALABAMA

GEORGIA

LOUISIANA

FLORIDA

Biscayne

Everglades

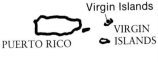

Virgin Islands

VIRGIN
ISLANDS

PUERTO RICO

AAA GUIDE TO THE NATIONAL PARKS

Acadia National Park is the only national park in New England. Luckily, it encompasses much of the charm and beauty associated with this part of the country. Here are rich evergreen forests, impressive coastal mountains, rugged rocky coastlines, and the restless Atlantic Ocean, dotted with islands and lobster buoys bobbing in the waves. The majority of Acadia is on Mount Desert Island, but sections of Isle au Haut and the Schoodic Peninsula (including Schoodic Point) are part of the park as well.

Water is ever present in Acadia. The relentless sea pounds away at the rocks along the coast, while mist and fog often set the mood. Probably the most famous inhabitant of the ocean waters here is the lobster, an important product for Maine's fishing industry. Other marine life includes Atlantic bottle-nosed dolphins, crabs, northern starfish, green sea urchins, seals, and common eider, oceanic ducks that live here year-round. The park is also home to 300 species of birds, including the herring gulls that often follow fishing boats for scraps.

Situated between the ocean and the forests is an unusual habitat known as the tidal zone. Twice a day, it is exposed to air and covered by water as the tide rises and recedes. The tide varies from around 9 to 14 feet but averages 11 to 12 feet. Living in this rock-and-water habitat are specially adapted organisms, including the hardy barnacles that cling for life to the coastal cliffs.

In most coastal areas, you will find the sea giving way to sand and marsh before any forest growth begins. Here at Acadia, the forest—of spruce, pine, balsam firs, and other conifers—comes nearly down to the water. From the top of Cadillac Mountain, the tallest mountain in the park and, in fact, the tallest peak on the eastern coast of the United States, you can get a spectacular view of the trees giving way to the sea.

The landscape of Acadia today was shaped by glaciation during the last ice age. A sheet of ice up to two miles thick moved down to cover the area and eventually extended 300 miles out to the continental shelf. As it moved, it ripped and gouged out the land, turning the east–west mountains of before into the north–south mountains of today. The ice was also responsible for the rounded tops of the mountains. After it melted, the water level rose and created the islands. Somes Sound, the only fjord on the eastern coast of the United States, was a glacial river valley filled in by the sea. The pounding of the water on the rocky shores continues to erode the shape of the land today.

The Abnaki Native Americans lived on the mainland here but often came to Pemetic, as they called Mount Desert Island, to fish. The first European in the area was Frenchman Samuel de Champlain, who ran aground here in 1604 and gave the island its present name. The French, who fought with the English for possession of North America from 1613 until 1763, used Frenchman Bay as a hiding place for their ships. After their victory in 1763, the En-

NATIONAL PARK SERVICE

glish began to colonize the area. Farming and lumbering eventually gave way to fishing and boat-building as commercial endeavors. By the mid-1800s, with the arrival of regular steamship runs, the area became known as a retreat for the wealthy and the artistic who would summer here. Yacht racing became a popular pastime. Commercial fishing remains an important Maine industry, however, and boat-building continues on the island and Schoodic Peninsula.

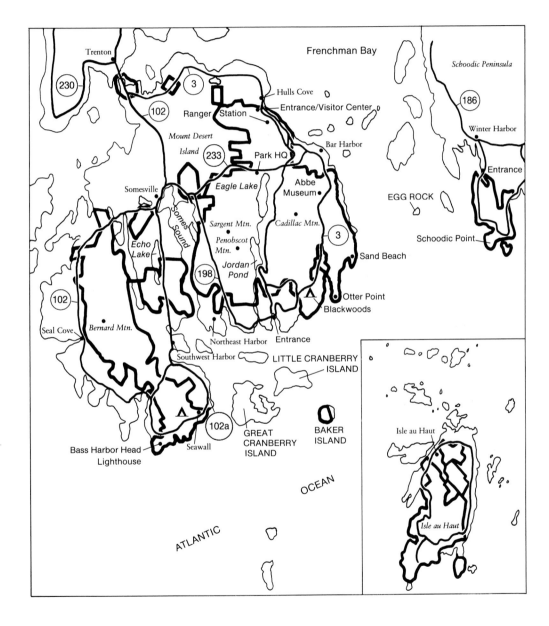

Further Information

Write or call: Superintendent, Acadia National Park, P.O. Box 177, Bar Harbor, ME 04609; (207) 288–3338

Visitor Information

Hulls Cove Visitor Center: On Highway 3 south of Hulls Cove; 15-minute film about the park; self-guiding tape tour of the park to buy or rent; information about park routes and about the cultural and natural history of the area. (Closed November to April.)

Park Headquarters: On Highway 233 three miles west of Bar Harbor; serves as the winter visitor and information center.

Nuts and Bolts

Entrance Fee: $5/vehicle or $2/person arriving by other means. Good for seven days.
Park Open: All year.
Permits: Maine fishing license is required for freshwater fishing (none needed for saltwater fishing).
In Emergency: Call ranger station at 288–3369.
Acreage: 41,408.63

Practical Advisory

Seasons

Changeable weather conditions; rain and fog are possible at any time. In the summer, high temperatures are usually in the 70s and 80s. Fog is common. Spring and fall are cooler, with highs usually in the 50s and 60s. In the winter, which lasts from November to April, highs are normally in the 30s; nighttime lows may be below zero. Snow falls occasionally.

Special Advisories

- Be careful along the shores. Ledges and rocks below the high-tide line are slippery with algae; walk carefully. In spring and autumn, watch out for storm waves. A large one could knock you down and sweep you out to sea.
- On trails, beware of loose stones and poison ivy.
- Mosquitoes and blackflies are common during June.

Facilities for Disabled

Accessibility guides are available at the visitor center.

Travel Advisory

Entrances

Mount Desert Island: U.S. 1 to Highway 3 for 48 miles from Bangor.

Schoodic Peninsula: U.S. 1 to Highway 3 to Highway 186 for 58 miles from Bangor.

Isle au Haut: Highway 3 to Highway 172 to Highway 15 for 70 miles from Bangor to Stonington. From there catch a passenger ferry.

Transportation

Airports: Airlines fly to Bar Harbor Airport, 10 miles from Bar Harbor.

Bus Service: Greyhound Bus Service operates between Bangor and Bar Harbor during the summer months. Downeast Transportation runs a local service that connects Mount Desert Island towns and Ellsworth.

Train Service: Not available.

Rental Cars: Major rental-car companies have offices at Bar Harbor Airport and in Ellsworth.

Attractions

One of the most popular features of this coastline park is *Cadillac Mountain*. You can drive to the top for spectacular views. Other major features of the park are water-related, including *Somes Sound*, the only fjord on the eastern coast of the United States; the island-studded *Frenchman Bay*; and *Eagle Lake*, which is encircled by a carriage road. *Sand Beach* is the only park beach on the ocean for swimming. Other scenic spots include *Otter Point* and *Seawall*. The carriage roads offer an unusual way to see much of the park. And, although it is out of the way of Mount Desert Island, the *Schoodic Peninsula* is quite scenic and worth the short drive.

Other Points of Interest (Museums, Historic Sites, etc.)

The *Abbe Museum*, at Sieur de Monts Spring, contains artifacts of and exhibits about the Abnaki tribe, who lived in the area when Samuel de Champlain first arrived. Take the ferry to Little Cranberry Island to see the *Islesford Museum*, with ship models, tools, and pictures that tell about island life in the 19th and early 20th centuries. The U.S. Coast Guard maintains five *lighthouses* in the area, at Bear Island, Baker Island, Bass Harbor Head, and Egg Rock.

Accommodations

The park contains no lodgings. There are lodgings in nearby Bar Harbor, Northeast Harbor, Southwest Harbor, and Winter Harbor.

Campgrounds and Picnic Areas

Fires and camping are permitted only in designated sites; no backcountry camping. There is a 14-day limit. Campsites accommodate trailers up to 35 feet.

Blackwoods Campground: Off Highway 3, five miles south of Bar Harbor; 306 sites, toilets, water, dump station, picnic tables, fire rings, amphitheaters; open all year, with limited facilities in winter; $12/night from mid-June to mid-September; $10/night from mid-May to mid-June and from mid-September to mid-October; free mid-October to mid-May. Reservations are required; call MISTIX, (800) 365–2267.

Seawall Campground: Highway 102A, four miles south of Southwest Harbor; toilets, water, dump station, picnic tables, fire rings, amphitheater; open late May to late September; first-come, first-served, no reservations; $10/night for drive-up campsites and $7/night at walk-in campsites.

Picnic Areas: At Bear Brook, Fabbri, Seawall, Pretty Marsh, Thompson Island, and Frazer Point on Schoodic Peninsula. Tables.

Restaurant

Jordan Pond House: Tea and popovers served in the afternoons on the lawn.

Activities

Scenic Drives

The 20-mile Park Loop Road connects Mount Desert Island's lakes, mountains, and seashore. At stops along the road you can see glacier-carved valleys and lakes, surf-pounded cliffs, and magnificent coniferous forests. You can also drive up Cadillac Mountain to the highest point on the Atlantic Coast for panoramas of the coast and of the island-studded Frenchman, Blue Hill, and Penobscot bays. Or visit the Bass Harbor Head Light by other state roads. There are parking areas and rest rooms along all the roads.

Hiking

The more than 120 miles of trails in the park range from short, level surf walks or easy lowland paths to rugged mountain routes, including the steep Precipice Trail. Connecting trails enable hardy hikers to scale several Acadia peaks in one trip. An extensive system, 57 miles long, of broad, smooth, graveled carriage roads connected by 16 stone bridges travels through the woodlands and is free of motor vehicles. You can encircle Jordan Pond and Eagle Lake and wind around the foothills of Sargent and Penobscot mountains. The carriage roads offer stunning views of Somes Sound and Frenchman Bay.

Bicycling

The carriage roads are open to bicyclists. The loop around Eagle Lake is a bicycle path. Bicycles may be rented in Bar Harbor, Northeast Harbor, and Southwest Harbor.

Boating

Villages offer boat rentals, charters, cruises, and ferry service. Information can be found at the visitor center. There is courtesy mooring at Valley Cove on Mount Desert Island and Frazer Point on Schoodic Peninsula.

Fishing

State laws govern fishing. Freshwater fishing is allowed in all the ponds.

Swimming

Lifeguards are on duty in the summer at Echo Lake (fresh water) and Sand Beach (salt water). Beware: The ocean is cold.

Horseback Riding

A portion of the carriage roads is open for horseback riding. Carriage rides are available starting in mid-June.

Winter Activities

Cross-country skiing, snowmobiling, ice fishing, and winter hiking are popular. The carriage roads are open for these activites.

Sightseeing

Local businesses operate bus tours of the park, and scenic boat trips.

Naturalist Programs

From mid-June through early October naturalists lead seashore, woodland, and mountaintop walks, boat cruises, and evening programs at the campgrounds. Schedules are posted at park headquarters, the visitor center, and park campgrounds. Two examples: tide-pool walks that teach about plants and animals in the microhabitats between land and sea, and cruises during which you may see porpoises, seals, and eagles.

Only recently authorized by Congress—in 1988—American Samoa is the newest of the nation's national parks and the only one south of the Equator. Before Congress acted, Samoan chiefs had agreed in principle to lease portions of their lands for a national park. However, until final arrangements are made between the National Park Service and the American Samoa government to lease those communally owned village lands for public use, all lands within the authorized boundaries of the park remain under the control of the affected villages. So at present this is a "potential" or "project" national park.

The wild and scenic park land is in three units on widely separated islands in the South Pacific. The Ta'u, Tutuila, and Ofu units consist of a superb native rain forest extending from the ocean's edge up to the mountaintops; miles of some of the most scenic shoreline on earth; long white-sand beaches; sea cliffs; sheltered coves; and the blue tropical ocean, out to the edge of the fringing coral reefs. Ta'u, Tutuila, and Ofu also provide important habitat for two species of flying foxes. These large, soaring fruit bats act as pollinators of rain-forest plants. Along with this varied and wonderful natural scene comes a 3,000-year-old culture. Archaeological sites, many yet to be discovered, abound in the islands.

The unit on the island of Ta'u is the largest, and is mostly undisturbed rain forest. The spectacular sea cliffs along the south coast drop from the top of Lata Mountain, at 3,100 feet American Samoa's highest peak, down to the rugged coast. The Tutuila unit contains a major expanse of undisturbed rain forest, as well as the most significant seabird nesting site on Tutuila. The shoreline along the north coast includes sheer cliffs, knifelike ridges, and sheltered coves. The Ofu unit of the park consists primarily of what many call one of the South Pacific's loveliest beaches and one of the Pacific's best examples of a healthy coral reef.

NATIONAL PARK SERVICE

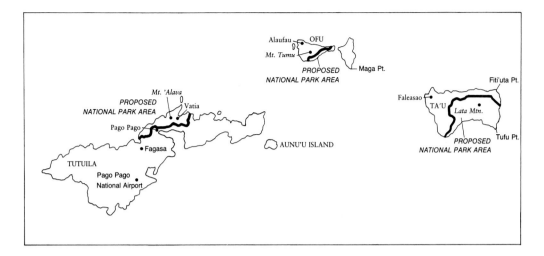

Further Information

Write: Superintendent, National Park of American Samoa, Pago Pago, American Samoa 96799

Visitor Information:

Park Office: Pago Plaza, Suite 214. There will be only one ranger present until the park is officially established. The ranger can be reached only from within the island at 633–7082.

Nuts and Bolts

Acreage: Nearly 8,000

Practical Advisory

Seasons

Weather is warm and humid year-round. During the Southern Hemisphere's winter—April through September—it is slightly cooler and drier than in summer, October through March. But heavy rains can occur anytime.

Special Advisories

- A hat, mosquito repellent, rain gear, and sunscreen are recommended.
- There are no poisonous snakes or plants to worry about.

Travel Advisory

There are several flights each week to Pago Pago from Honolulu; the trip takes about 5½ hours. Ta'u and Ofu islands can be reached from Pago Pago; the flights are 35 minutes long.

Tau

Hikers can reach the park from the newly completed Fiti'uta airport. An easy 1½-hour walk will get you to the south side of Ta'u.

Tutuila

Access by car only to the village of Vatia. Or hike in: The trail starts at Fagasa Pass.

Ofu

Easily accessible from the airport or from Va'oto Lodge, by the coastal road. Walking time is about 10 minutes.

Attractions

The major natural features in all three units of the mostly wild park are native *rain forests*, sandy *shorelines* marked by cliffs and coves, and beautiful *coral reefs* offshore. Signs of a 3,000-year-old culture can be found in *archaeological sites* amid the wilderness as well. You are on your own in discovering the beauty of the park.

Accommodations

Food and lodging are not available in the park, but can be found on each of the islands near the park.

Activities

Hiking

The Ta'u portion of the park can be reached by an easy trail running about three miles along the coast from Fiti'uta airport. Day hikes farther into the park are possible but are more difficult: The trail deteriorates, so you are hiking cross-country. The uplands lack trails and are nearly inaccessible at present. On Tutuila, a moderately strenuous trail runs from Fagasa Pass along the ridge to the top of Mount 'Alava. The spectacular views are worth the effort.

There is a region in southeastern Utah's red-rock country that contains more natural arches than any other place on earth. Appropriately named Arches National Park, this quiet and austere rock landscape offers an unrivaled variety of more than 1,500 such sandstone formations, from the smallest to one of the largest in the world.

Some of the most outstanding arches are named and noted on park maps. Delicate Arch, the most famous and probably the most remarkable, stands by itself with the La Sal Mountains forming a beautiful backdrop for its 32-foot-tall grandeur. Landscape Arch, spanning 306 feet from base to base, is one of the longest in the world. Not to be overlooked are the other rock formations, such as spires, pinnacles, and balanced rocks, scattered throughout the park; these are just as spectacular as the arches.

A sea existed in this area about 300 million years ago. When it evaporated, it left a salt bed that was covered with residue over the course of millions of years. Eventually the residue was compressed into rock, which exerted pressure on the salt bed. Since salt is unstable under pressure, this bed buckled and moved, thrusting the earth upward into domes. Eventually this earth cracked and eroded into narrow sandstone walls, or "fins."

Frost, snow, and rain soaked into the pores of the sandstone, crumbling and dissolving it and eventually cutting through some of the fins. In this process of differential erosion, the softer places in the rock eroded more quickly than the harder, denser places. Strange shapes, including holes in the rock, resulted. These holes were then enlarged to arches by further erosion. This is a never-ending process: Arches eventually collapse, leaving only their vertical buttresses, which in time erode down to rocks and pebbles. The arches seen in the park are all in different stages of formation and destruction. If you came back in ten years, they might not look the same.

Most of the early explorers of this region passed north of Arches, on the easier path that roads and the railroad follow today. But one trail, used by trappers and traders headed for California, came from New Mexico, crossed the Colorado River at Moab, and traveled directly past the present-day park. It was called the Old Spanish Trail, although it was used most heavily by Mexicans and Americans in the 1830s and 1840s. A remnant of the trail in the park provides a bit of historical interest.

Wolfe Ranch adds another piece of history. In 1888, John Wesley Wolfe, a disabled Civil War veteran, settled here with his son on the bank of Salt Wash below Delicate Arch. A weathered log cabin, root cellar, and corral remain as evidence of their primitive ranch, a typical early frontier cattle operation.

This high desert country offers a challenging environment for its inhabitants. Dryland piñons and gnarled juniper trees grow throughout the park, and cottonwoods sprout along the washes. Colorful

wildflowers bloom from May to August. Because of the heat of the day, most of the animals living here are nocturnal. You may spot mule deer or kit foxes, or, more likely, cottontails, rock squirrels and other rodents, and small reptiles. Coyotes, bobcats, and foxes come out at dusk or later. Mountain bluebirds and many other bird species are migratory visitors, while golden eagles, red-tailed hawks, and flocks of blue piñon jays reside here.

Further Information

Write or Call: Superintendent, Arches National Park, P.O. Box 907, Moab, UT 84532; (801) 259–8161

Visitor Information

Park Headquarters/Visitor Center: At park entrance; information on road and trail conditions; weather forecasts; slide program for orientation; geology museum; history exhibit. Books and area maps for sale.

Nuts and Bolts

Entrance Fee: $4/vehicle for seven days; $2/person arriving by other means.
Park Open: All year. Visitor center is closed December 25 and January 1.
Permits: Required for backcountry camping.
In Emergency: Contact a park ranger or call 911.
Acreage: 73,378.98

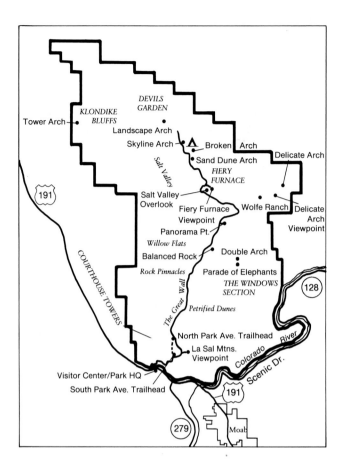

Practical Advisory

Seasons

Summer daytime temperatures can reach 95°.
Spring winds are common and sometimes
blow considerable dust and grit. Winter daytime temperatures are generally comfortable;
nighttime temperatures drop below freezing.
Winter can be very pleasant or very cold, with
snow on the trails and rocks making hiking
risky. Annual snowfall averages 4½ inches.

Special Advisories

• Sandstone slickrock can be dangerous; it
  crumbles and breaks easily. Climbing down
  after an ascent may be impossible.
• Avoid crushing the life-giving microbiotic
  crust on the ground: Stay on the trails.

Facilities for Disabled

The rest room at the visitor center, and the toilets at the campground, at Devils Garden Picnic Area, and at Windows Trailhead are wheelchair-accessible. A short trail at South Park Avenue is wheelchair-accessible. One wheelchair-accessible campsite at Devils Garden Campground is level and has an accessible picnic table adjacent to an accessible rest room.

Travel Advisory

Entrance

U.S. 191 northwest for five miles from Moab.

Transportation

There is no public transportation from the Grand Junction airport or the bus or train station to Moab. Travelers can get additional information by calling Tag-A-Long Tours and Travel Agency in Moab, (801) 259–8946.

Airports. The nearest metropolitan airport is in Grand Junction, Colorado, 120 miles northeast of Moab. It is served by major airlines.

Bus Service: The nearest Greyhound station is at the West Winds Truck Stop in Green River, Utah, 50 miles northwest of Moab.

Train Service: The nearest Amtrak station is at Thompson Springs, Utah, 40 miles northeast of Moab.

Rental Cars: Several locations in Moab.

Attractions

The beautiful sandstone *arches* are the most important feature of the park. You can drive the park roads for views of many of them, or get out of the car and hike to see them up close. You'll have to hike to get close to *Delicate Arch*, the most famous, and *Landscape Arch*, one of the longest in the world. Other worthwhile arches and rock formations include *Skyline Arch, Broken Arch, Sand Dune Arch, Balanced Rock, Park Avenue*, and *Courthouse Towers*. The *Windows Section* can be reached via a spur road off the main road; it includes the spectacular *Double Arch*. *Panorama Point*, off the main road, offers great views, as do the *Salt Valley Overlook* and the *Fiery Furnace Viewpoint*.

Other Points of Interest
(Museums, Historic Sites, etc.)

A weathered log cabin, root cellar, and corral remain from *John Wesley Wolfe's primitive 1888 ranch*, a typical early cattle operation. They are open to visitors.

Accommodations

There is no food or lodging in the park.

Campgrounds and Picnic Areas

Wood-gathering is prohibited; bring fuel for the grills provided or bring a stove.

Devils Garden Campground: 53 sites; first-come, first-served, no reservations; tables, grills, toilets, water (mid-March through October only; no fee when no water); $7/night.

Picnic Areas: Near the visitor center, Balanced Rock, and Devils Garden. With tables. Two have pit toilets; the area near the visitor center has a rest room. The visitor center has water all year; Devils Garden has water in summer.

Activities

Scenic Drives

From the park's main paved road (18 miles), spur roads off it, and some unpaved roads, you can see many popular features, including Delicate Arch; Balanced Rock; Park Avenue; Courthouse Towers; the Windows Section, including the Double Arch; Panorama Point; Salt Valley Overlook; Fiery Furnace Viewpoint; Skyline Arch; and Broken Arch.

Hiking

In order to see more of the arches, spires, balanced rocks, and sandstone fins, you need to walk. There are 11 trails in the park, ranging from easy to strenuous; they are marked with cairns (piles of rocks). There are no designated backcountry trails; a United States Geological Survey map is recommended.

Bicycling

Bicycles are allowed on established roads only. Do not take them on trails or in the backcountry. Bicycles can be rented in Moab.

Rock Climbing

Technical climbing is allowed only for experienced climbers. The named arches, Balanced Rock, and a few other locations may not be climbed. Check at visitor center for more information.

Horseback Riding

Guided day rides are available from park concessioner: Ken Sleight Expeditions, Pack Creek Ranch, Box 1270, Moab, UT 84532; (801) 259–5505.

Concessioner Trips

Outfitters in Moab offer a variety of sightseeing trips in the park. Check with the park for a list.

Naturalist Programs

Naturalists lead walks through Fiery Furnace and other locations and give campfire talks in spring, summer, and fall.

Within the grassy prairie land of southwest South Dakota lies a spectacularly eroded landscape of steep canyons, sharp ridges, cliffs, and spires. To the native Sioux, this land was *mako sica* ("bad land"). To early French-Canadian trappers who visited the region it was *les mauvaises terres à traverser* ("bad lands to travel across"). We now know the area simply as the Badlands.

Erosion of the soft rock that created the landscape of the Badlands began about 500,000 years ago and still continues. At first glance, this stark landscape is rather grim, seemingly barren, and nearly devoid of life. But despite temperatures that may top 100° in summer and can reach −20° in the winter, some hardy plants and animals find the Badlands a hospitable place to live.

Annual precipitation in the park is only 16 inches, but that is just enough to sustain the grasses, over 50 species of which grow intermixed in the Badlands. The most prevalent are buffalo grass, blue grama, Western wheat grass, and needle-and-thread. Yucca and juniper dot the landscape, as do cottonwoods, wild roses, and skunkbush sumac. And in springtime, wildflowers bring a refreshing dose of brilliant color.

Hundreds of prairie dogs live on the plains in their socially ordered "towns." Jackrabbits and cottontails travel swiftly through the grasses, where pronghorns, the fastest mammals on the continent, graze. Within the canyons, mule deer, coyotes, and badgers can be found. Nesting in the rocky cliffs are white-throated swifts, swallows,

rock wrens, and an occasional golden eagle. Bison and bighorn sheep, which had vanished from the Badlands for a time, have been reintroduced by the National Park Service and have multiplied. Now, in the Sage Creek Basin of the Badlands, they roam and graze freely and fully protected.

Around 37 million years ago, at the beginning of the "Golden Age of Mammals," the land here was populated by many species of early mammals, including giant pigs, oreodons, saber-toothed tigers, and others. Many of the animals' remains have been converted into fossils, and now constitute one of the richest fossil beds known to man. Nowhere else are these fossil mammals found in such abundance and variety. In fact, scientists continue to find fossils from this period in the constantly eroding soft rock of the Badlands.

The Lakota, or Sioux, were the first people to really thrive in this area. By the mid-18th century, their culture, based on bison hunting, was flourishing. The Stronghold Area of the park is the scene of much important Sioux history, including struggles with the U.S. Army. The famous massacre at Wounded Knee in 1890 took place 25 miles south of here; it was preceded by the Ghost Dances at Stronghold Table within the park's territory.

Homesteaders and ranchers were next to try and make a go at living on the harsh land, but many were happy to abandon the area by 1939, when the federal government decided the Badlands was worthy of preser-

BADLANDS NATIONAL PARK

vation. The Pine Ridge Reservation, administered by the National Park Service in agreement with the Oglala Sioux Tribe, was added later to the park. Today, the park land includes both the 200-foot-high band of varicolored ridges, hills, and cliffs (the park's scenic landscape) and the surrounding prairie grasslands.

Further Information

Write or call: Superintendent, Badlands National Park, P.O. Box 6, Interior, SD 57750; (605) 433–5361

Visitor Information

Park Headquarters/Ben Reifel Visitor Center: Highway 240; park video, Touch Room (with fossils, rocks, bones, and plants for handling), natural-history and cultural-history exhibits.
White River Visitor Center: In the Stronghold Unit, Highway 27; Oglala Sioux cultural exhibits and video. (Closed fall to spring.)

Nuts and Bolts

Entrance Fee: $5/car or $3/person arriving by other means.
Park Open: All year.
Permits: None needed.
In Emergency: Contact park ranger or call 433–5361.
Acreage: 243,244.48

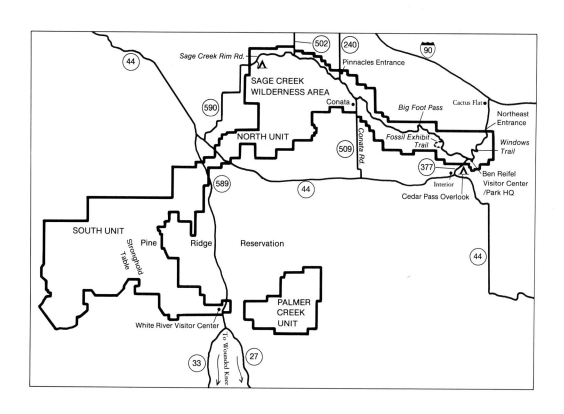

Practical Advisory

Seasons

Summer: Most days sunny with highs in the 90s. A few days top 100°. Thunderstorms bring high winds, hail, and lightning. Fall: Mild and pleasant with wet snow a possibility in late September. Winter: Some days mild and sunny, many cold. Blizzards bring snow and wind and temperatures as low as −20°. Spring: Warming begins in March, though freezes and blizzards are possible through April. April and May are usually wet.

Special Advisories

- Climbing rock formations can be dangerous: Slopes are steep and crumbly and give way under your feet.

- Cactuses are hidden in prairie grass.
- Watch for prairie rattlesnakes; they are fairly common.

Facilities for Disabled

Fossil Exhibit Trail and Window Trail are wheelchair-accessible. Both visitor centers, including displays and rest rooms, are wheelchair-accessible. The park orientation video is captioned. Two rest rooms in the Cedar Pass campground are wheelchair-accessible.

Travel Advisory

Entrances

North: I-90 50 miles east of Rapid City to exit 110; eight miles south on Highway 240 to Pinnacles entrance.

Northeast: I-90 71 miles east of Rapid City to exit 131; four miles south on Highway 240.

South: Highway 377, two miles east of Interior.

Transportation

Airport: Rapid City.

Bus Service: Jackrabbit Bus Lines serves Wall, which is approximately seven miles from the park entrance.

Train Service: Not convenient to park.

Rental Cars: Available at Rapid City airport.

Attractions

The major feature of the park is the fabulously eroded and colored *ridges*, *hills*, and *cliffs* that stretch in a 200-foot-high band across the park. Also of importance is the surrounding *prairie grassland*, including the *Sage Creek* *Wilderness Area*, and the bison that graze there. A drive on the park road will give you good views of the landscape; much of the park is accessible only by foot, however.

Accommodations

Lodge

Cedar Pass Lodge: Highway 240; lodging; available from April to October. For reservations: Box 5, Interior, SD 57750; (605) 433–5460. Check for off-season schedule.

Campgrounds and Picnic Areas

Campfires prohibited throughout the park.

Cedar Pass Campground: In summer, first-come, first-served; 14-day maximum; water, rest rooms, tables, dump station; $8/night. In winter, pit toilets, no water; free.

Sage Creek Primitive Campground: First-come, first-served; 14-day maximum; tables, pit toilets; free.

Picnic Areas. At Big Foot and Conata; tables, pit toilets.

Restaurant

Cedar Pass Lodge: Highway 240; dining room; available from April to October. Check for off-season schedule (see "Lodge," above).

Activities

Scenic Drives

There are scenic overlooks with exhibits all along Highway 240, the loop road through the park, that give a very good orientation to the Badlands. Sage Creek Rim Road is an unpaved road that continues after Highway 240 ends.

Hiking

Hiking is permitted everywhere in the Badlands. There are eight trails in the Cedar Pass area, ranging from easy to moderately difficult (some are self-guiding), and two trails in the Stronghold Unit (only accessible by a difficult unpaved road). Backcountry hiking is possible in the Sage Creek Wilderness Area. Use a topographic map, available for purchase at the visitor centers, to find your way around. Before camping, check with a ranger.

Naturalist Programs

In summer, park naturalists and rangers give guided nature walks and nightly programs at the Cedar Pass campground. Activity schedules are posted in the visitor center and at the campground.

Big Bend National Park is named for the quick turn, or bend, the Rio Grande makes along the southern border of the park. But the river is only part of the story here; the park also contains desert and mountains. The interplay among these three natural environments makes for an interesting landscape that can be both harsh and lush.

Although intensely hot and dry, the Chihuahuan desert land in the park is not a barren wasteland. It is full of plants and animals that have developed elaborate systems for finding and storing water and surviving under the relentless sun. Standing as a cool counterpoint to the flat desert and grasslands are the Chisos Mountains, the central feature of the park. And winding around the desert and through some of the mountains, where it has carved deep canyons, is a stretch of the green Rio Grande, or "Big River," the southern boundary of the park for 107 miles.

Plant life in the park varies with the climate. The desert is full of beautiful flowering plants, many of which bloom in the spring, including Big Bend bluebonnets, a member of the Texas state flower's family; ocotillo; sotol; and more than 60 cactus species, including many kinds of prickly pear. In contrast, the higher and cooler elevations of the mountains are home to forests not at all like the vegetation on the desert floor. Growing here are masses of junipers, small oak trees, piñons, ponderosa pines, Douglas firs, quaking aspens, and madrones. One of the more unusual plants

in the park is the lechuguilla. Native only to this area, this plant can be found at nearly any elevation in the park. It is known for its needle-sharp spines, which can be hazardous to hikers and can even, when the lechuguilla has grown in dense thickets in the grasslands, make walking impossible.

Mammals living in the park include beavers, coyotes, gray foxes, pronghorns, rock squirrels, mule deer, kangaroo rats, and mountain lions. Local jackrabbits have extra-large ears that can be used as radiators, transferring heat out of their bodies to keep them cool. Over 430 species of birds have been seen in the park. White-winged doves, mockingbirds, summer tanagers, blue grosbeaks, painted buntings, vermilion flycatchers, and cardinals can be seen near the river. Ducks and other water birds are abundant. And the roadrunner, a large member of the cuckoo family that prefers to run rather than fly, can be seen racing throughout the desert.

Most likely the earliest settlers in the area were prehistoric Native Americans who lived here 10,000 or more years ago. Several other tribes, mostly hunters and gatherers, followed the first. By the early 1500s, Spanish explorers searching for riches had moved in and enslaved the local Native American population. They referred to the Big Bend region as *El Despoblado*, "the Uninhabited Land." In the next few centuries, Apaches and then Comanches moved in; they constantly struggled for dominance, both with each other and with the Spanish. Raids on

NATIONAL PARK SERVICE

Mexican—and, later, U.S.—settlements were frequent.

The Spanish, never really able to conquer the Big Bend country, eventually relinquished it to newly independent Mexico in 1821. Fifteen years later, the territory became part of the Lone Star Republic of Texas, although raids and fighting continued. Real exploration of the river didn't begin until 1852, with a boundary survey conducted by the U.S. Army. The land was established as a park in 1944.

Further Information

Write or Call: Superintendent, Big Bend National Park, Big Bend National Park, TX 79834; (915) 477–2251

Visitor Information

Park Headquarters/Visitor Center: At Panther Junction; information.
Visitor Center: At Rio Grande Village; information, books, maps, and videos.
Visitor Center: In the Basin; information, books, maps, and videos.
Visitor Center: At Persimmon Gap; information, books, maps, and videos.

Nuts and Bolts

Entrance Fee: $5/vehicle or $2/person arriving by other means; good for seven days. Children under 17 free.
Park Open: All year.
Permits: Required for backcountry camping and floating the river.
In Emergency: Call (915) 477–2251
Acreage: 801,163.02

Practical Advisory

Seasons

Sunshine is abundant all year and relative humidity is usually quite low. The annual precipitation in the desert is about eight inches, and in the mountains about 15–20 inches. The temperature is always 5°–10° higher along the river and 5°–10° lower in the mountains. Summer: Temperatures are in the 90s, often topping 100° in the daytime; they fall to the 60s and 70s at night. During the rainy season, from mid-June through October, there can be locally heavy thunderstorms and some flash flooding. Winter: Temperatures are in the 60s during the day; they fall to the upper 20s or 30s at night. There are infrequent and brief periods of cloudy weather. Snow falls very rarely and is generally light, lasting only a short time.

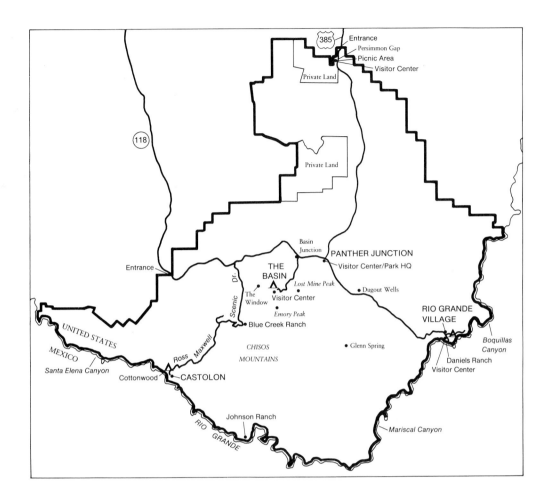

Special Advisories

- The rock throughout the park is unstable; climbing is not recommended.
- Spines and thorns of cacti and other plants can be a serious hazard; be careful if you hike off trails, and carry tweezers to remove spines too small to be removed by hand.
- The Rio Grande is dangerous because of strong currents, submerged snags, and sudden drop-offs; swimmers and waders beware.
- If water crossings are flooded, wait out the high water, or your vehicle may be swept downstream.

Facilities for Disabled

Window View Trail, a ¼-mile loop in the Chisos Mountains, is wheelchair-accessible.

Travel Advisory

Entrances

North: U.S. 385, 69 miles south of Marathon.

West: Highway 118, 103 miles south of Alpine.

Transportation

There is no public transportation to the park.

Airports: Airlines serve the Midland-Odessa and El Paso airports.

Rental Cars: Available at Midland and El Paso.

Attractions

The *Chisos Mountains* are the park's central feature; *Emory Peak* is the highest point in the park. A trail leads to the summit. The *Basin* at the base of the mountains is accessible by road. The *Rio Grande* runs along the southern border of the park and is the site of much of the life and activity in the park, including river running. The *Chihuahuan Desert* makes up much of the park and offers spectacular scenery.

Other Points of Interest (Museums, Historic Sites, etc.)

Historic sites in the park include the *Rio Grande Village* and *Castolon settlement*, as well as the *Johnson Ranch, Daniels Ranch, Blue Creek Ranch*, and *Glenn Spring ruins*.

Accommodations

Lodge

Chisos Mountains Lodge: In the Basin. For reservations and information write National Park Concessions, Inc., Big Bend National Park, TX 79834 or call (915) 477–2291.

Campgrounds and Picnic Areas

First-come first-served; 14-day limit. Wood and ground fires are prohibited; carry out all refuse.

Chisos Basin Campground: 63 sites; toilets,

water, tables, grills, overhead shelters, dump station; $5/night.

Rio Grande Village RV Park: The only campground in the park with hookups.

Rio Grande Village Class A Campground: 100 sites; toilets, water, tables, grills, some overhead shelters, dump station; $5/night.

Rio Grande Village Class B Campground: Used only when the Class A campground is full. Pit toilets, water; $3/night.

Cottonwood Campground: 35 sites; pit toilets, tables, grills, water; $3/night.

Backcountry Camping: Backcountry camping allowed throughout the park. Some roadside campsites available throughout the park; no services or facilities.

Picnic Areas: Five areas off the paved road; tables.

Restaurant

Chisos Mountains Lodge: In the Basin; dining room. See "Lodge," above.

Activities

Scenic Drives

The paved principal roads in the park lead to the major developed areas and sites of interest, including Rio Grande Village, the Basin, and Castolon, with several overlooks and viewpoints along the way. Improved dirt roads are usually in good condition and accessible to normal passenger cars except after rainstorms. Unimproved backcountry roads that go to the less used areas of the park generally require high-clearance and/or four-wheel-drive vehicles.

Hiking

Hiking is considered the best way to experience and appreciate the park. Walks and hikes cover a range of levels including short, self-guided nature trails, cross-park treks, and remote wilderness routes shown only in general terms on a topographical map. The Lost Mine Trail, one of the most popular, is a five-mile self-guiding nature trail named for stories about a lost silver mine. For an overview of the park, there is a hike to the summit of Emory Peak, the high point of the park, where you can look across the desert and grasslands to the river. Because of the unreliability of desert springs, you shouldn't try to plan an extended backpacking trip prior to your arrival. Wait until you arrive at the park to check on conditions.

Horseback Riding

Guided horseback trips are available. Saddle horses, pack animals, and guides can be arranged for in the Basin or by contacting Chisos Remuda, Basin Rural Station, Big Bend National Park, TX 79834; (915) 477–2374.

River Running

You can take float trips on open stretches of the Rio Grande or into the depths of the three great canyons. The Rio Grande Wild and Scenic River, a specially designated stretch of the river that extends along part of the park boundary plus an additional 127 miles downstream, is managed by the Park Service. Between the canyons, the river is generally slow and quiet. The canyons, however, are steep and sheer-walled; the considerable white water in certain locations can be very dangerous to the novice. A river guide is available at park headquarters. You can bring your own equipment or, if you need to rent, contact the park for a list of river outfitters. (There are no equipment rentals in the park.)

Fishing

Fishing is allowed in the Rio Grande; catfish are commonly taken.

Naturalist Programs

Nature walks, workshops, and evening slide programs are provided by park naturalists. Check bulletin boards and visitor centers for current schedule.

Looking at a map of Biscayne National Park, you may be surprised to see that the total park land consists of only a sliver of shoreline and some small islands south of Miami. That is because nearly 95 percent of the park is not land: It's water.

Extending east from the mangrove forests of the coast across Biscayne Bay to the living coral reefs at the outer edge of the barrier islands, this park is ideal for boaters, snorkelers, scuba divers, and water lovers of all types. The water in much of the park is so shallow that it is possible to see brilliantly colored tropical fish and coral just by snorkeling. Scuba divers can venture out to small patch coral reefs to explore the beautiful underwater landscape and its inhabitants. Of course, just cruising the waters on board a boat or watching the scene from the end of the jetty can be a blissful way to spend a day. The important thing is that, whatever your choice of vehicle, it is essential to head to the water to experience Biscayne.

The land within the park's boundaries includes the coastline on the mainland (the only part of the park accessible by car) and about 40 islands, or keys, offshore. Only three of the islands—Elliott, Adams, and Boca Chita Key—have areas set aside for public use. They are accessible only by boat and are available for hiking, picnicking, and limited camping.

Within this beautiful marine park's boundaries lies a unique ecosystem with a variety of life forms that are dependent on one another for their survival. The mainland mangrove trees serve as nurseries for and protectors of marine life; their tangled maze of roots, anchored in the mud, keeps out larger creatures. The forests of rare mahogany trees on the islands shelter migratory birds. And many plants and animals in the water thrive almost solely because of the food and protection provided by the coral reefs. The main coral reef itself creates a barrier that protects the islands from the full force of the sea. About 100,000 years ago, the islands themselves were part of a line of coral reefs, which dried out when sea level dropped about 25 feet.

The extraordinarily clean and clear water is home to an incredible variety of fish, shellfish, and other marine creatures including sponges, sea turtles, moray eels, sea urchins, starfish, octopuses, and sea horses. Some of the fish that may be spotted in the waters are parrotfish, surgeonfish, grunt, porkfish, butterflyfish, and queen angelfish. An especially beloved inhabitant of these waters is the manatee. About 10 feet long and weighing up to a ton, these slow-moving animals have an entire North American population of only about 1,000, almost all of it in the waters off Florida.

This stretch of southern Florida's coast is rich in history from the days when European and American trading ships sailed past here on their way to and from the Caribbean. Many ships were destroyed by underwater reefs, and sank. Possibly even more dangerous than the reefs, though, were the

NATIONAL PARK SERVICE

pirates that occupied these waters. One of the most famous, Black Caesar, apparently used the area that is now the park as his home base. Today, in his memory, the chan-nel between Elliott and Old Rhodes keys is named for him, as is a ledge where his crew often lurked while preparing surprise attacks.

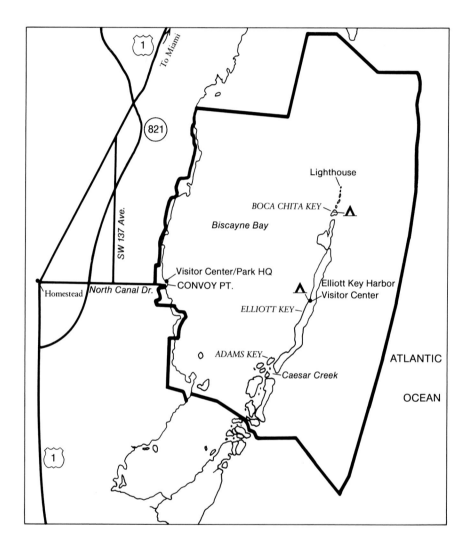

Further Information

Write or call: Superintendent, Biscayne National Park, P.O. Box 1369, Homestead, FL 33090-1369; (305) 247–PARK (7275)

Visitor Information

Park Headquarters/Visitor Center: Convoy Point, North Canal Drive; information, exhibits, slide presentations.
Elliott Key Visitor Center: Exhibits, slide presentation. Please note: The park sustained damage from Hurricane Andrew in 1992. Contact the park before you visit for information on availability of services.

Nuts and Bolts

Entrance Fee: None.
Park Open: All year.
Permits: Required for backcountry camping; saltwater fishing license is required.
In Emergency: Call 247–2400.
Acreage: 181,500

Practical Advisory

Seasons

Subtropical climate with abundant sunshine and high humidity year-round. Summer (May–October): Warm and wet with high temperatures around 84° and brief but frequent afternoon thunderstorms. Winter (November–April): Mild and dry with high temperatures of about 76°.

Special Advisories

- Anchor only on a sandy bottom and away from fragile corals and grass beds.
- The State of Florida requires that when you are diving you display a dive flag to alert other boaters to your presence.
- Mosquitoes can be a problem; be sure to carry insect repellent.

Facilities for Disabled

Both visitor centers (including rest rooms), boat-launching ramp, and part of the jetty near headquarters are wheelchair-accessible.

Travel Advisory

Entrances

West: Florida Turnpike or U.S. 1, south of Miami, to SW 137 Avenue (Tallahassee Road) to SW 328 Street (North Canal Drive) to mainland section of park.

All Directions: Access to the islands is by boat only. The mainland is also accessible by boat.

Transportation

Airports: Miami International Airport is 30 minutes north of the park.

Bus Service: Bus service is available to Homestead.

Train Service: Train service is available to Miami, 25 miles north of the park.

Rental Cars: Available at Miami airport and in Homestead.

Attractions

The highlights of the park lie in and around the waters of *Biscayne Bay*. The park is best experienced by boat, although there is a jetty available on the mainland for some activities. Of interest are the barrier islands or *keys*, three of which are open to the public; they are accessible only by boat. Also of interest are the living *coral reefs* fringing the islands, as well as the variety of *marine life* in the waters.

Other Points of Interest (Museums, Historic Sites, etc.)

Ther is a 65-foot ornamental *lighthouse* open to visitors on Boca Chita Key.

Accommodations

There are no lodgings or restaurants in the park.

Campgrounds and Picnic Areas

All campsites available on a first-come, first-served basis; 14-day limit. Bugs are considered by park rangers to be too intense in the summer for camping on the islands. All camping areas are accessible only by boat.

Elliott Key Campground: Primitive; tent sites with picnic tables and grills, rest rooms, cold-water showers, water.

Boca Chita Key Campground: Primitive; picnic tables and grills, rest rooms.

Picnic Areas: At Convoy Point and Adams Key; tables, grills, rest rooms. At Adams Key, rest rooms are in the recreation building of the former Cocolobo Club, a millionaires' hideaway in the early 1900s.

Activities

Boating

Visitors with their own boats can gain direct access to park waters from two county-operated parks and indirect access from many points north and south of park boundaries. Since navigation can be difficult, use of NOAA (National Oceanic and Atmospheric Administration) nautical charts is strongly recommended. They are sold at the Convoy Point

Visitor Center, or you can order by phone: (305) 247–1216. Free docking is available on Elliott Key at the 64-slip Elliott Key Harbor and at University Dock; on Adams Key; and on Boca Chita Key.

Fishing

Saltwater fish include marlin, snapper, sea trout, grouper, and Spanish mackerel. Crabs, lobster, and shrimp can also be taken. Florida's regulations regarding size, number, season, location, and method of take must be obeyed.

Snorkeling and Diving

Crystal-clear waters provide ideal conditions for snorkeling and diving; calm and sunny days are best. Park rangers request that boats be moored to a buoy so as not to disturb the patch reefs with an anchor; check with a park ranger for locations of mooring buoys. Diving-equipment sales and rentals are available; for information call (305) 247–2400.

Other Water Sports

There are few sandy beaches since most of the shoreline is exposed coral rock and is thick with mangroves. There are no lifeguards on the beaches. Swimmers, windsurfers, and water-skiers should be aware of boat traffic.

Boat Trips

A concessioner, located at the Convoy Point Visitor Center, offers glass-bottom-boat tours of the bay and reefs, family snorkeling and scuba-diving trips to the reefs, and island excursions for hiking and picnicking. Canoe rentals are also available. For information call (305) 247–2400.

Hiking

A short trail from Convoy Point on the mainland leads onto a jetty into Biscayne Bay. Elliott Key has a short boardwalk on the ocean side, at the end of which is a self-guided ⅓-mile trail through the center of the island. There is also an old road that runs the length of the island. On Adams Key there is a nature trail. Boca Chita Key has a nature trail that circles the island.

Bryce Canyon in southern Utah is not, strictly speaking, a canyon at all. It is more like a series of amphitheaters carved into the side of the Paunsaugunt Plateau. Filling these arenas are thousands of multicolored pinnacles, spires, columns, and figures of every description rising in bizarre and fantastic shapes toward the sky.

The approach to the canyon rim through the pine forest to its east reveals nothing of what is to come. Suddenly, the forest ends and the earth breaks away to reveal the strange and beautiful forms of the canyon. Many have been named for who or what they resemble, including castles, cathedrals, animals, and even miniature cities.

From this vantage point, the monuments seem to be almost delicate because of their precarious shapes. They also look pink; hence the name "Pink Cliffs." They are actually a mixture of pink, red, and orange, blended with white, brown, and gold and in some places striped with lavender and blue. The colors are those of minerals, mainly iron and manganese oxides, in the rocks. The scene changes with the shifts of the sun and with every passing cloud or summer shower. It is possible to go down into the heart of the canyon on one of the trails and get a closer look at these unusual rock formations, which were millions of years in the making.

Sixty million years ago, layers of sand, silt, and lime deposited by lakes and seas in this area were being compacted into rock. Later, beginning about 16 million years ago, the rock was gradually lifted up to mountainous heights, almost two miles above sea level. Huge blocks, including the Paunsaugunt Plateau, were broken off and formed distinct plateaus or tablelands.

Over the next centuries, rain, frost and thaw, thunderstorms, snowmelts, and plant roots that forced themselves deeper into the cracks widened gaps and fractures in the plateau. Trickles and streams of water cut through the Pink Cliffs and slowly shaped the incredible sculptures that line the canyon today. The sedimentary rocks that formed the different layers were of varying degrees of hardness, so they eroded at different rates, forming these unusual shapes. Some of the spires, like the famous Thor's Hammer at Sunset Point, are capped by hard layers that have resisted the erosion. The head of Thor's Hammer rests on a slim handle that will eventually be eaten away—as, in time, will all of Bryce Canyon.

The pine forests of the plateau consist mainly of fir and spruce to the south, but ponderosa pines dominate in the northern area, interrupted by grassy meadows of elderberry and creeping barberry. There are chipmunks, marmots, and ground squirrels scurrying about; mule deer and a large assortment of birds can also be seen.

In the canyon area, ponderosa pines are widely scattered close to the rim. Farther down into the canyon are piñons, sagebrush, junipers, and desert scrub dotting the slopes. Grasses, sagebrush, cactus, and yucca flourish on the floor of the valley. Skunks, gray foxes, deer, porcupines, and bobcats may be seen. Bird species in the park include hawks, owls, and doves.

NATIONAL PARK SERVICE

Further Information:

Write or call: Superintendent, Bryce Canyon National Park, Bryce Canyon, UT 84717; (801) 834–5322

Visitor Information

Park Headquarters/Visitor Center: Highway 63; exhibits on geology, animals, cultural history, night skies, and natural history. Small auditorium offers ranger talks and films. Books and tapes are sold.

Nuts and Bolts

Entrance Fee: $5/car or $3/person arriving by other means.
Park Open: All year.
Permits: Required for backcountry camping, and winter activities.
In Emergency: Call the Garfield County sheriff's office at 676–2411.
Acreage: 35,835.08

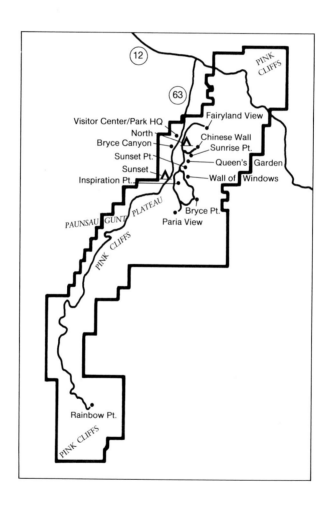

Practical Advisory

Seasons

Extreme weather is possible at any time of year. There is usually a 30° temperature difference between days and nights. Summer: Temperatures usually reach the upper 70s to low 80s, with lows in the upper 40s to low 50s. Winter: Comes early and stays late. Temperatures range from highs in the upper 20s to low 30s, to lows in the low teens. Temperatures of below zero are possible from October to April.

Special Advisories

• Popular overlooks along the rim range from 8,000 to 9,000 feet in elevation. Those with heart conditions or other medical problems should keep this in mind; all should pace themselves.

Facilities for Disabled

Most park buildings, rest rooms, and viewpoints are wheelchair-accessible, as is the paved, fairly level trail between Sunrise and Sunset points. In the summer, two North Campground campsites are reserved until six P.M. each day for mobility-impaired campers. Some of the ranger-led interpretive activities are accessible to all visitors. For complete information, contact the park for a copy of the "Bryce Canyon Access Guide."

Travel Advisory

Entrance

U.S. 89 to the junction seven miles south of Panguitch, east on Highway 12 to Highway 63 for 17 miles.

Transportation

There is no scheduled public transportation to the park.

Airports: Bryce Canyon Airport is four miles from the park. Air Nevada Airlines offers flights between here and Las Vegas's McCarran International Airport between April and mid-November. Call for information: (800) 634–6377. Private planes are also permitted. Other commercial airports are in Cedar City, 78 miles away, and Salt Lake City, 260 miles away.

Rental Cars: Rental-car agencies are at Bryce Canyon, Cedar City, and Salt Lake City airports.

Attractions

The major features of the park are the *Paunsaugunt Plateau*, its *Pink Cliffs*, and the many multicolored *rock formations* rising from the floor of the canyon. Some of the best-known of the pinnacles, spires, columns, and other formations include *Thor's Hammer*, the *Queen's Garden*, the *Chinese Wall*, and the *Wall of Windows*. A variety of overlooks from the park roads offer spectacular views. You must go by trail, however, to get down into the canyon for up-close looks.

Accommodations

Lodge

Bryce Canyon Lodge: Cabins and motel rooms; available May to mid-October. For information and reservations: TW Recreational Services, Inc., P.O. Box 400, Cedar City, UT 84720; (801) 586–7686.

Campgrounds

Buy or bring your own firewood; no wood gathering is allowed within the park.

North Campground and Sunset Campground: Total of 206 sites; open mid-May through October; first-come, first-served. Generally full every night from mid-May through mid-September; 14-day limit; dump station near North Campground; $6/night. Loop A of North Campground is open all winter and has heated comfort station.

Restaurants

Bryce Canyon Lodge: Dining room; open May to mid-October.

Snack Bar: In the General Store near Sunrise Point.

Activities

Scenic Drives

Twenty miles of main roads and four major spur roads lead to the park's 13 overlooks. Views are best from Fairyland View, Sunrise, Sunset, Inspiration, and Bryce points, and Paria View. Overlooks along the road south of the Inspiration/Bryce/Paria intersection offer panoramic views to the east and south. Rainbow Point, at the south end of the park, provides a 270° panoramic view of the plateau and canyon country. No trailers are allowed beyond Sunset Campground.

Hiking

There are many day-hike trails, ranging from easy to strenuous and from one to five hours' round-trip time. There are also two back-country hike trails; these are strenuous and require one to three days each to do round-trip.

Bicycling

Bicycles are permitted on park roadways only.

Horseback Riding

Horseback trips, available April through October, are led by concession wranglers and begin at the corral near the lodge. Advance reservations may be made by calling (801) 679–8665.

Cross-country Skiing

Available in wintertime throughout the park. Fairyland and Paria roads are not plowed and are used as ski trails. Cross-country ski equipment is available for rental outside the park.

Snowshoeing

An excellent way to see the park during wintertime. Snowshoes are available in the visitor center and are loaned free of charge on a first-come, first-served basis.

Ranger-Led Programs

In the summer, the park staff offers campfire programs, geology talks, hikes into the canyon, and rim walks. Current schedules are available at the visitor center.

The word "surreal" has often been used to describe the arid landscape of Canyonlands National Park. The steep-walled canyons, flat-topped mesas, and sloping buttes in intense reds, browns, and oranges can seem impenetrable upon first sighting. In fact, much of the park land remains undeveloped and is difficult to reach. Most roads are still unpaved and many parts of the backcountry can only be seen on foot, on horseback, or in a four-wheel-drive vehicle.

The winding Colorado and Green rivers separate the park into its four very distinct sections: Island in the Sky, to the north; the Needles, to the southeast; the Maze, to the west; and the rivers themselves. These sections are so separate, in fact, that the only way to get from one to another by road is to exit the park and drive, going as much as 100 miles.

Island in the Sky is made up of flat-topped mesas of mostly bare rock. The Needles is named for its thousands of pillars, spires, and colorful rock formations. In the Maze, the most remote area of the park, eroded buttes and towers of stone stand among a complex mix of canyons that turn in every direction. Wandering slowly through the canyons of the park, the two rivers come together at the Confluence, the heart of Canyonlands, where the Green River flows into the Colorado. Once joined, the river speeds up into Cataract Canyon, 14 miles of treacherous white water.

The park, with its forbidding desert terrain, may appear barren. But creatures have adapted in order to survive in this harsh environment. Piñons and junipers are the most widespread plants in the park. Deer, coyotes, bighorn sheep, mountain lions, and foxes are among the animal inhabitants. They are rarely seen, however; some are nocturnal, to avoid the heat of the day.

The Colorado Plateau from which the park is carved is made up of sandstone, shale, siltstone, mudstone, and limestone. It took many of nature's forces, including the Green and Colorado rivers with the help of other streams, rain, and frost, to slice through the layers of rock and produce the landscape of today. Pure salt from an evaporated ancient sea, 3,000 feet thick and one mile below the surface, also helped shape the land. As underground water dissolved away the salt, blocks of sandstone above it slowly settled into the spaces where the salt was, forming long, straight canyons.

Upheaval Dome is one of the most unusual geologic features in the park. Measuring 1,500 feet deep, the Dome does not look like a dome at all, but rather like a crater. There are many theories of how it was created. One popular theory suggests that slow-moving underground salt deposits pushed layers of sandstone upward, and then later erosion created the jagged-edged crater seen today. Another popular and more recent theory suggests that the Dome was created when a meteor hit. If this is true, Upheaval Dome is the only meteor-impact site preserved in a national park in this country.

NATIONAL PARK SERVICE

Signs of ancient Native Americans in the park include ruins of their stone and mud dwellings and storehouses, and petroglyphs and pictographs, some considered to be among the finest prehistoric rock art in the country. In 1869, Major John Wesley Powell explored the area. In the decades following, other explorers came and went, including prospectors looking for gold or silver, cowboys herding cattle, and in the 1950s, uranium prospectors. Because Canyonlands is so inaccessible, it has only very recently become well known outside of southern Utah.

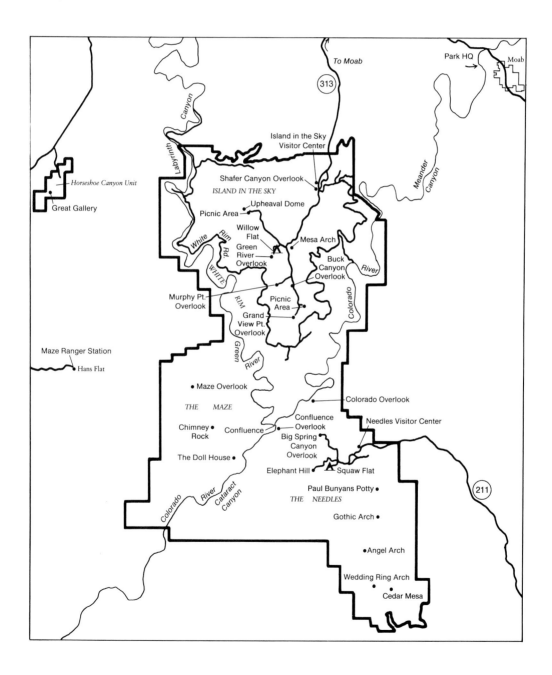

Further Information

Write or call: Superintendent, Canyonlands National Park, 125 West 200 South, Moab, UT 84532; (801) 259–7164

Visitor Information

All of the following offer information, exhibits, publications, and maps.
Park Headquarters: Outside the park in Moab.
Island in the Sky Visitor Center: Two miles inside the park boundary.
Needles Visitor Center: Three miles inside park boundary.
Maze Ranger Station: At Hans Flat, 46 miles (on dirt road) east of Highway 24.

Nuts and Bolts

Entrance Fee: $4/car or $2/person arriving by other means. Good for seven days. No fee November through February.
Park Open: All year.
Permits: Required for backcountry camping, boating, technical rock climbing, and horseback riding.
In Emergency: There are no accessible phones within the park; contact a park ranger.
Acreage: 337,570.43

Practical Advisory

Seasons

Summer: Very hot with average daytime temperatures ranging from 80° to 100° and nighttime temperatures of 50° to 60°. Spring and fall: Long and pleasant, with daytime temperatures of 60° to 80° and nighttime temperatures of 20° to 50°. High winds are common and are sometimes accompanied by blowing sand. Winter: Short and cold, with daytime temperatures of 30° to 50° and nighttime temperatures of 0° to 20°; light snowfall.

Special Advisories

- Use caution in climbing on sandstone; it can be slippery and crumbles easily.
- Never camp in a dry wash, and never drive across a wash during a flash flood.

- Stay on trails to avoid stepping on fragile microbiotic crust. This black, crunchy soil is actually a delicate living community that plays a vital ecological role.

Facilities for Disabled

The Island in the Sky and Needles visitor centers and rest rooms are wheelchair-accessible. Headquarters in Moab is fully accessible, including the rest rooms. Grandview Point and Buck Canyon overlooks (Island in the Sky) are paved with curb cuts and designated parking areas; assistance may be needed. Both campgrounds have accessible rest rooms but only Squaw Flat (Needles) has paved pullouts. Assistance is required for most.

Travel Advisory

Entrances

Island in the Sky: U.S. 191, 9 miles north of Moab, to Highway 313 for 26 miles southwest.

The Needles: U.S. 191, 14 miles north of Monticello, to Highway 211 for 35 miles west or 41 miles south of Moab, to Highway 211 for 34 miles west.

The Maze: I-70, west of Green River, to Highway 24 for 24 miles south to two-wheel-drive dirt road for 46 miles east to Hans Flat Ranger Station.

Transportation

Airports: Commuter airport, Redtail Aviation, is 15 miles north of Moab. Alpine Air provides service from Salt Lake City. Closest major airport is Grand Junction, Colorado, 115 miles east.

Bus Service: Greyhound buses serve Green River, Utah, 55 miles from Moab.

Train Service: Amtrak trains serve Thompson, Utah, 40 miles from Moab.

Rental Cars: Rental cars are available at the airports and in Moab.

Attractions

The highlights of the park include the many *cliffs*, *canyons*, and *rock formations* throughout the three sections. Island in the Sky is the most accessible by paved roads; the Maze section has no paved roads. The major features most easily reached by road are overlooks at *Shafer Canyon* and *Buck Canyon*, as well as *Elephant Hill* in Needles. Many important features, including *Upheaval Dome*, the *White Rim*, *Mesa Arch*, *Angel Arch*, and *The Doll House*, can be reached only by trail or four-wheel-drive road. The dividers of the park— the *Colorado and Green rivers* and their *confluence*—offer exciting opportunities for river running.

Other Points of Interest (Museums, Historic Sites, etc.)

Pictographs on the walls of *Horseshoe Canyon*, a detached unit of the park reachable by dirt road, are considered among the finest *prehistoric rock art* in the country. The *Great Gallery* is the best known and most spectacular of the panels.

Accommodations

There is no food or lodging available in the park.

Campgrounds and Picnic Areas

Collecting firewood is prohibited. First-come, first-served, seven-day limit.

ISLAND IN THE SKY

Willow Flat Campground: 12 sites; tables, fireplaces, pit toilets; free.

Backcountry Camping: Primitive campsites available off four-wheel-drive White Rim

Road. Reservations are recommended: White Rim Reservations, Canyonlands National Park, 125 W. 200 S., Moab, UT 84532. Free.

Picnic Areas: Grandview and Upheaval Dome; tables, pit toilets, fireplaces.

THE NEEDLES

Squaw Flat Campground: 25 sites; water, tables, fireplaces, pit toilets; $6/night.

Backcountry Camping: Primitive campsites available off four-wheel-drive roads; free.

THE MAZE

Backcountry Camping: Primitive campsites available off four-wheel-drive roads; free.

Activities

Scenic Drives

Driving can be a comfortable ride on a paved road or a tortuous four-wheel-drive climb up a steep, rocky road. Paved roads and two-wheel-drive dirt roads on Island in the Sky and in the Needles lead to interesting natural features, overlooks, and trailheads. Four-wheel-drive roads wind throughout the park, offering trips as short as a day or longer than a week. One of the most popular, the 100-mile White Rim Trail, can be driven in two days or leisurely explored over many days. Primitive campsites are located along many of the roads.

Hiking

Both short walks and long hikes lead to some of Canyonlands' outstanding features. Short trails (less than a mile) on the Island and in the Needles will take you to overlooks, to arches and other geologic features, and to Native American ruins. Some trails have wayside exhibits; brochures about trails can be picked up at trailheads or visitor centers. Longer trails penetrate wilder regions. Trails are generally primitive, marked only with rock cairns. They are rugged and require strenuous exertion. Carry a map.

Boating

Boating is popular on the Green and Colorado rivers. River access points for those with their own boats are near the town of Green River for the Green River and near Moab for the Colorado River. There are no services along the rivers. The best times for trips are spring, summer, and fall. Canoes, kayaks, and rafts are available for rent, and guided rafting trips are offered by concessioners in nearby towns. Request information for calm-water float trips by calling (800) 635–6622.

Bicycling

Bicycles are allowed on paved and dirt roads only, not on foot trails or off-road. Bicycle tours and bicycles for rent are offered by concessioners in nearby towns.

Driving Tours

Tours on four-wheel-drive roads are offered by outside concessioners.

Horseback Riding

Horses may be ridden on dirt roads and within specific roadless areas designated for such use. Loose herding and grazing are prohibited. A copy of the regulations is available from the superintendent. Contact the park before arriving to determine current conditions and any policy changes. Horseback trail rides and horses for hire are available from outside concessioners.

Rock Climbing

Climbing named features is restricted. The Salt Creek Archaeological District in the Needles is closed to all technical climbing. Chalk and webbing left at permanent anchor points must closely match the color of the rock.

Ranger-Led Programs

Rangers conduct campfire talks and guided walks from mid-March to mid-October in Island in the Sky and Needles. Schedules are posted at visitor centers and park offices.

Among the many wonders of colorful Capitol Reef National Park are spectacular rock formations, gigantic natural arches, and archaeological sites. But defining the land the Navajos called "Land of the Sleeping Rainbow" is the Waterpocket Fold, a 100-mile-long strip of multicolored rock layers created when the earth's crust buckled.

Each of these layers of rock, with its own color and texture, was laid down separately over 125 million years ago. Millions of years later, an enormous collision occurred between the continental plate beneath North America and the plate beneath the Pacific Ocean; the pressure from the collision caused the land here to wrinkle. These thick layers of rock slowly arched upward; they were torn off, broken up, and eventually eroded into tiny pebbles. Only jutting pieces of brilliantly colored rock remained. Since then, further erosion has carved the land into towers, domes, and pinnacles more than 1,000 feet high. Seventy-two miles of the Waterpocket Fold are in Capitol Reef National Park, which was named for the white, dome-shaped formations, on the top of the Fold, that resemble the Capitol Building.

This is harsh, dry desert land. Although occasional thunderstorms will briefly flood the area, the myriad plants and animals here usually must find water near streams and even in dry washes. Among the plants growing here are cottonwoods, box elders, willows, junipers, piñons, and sego lilies.

Sagebrush grows in the open desert. The exotic tamarisk is one of the most dominant trees in some areas. Animal inhabitants of the park include canyon wrens, golden eagles, swifts, and swallows in the air, and badgers and coyotes as well as salamanders, canyon tree frogs, and snakes on the ground. There is a dense deer population near Fruita.

Because the area is fairly isolated and difficult to get to, it has been relatively unexplored until quite recently. Even today, the few roads that go to the more remote parts of the park are unpaved and often require a four-wheel-drive vehicle. The Fold can be crossed only in three places.

Some of the more interesting formations in the park include Twin Rocks and Chimney Rock near the west entrance on the paved road. For those willing to explore farther than the paved road, Cathedral Valley, in the northern end of the park, has spectacular sandstone monoliths 400 to 700 feet high. Other interesting formations that are reachable by road or trail are Grand Wash, with 1,000-feet walls; Hickman Natural Bridge, which is 72 feet high and has a 133-foot span, and Cohab Canyon. Capitol Gorge was originally the only route through Capitol Reef.

The earliest inhabitants of this area were the Fremont people, who lived here from about A.D. 700 to A.D. 1275. They left irrigation ditches, baskets, pottery, and also the pictographs and petroglyphs painted and

NATIONAL PARK SERVICE

chiseled on many of the cliffs near Fruita. It is believed that the outlaw Butch Cassidy may have used the area as a hiding place; Cassidy Arch is named after him. In the early 1880s, Mormons settled along the Fremont River. They founded the settlement of Fruita, named for the orchards they planted. The orchards still bear fruit.

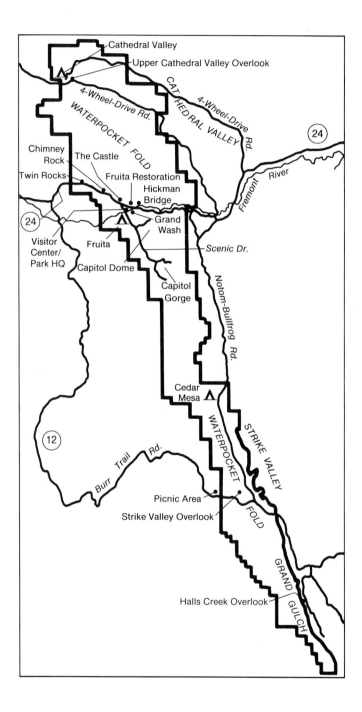

Further Information

Write or call: Superintendent, Capitol Reef National Park, Torrey, UT 84775; (801) 425–3791

Visitor Information

Park Headquarters/Visitor Center: Highway 24; orientation program; exhibits and displays concerning the Native American and Mormon settlers; publications; audiovisual programs.

Nuts and Bolts

Entrance Fee: $4/car for access to Scenic Drive.
Park Open: All year.
Permits: Required for backcountry camping.
In Emergency: Contact a park ranger.
Acreage: 241,904.26

Practical Advisory

Seasons

Flash floods are common. Summer: Daytime temperatures are in the 80s and 90s, with 100° temperatures not uncommon in June and July. Nights are generally cool, in the 50s or 60s. Winter: Cold weather from mid-December through February with daytime temperatures averaging below 50° and often below freezing, and dropping below freezing—sometimes below 0°—at night. Although snowfall is usually light, heavy snows are not uncommon.

Special Advisories

• Never park in a shallow lowland area or enter a gorge while it's raining: Flash floods do occur.

Facilities for Disabled

Wheelchair-accesible rest rooms are available at the visitor center and in the campground.

Travel Advisory

Entrances

West: U.S. 89 south of Salina to Highway 24 southeast for 69 miles.

East: I-70 west of Green River to Highway 24 southwest for 70 miles.

Transportation

There is no regularly scheduled public transportation to the park.

Airports: Cedar City airport, which is approximately 180 miles from the park.

Rental Cars: Available at airport.

Attractions

The *Waterpocket Fold* with its multicolored rock layers is the major feature of the park. Beautiful views of the Fold can be had from the main park road. Off this road are also some of the best-known rock formations in the park, including *Twin Rocks*, *Chimney Rock*, *the Castle*, *Hickman Bridge*, and *Capitol Dome*. Also of interest are *Capitol Gorge*, *Grand Wash*, and *Strike Valley*, areas that can be reached by unpaved roads. Scenic *Cathedral Valley* can be reached only with a four-wheel-drive vehicle.

Other Points of Interest
(Museums, Historic Sites, etc.)

The *Fruita Restoration* has the Mormons' old one-room schoolhouse, part of the original orchards, a pioneer dwelling, barn, blacksmith shop, and smokehouse. Fruit may be picked in the orchards.

Accommodations

There is no food or lodging available in the park.

Campgrounds and Picnic Areas

First-come, first-served, 14-day limit, open all year.

Fruita Campground: One mile south of the visitor center; 71 sites; water, rest rooms, tables, grills; $6/night.

Cedar Mesa Campground: Five sites; primitive; pit toilets, tables, grills; free.

Cathedral Valley Campground: Five sites; primitive; pit toilets, tables, grills; free.

Backcountry Camping: Allowed throughout the park; open fires and wood fires are prohibited.

Picnic Areas: Near visitor center; tables, grills, rest rooms, water. On Burr Trail; tables.

Activities

Scenic Drives

You can enjoy splendid views from the paved Highway 24, which passes through the park from east to west, and the Scenic Drive, which travels into the canyons. Guides are available at the visitor center for the Scenic Drive as well as for road tours of Cathedral Valley and Strike Valley. Unpaved roads designated for travel by all passenger vehicles, including the Scenic Drive and roads to remote areas south

of the Fremont River, are usually passable without difficulty. Because they are rough, other unpaved backcountry roads are suitable only for four-wheel-drive vehicles. Rain or snow may make some roads impassable from time to time.

Hiking

There are a number of trails leading to arches, bridges, overlooks, and narrows. Trails offer a slower, more intimate way to discover the park. They travel near the Fremont River, twist and turn through steep-walled canyons, allow for views of the Waterpocket Fold, and take you up close to formations such as Hickman Bridge. Trails range from short strolls to strenuous hikes over rough terrain requiring a day or more. Topographic maps are available at the visitor center.

Horseback Riding

Horses are permitted on some of the trails and in some areas of the park. Contact the superintendent for a copy of the regulations regarding horse use and in order to determine current conditions and any possible policy change.

Bicycling

Bicycling is allowed only on established roads. Suggested routes are Scenic Drive, Cathedral Valley loop, South Draw, and the Notom Road–Burr Trail–Boulder Mountain loop.

Ranger-Led Programs

Rangers offer guided walks, campfire programs, and workshops from May to September. Schedules are posted at the visitor center.

To enter the subterranean wonder that is the Carlsbad Caverns is to leave the known world behind with the New Mexico sunshine. Hidden beneath the foothills of the Guadalupe Mountains, these are the most outstanding limestone caverns in the country, a separate universe of spectacular silent beauty.

The caverns comprise a vast series of underground rooms and corridors fantastically decorated over millions of years by nature's hand. More than 20 miles of the caverns have been explored so far, but only part of that is available for touring. Among the many fantastic chambers you can see are the Green Lake Room, featuring thousands of stalactites and an eight-foot-deep pool of water; the Papoose Room, known for its stone draperies; the Queen's Chamber, 829 feet below the surface; and the Bottomless Pit, a black hole 140 feet deep.

Probably the most extraordinary chamber is the Big Room, a cross-shaped room at a depth of 750 feet. Measuring 1,800 feet at its longest, 1,100 feet at its widest, and 255 feet at its highest, it is one of the largest underground chambers in the world, big enough to contain 14 football fields and high enough to fit an 18-story building. It takes an hour and a half just to stroll through the entire room. This chamber is filled with stalagmites, stalactites, columns, draperies, and flowstone formations. The largest formation is the Giant Dome, Carlsbad's biggest stalagmite, a massive column 62 feet high and nearly 16 feet thick.

The wonderful underground landscape at Carlsbad Caverns was begun about 250 million years ago when an inland sea evaporated, leaving a reef covered in salt deposits. Erosion and a lifting of the earth's surface uncovered the buried rock reef a few million years ago. As rainwater, made slightly acidic by the air and soil, seeped down into the cracks in the reef, the limestone slowly dissolved, and the large underground chambers formed. When the water table lowered, these chambers filled with air; it was then that their decoration began. As new rainwater seeped from the surface, it picked up limestone along the way and absorbed some calcite, the basic ingredient in most cave formations. Wherever the drip was slow enough, the water evaporated and a crystal of calcite was deposited. Billions and billions of drops later, thousands of cave formations have been formed.

A phenomenon almost as fascinating as the caverns themselves is the spectacle of the flight of the bats. Each summer evening at sundown, swarms of Mexican free-tail bats fly out of the Bat Cave, 200 feet inside the cavern's entrance. Filling the sky at the rate of 300 per second, they head out for a night of feeding. They will return before sunrise to sleep away the next day. This scene of mass exodus can be viewed from the outdoor amphitheater at the cave's natural entrance. The bats, who moved in about 17,000 years ago, have numbered as many as 9 million at a time, but today the park is home to only about 300,000.

Prehistoric Native Americans ventured into the Carlsbad Caverns more than a thousand years ago and left drawings on the cave walls near the natural entrance. Much later, in the 1800s, settlers were drawn here by the sight of the bats. Some of them mined bat guano to sell as a natural fertilizer. In the early 1900s, visitors began touring the caverns, and the public's interest eventually drew the attention of the government. Exploration of the more than 70 caverns in the park continues today.

Further Information

Write or call: Superintendent, Carlsbad Caverns National Park, 3225 National Parks Highway, Carlsbad, NM 88220; (505) 785-2232

Visitor Information

Park Headquarters/Visitor Center: On Highway 7. Tours of Carlsbad Caverns begin here; radio tour guide, park information, exhibits (including a three-dimensional model of the caverns); nursery and kennel.

Nuts and Bolts

Entrance Fee: $5/adult, $3/ages 6–15, free for children under age six; $2.50/seniors. Separate fee for Slaughter Canyon Cave (New Cave).
Park Open: All year except December 25.
Permits: Required for backcountry camping.
In Emergency: Call (505) 785-2232.
Acreage: 46,755.33

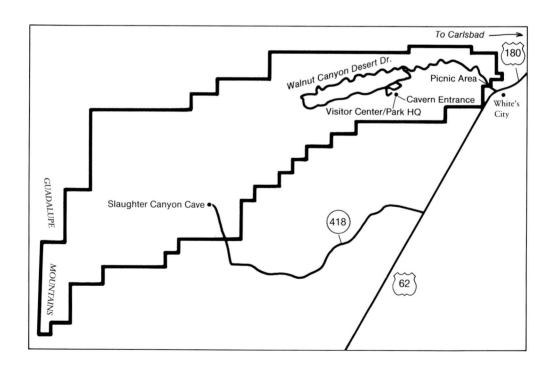

Practical Advisory

Seasons

In the Caves: The caves's temperature is a constant 56°.

Aboveground: Summer: Hot, average highs in the 90s. Intense thunderstorms bring lightning to higher areas and flooding to low-lying areas. Winter: Mild; average high temperatures are in the 50s and 60s but there is the possibility of a short snowstorm or a cold front. Spring: Winds can be strong.

Special Advisories

In the cave:

- Stay on trails (even for picture-taking); beyond them are steep dropoffs where you could fall, and unlighted passages where you could get lost.

- Touching cave formations can damage them and is prohibited.
- You may not use tobacco, eat, or drink in the cave. Baby strollers are not permitted.
- It is forbidden to throw anything into the cave pools.
- Photography is not permitted when you accompany a ranger-guided tour.
- Do not rest tripods or other camera equipment on formations.
- Wear low-heeled, nonskid shoes for walking on the sometimes steep and slippery paved trails, and use handrails where available.
- Bring a sweater or jacket into the cave.

Facilities for Disabled

The visitor center, including the rest rooms, is accessible, as is the picnic area. A portion of the Red Tour of the cavern is accessible to wheelchairs.

Travel Advisory

Entrance

U.S. 62-180, 22 miles southwest of Carlsbad to Highway 7.

Transportation

Airports: Carlsbad, 27 miles from the visitor center, and El Paso, Texas, 150 miles from the visitor center.

Bus Service: Buses travel from Carlsbad to White City, and from El Paso, Texas, to White City; a shuttle bus is available from White City to the visitor center seven miles away.

Train Service: Trains serve El Paso, Texas, 150 miles from the visitor center.

Rental Cars: Carlsbad, New Mexico, and El Paso, Texas.

Attractions

Carlsbad Caverns is the major feature of the park. It can be viewed on one of two tours. The more notable chambers are the *Big Room,* the *Green Lake Room,* the *Papoose Room,* the *Queen's Chamber,* and the *Bottomless Pit.* The *Giant Dome* is the largest stalagmite in the cavern. The evening *flight of the bats* is fascinating to witness.

Accommodations

There are no lodgings or campgrounds in the park.

Picnic Areas

Picnic tables are available near the visitor center and Rattlesnake Springs.

Restaurants

Visitor Center Restaurant: Dining room.

Underground Lunchroom: Sandwiches, box lunches, drinks, and rest rooms. Only facilities available underground.

Activities

Cave Tours

There are two cave-tour routes, the Blue Tour and the Red Tour. Both follow paved, well-lighted trails. Exhibits are located along the trails and park rangers are there to answer questions and give assistance. The tours are continuous, and may be started at any time during the hours posted. They are always self-guided, except that the first half of the Blue Tour is ranger-guided during November, the first two weeks in December, most of January, and February. Visitors may rent radio receivers for further information.

Blue Tour: Three miles and 2½ to three hours long. Includes all the chambers of Carlsbad Caverns that are open to the public—the Main Corridor, the Scenic Rooms, and the Big Room. The route is strenuous and is not recommended for persons with walking, breathing, or heart problems.

Red Tour: 1¼ miles and one to 1½ hours long. Explores the Big Room, which is reached by elevator. Most of the route is fairly level.

New Cave Tour: More primitive ranger-guided tours of Slaughter Canyon Cave, a cavern still under exploration, are available daily in the summer and on weekends the rest of the year. The tour is two hours long. Reservations must be made. Flashlights and water are required.

Bat Flight Program

You can see the Mexican free-tail bats leaving the cave from an outdoor amphitheater at the cave's natural entrance. The bats fly in front of the seating area but away from the visitors. Check at the visitor center for the anticipated time. May through October (approximately).

Scenic Drive

The 9½-mile, gravel-covered Walnut Canyon Desert Drive is a one-way loop through beautiful desert mountain country. Not recommended for trailers or motor homes.

Hiking

The park's trail system includes a short nature trail and, for experienced hikers, more than 50 miles of primitive backcountry trails. Trailheads are located along each of the park roads. A topographical map is recommended for backcountry hiking.

Ranger Talks

Park rangers' talks about the cave take place at the seating area near the Top of the Cross inside the Big Room.

Out in the Pacific Ocean, directly off the coast of Southern California, are eight small islands known as the Channel Islands. Five of the eight—Anacapa, Santa Cruz, Santa Rosa, San Miguel, and Santa Barbara—and their surrounding nautical mile of ocean make up Channel Islands National Park. Although physically so close to the coast that they can be seen quite plainly on a clear day, these islands could not be farther away in spirit from the densely populated and highly developed mainland.

These harsh and windblown land masses offer a wild environment combining sea, land, and the intertidal zone in which a variety of marine life thrives. The sights and sounds of this unusual and delicate balance of nature make the challenge of crossing the rough waters of the Santa Barbara Channel worth the effort.

An unusual variety of animal species live here. Harbor seals, seabirds, and sea lions use the islands for resting. Whales travel the waters nearby on their migratory routes. And the distinct geography inland has fostered the development of slight differences between native animals and their mainland relatives, created over many years of isolation. For example, the islands' largest land mammal, the native island fox, is closely related to the mainland's gray fox, but has evolved into a much smaller animal.

Although the islands are similar, each has its own distinctive environment. Anacapa Island is the closest to the mainland, at about 14 miles from Ventura. Anacapa is actually three small islets, accessible from one to another only by boat. From January through March, migrating whales can be seen in the waters nearby. West Anacapa, the primary West Coast nesting site for the brown pelican, is closed to the public. Santa Cruz, the largest of the Channel Islands, has the most diverse habitats; residents include nesting seabirds, more than 600 plant species, 140 land bird species, and a distinct group of land animals. Since the early 1800s, this island has been privately owned and access is limited.

Grasslands cover close to 85 percent of Santa Rosa Island. The sandy beaches are a breeding ground for harbor seals, and the island is surrounded by large kelp beds. San Miguel Island is primarily a plateau, 400 to 500 feet in elevation, with two rounded hills. It is known mostly for its caliche, a fascinating natural phenomenon created by a chemical reaction that hardened the windblown sand covering the island plants. When the plants inside the hardened sand eventually decayed, the hollow sand "sculptures" remained. Santa Barbara Island, the smallest at 640 acres, is home to a large rookery of sea lions. During World War II the U.S. Navy used it as an early-warning outpost.

The northern Channel Islands were once part of one large island geologists call Santarosae. The sea level was much lower at that time. Then, when the continental ice sheets melted, the islands were separated by the rising waters. Over thousands of years

NATIONAL PARK SERVICE

the sea, wind, and rain have eroded the islands to their current size.

The Chumash tribe had early villages on the larger islands, but by the early 1800s the people were removed to mainland missions. Juan Rodriguez Cabrillo, a Portuguese navigator in service to Spain, was one of the earliest European explorers in the area, which he visited in 1542. Fur traders were the first to try to profit off the land, but by the mid-1800s ranchers took over, producing sheep, cattle, and more. During the 1900s, the islands played an important part in California's coastal defenses.

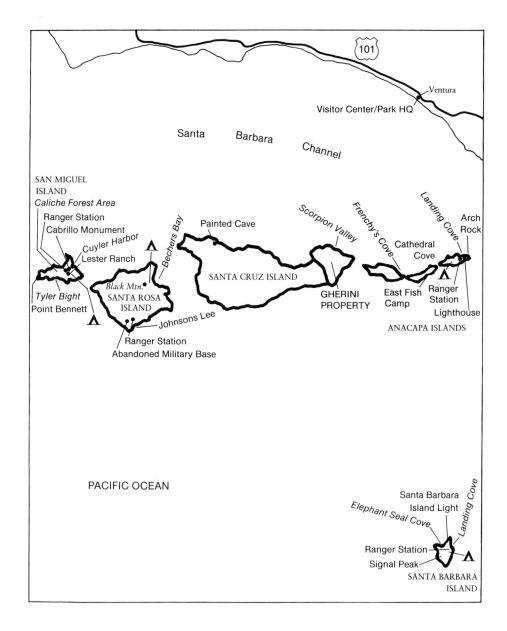

Further Information

Write or call: Superintendent, Channel Islands National Park, 1901 Spinnaker Drive, Ventura, CA 93001; (805) 658-5730

Visitor Information

Park Headquarters/Visitor Center: On the mainland, Spinnaker Drive in Ventura; 25-minute film, photo displays, exhibits, Chumash Native American artifacts, indoor tidepool, native-plant display.

Nuts and Bolts

Entrance Fee: None.
Park Open: All year. Visitor center closed on Thanksgiving, December 25.
Permits: Required for camping on Anacapa, Santa Barbara, Santa Rosa, and San Miguel islands and for landing on Santa Rosa, San Miguel, and Santa Cruz islands. California fishing license required.
In Emergency: Contact a park ranger or the U.S. Coast Guard on channel 16 of a marine-band radio.
Acreage: 249,353.77

Practical Advisory

Seasons

This is a harsh environment. The wind often blows for several days at a time, even in the summer, at speeds up to 30 miles per hour. Long periods of wet fog are not uncommon. Winter and spring rains turn the trails and campgrounds into sticky mud.

Special Advisories

- Check the current and forecast weather and sea conditions before boating, and know your vessel's limitations.
- Observe the surf and surge conditions before attempting to land.
- Anchoring may be difficult because the harbors are small and the sea floor slopes.
- Dress in layers to adjust to rapid changes in weather.
- Stay away from cliffs when hiking.
- Stay away from the lighthouse on East Anacapa Island; its high-intensity foghorn could permanently damage your hearing.
- Screeching and diving birds indicate you are near breeding activity; stay away from nests.
- Smoking is prohibited except at the dock/landing and picnic areas.

Facilities for Disabled

The visitor center is wheelchair-accessible. Because of difficult landing conditions, islands are not wheelchair-accessible. Assistance from the park staff is available to those in need on the islands upon request.

Travel Advisory

Entrances

U.S. 101 to Ventura; follow signs to visitor center. The islands can be reached only by boat or, rarely, by plane. For those without a boat, a park concessioner offers regular boat trips throughout the year to all the islands. Reservations are recommended: (805) 642-1393. Channel Islands Aviation flies visitors to Santa Rosa Island for camping or day trips. Call (805) 987-1301.

Transportation

Airports: Los Angeles International; Burbank; Oxnard; Santa Barbara.

Bus Service: Available to Ventura.

Train Service: Amtrak serves Santa Barbara and Oxnard.

Rental Cars: Available in all local communities and at all airports.

Attractions

Each island has its own special features.

On Anacapa: *Cathedral Cove* is a popular area for diving. On the west island, *Frenchy's Cove* and the *beach* are scenic. *Arch Rock* is on the tip of the island. Look for *sea lions* and *migrating whales*.

On Santa Cruz: This island is known for its *nesting seabirds*. There is also an *1850s ranch* on the island.

On Santa Rosa: *Bechers Bays* is most scenic. Look for *harbor seals* and *large kelp beds* offshore. There are over 180 *archaeological sites*, including *Chumash villages*, the *camps of* early explorers and fur hunters, and an *1850s cattle ranch*, still in operation.

On San Miguel: This island is most known for its *caliche*. *Cuyler Harbor* is popular; *Point Bennett*, at the western tip of the island, is scenic. There are more than 500 *archaeological sites* on the island. The *Lester Ranch Area* belonged to island caretakers in the 1930s and early 1940s. Also on the island is *Cabrillo Monument*, in honor of the explorer Juan Rodriguez Cabrillo.

On Santa Barbara: There is a *sea lion rookery* offshore. *Elephant Seal Cove* is scenic. *Signal Peak* is the high point of the small island.

Accommodations

There is no food or lodging available in the park.

Campgrounds and Picnic Areas

Reservations are required. No fees. No open fires permitted; bring a stove for cooking, and take trash with you.

East Anacapa Campground: 14-day limit; fire pits, tables, latrines. You must climb 154 steps from the landing cover to the island top and walk ¼ mile to get to the campground.

Santa Barbara Campground: Nine sites; tables, latrines.

San Miguel Campground: Four sites; two-night limit, 30-camper limit; pit toilet.

Santa Rosa Campground: 14-day limit, 30-camper limit; latrines, tables.

Picnic Area: On East Anacapa; latrines.

Activities

Hiking

There is a self-guiding nature trail, 1½ miles long, in East Anacapa. On San Miguel, once you hike from the beach to the island's top, it is about 3½ miles from the ranger station to the caliche forest; there is also a 15-mile round-trip hike across the island to Point Bennett, where you may see breeding seals and sea lions. Hikers must be accompanied by a ranger. On Santa Barbara there are 5½ miles of trails, including the Canyon View self-guiding nature trail. A trail booklet is available. Hiking and guided walks are available on Santa Rosa Island by request.

Boating

Boaters should refer to NOSC (National Ocean Survey Charts) 18720, 18729, and 18756. The channel is subject to sudden changes in sea and wind conditions; anchoring can be hazardous. To go ashore on the islands requires a skiff, raft, or small boat. Cruising guides are available at the visitor center.

Anacapa: Anchorages include East Fish Camp and, in good weather, Frenchy's Cove.

Santa Barbara: Anchoring is usually confined to the east side because of prevailing winds and waves.

San Miguel: You can anchor on the north side at Cuyler Harbor, or on the south side at Tyler Bight. Cuyler Harbor is usually a safe anchorage under normal weather conditions and is the only landing area on San Miguel. Sea conditions are often rough; only experienced boaters with sturdy vessels should attempt the trip.

Santa Rosa: Depending on sea conditions, you can anchor in Bechers Bay or Johnsons Lee.

Scuba Diving

There are many fine scuba-diving areas around the islands. Divers can explore caves, coves, and shipwrecks including the steamer *Winfield Scott*, grounded and sunk in 1853. Be aware of changing current and wind conditions when diving. All artifacts are protected by law and must be left in place.

Swimming

Beaches on East Anacapa are not accessible, but on calm summer days you may swim in the landing cove. At West Anacapa's Frenchy's Cove there is a beach and a fine snorkeling area. On San Miguel, there is a beach area at Cuyler Harbor.

Fishing

California fish and game regulations apply. Regulations are available at park headquarters.

Authorized Trips to Santa Cruz Island

The Nature Conservancy conducts day trips to Santa Cruz Island for both organized groups and the general public. For information: Nature Conservancy's Santa Cruz Island Project, 213 Stearns Wharf, Santa Barbara, CA 93101; (805) 962-9111. Island Packers, Inc., is authorized to provide guided boat trips for the general public to Scorpion Valley on the east side. Call (805) 642-1393.

Ranger-Led Programs

There are guided walks and evening programs given by rangers on East Anacapa. Guided walks are available by request on Santa Rosa, San Miguel, and Santa Barbara islands.

Crater Lake is high up on the crest of the Cascade Mountains in southern Oregon. The only way to see it is to take a road that climbs close to the rim, where it is possible to look down inside steep slopes that drop about 1,000 feet to a view of the lake. This enormous body of water is one of the most startling blues anywhere. At 1,932 feet, it is also the deepest lake in the country.

Surrounded by mountains, forests, and volcanic peaks, the lake lies inside the top of Mount Mazama, which was once a volcano. About 7,700 years ago, the volcano had its fiercest eruption ever, causing the support of the mountain's peak to be destroyed and the top of the volcano to collapse. Only the base of the mountain was left, and inside that a huge basin-shaped volcanic depression, or caldera. As volcanic activity subsided, water from rain and snow filled the caldera, and the giant lake was formed, growing eventually to its current size: 26 miles in circumference and six miles in diameter at its widest point. Evaporation and seepage offset the water flowing into the lake today, so its depth remains fairly constant, varying by less than three feet a year.

Since no other body of water runs into or out of Crater Lake it is considered a closed ecological system. The National Park Service has introduced six different species of fish to the lake over time. Of these six, only two remain: rainbow trout and kokanee salmon. To protect the natural system

in place at the lake, fish have not been stocked since 1941.

Most of the park land surrounding the lake is covered with forest species including mountain hemlocks, Shasta red firs, white-bark pines, lodgepole pines, and ponderosa pines. With the arrival of summer, the deep greens of the forest are patched with bright displays of wildflowers including phlox, monkeyflower, Indian paintbrush, lupine, knotweed, and aster. But the flowers have a quick blooming season, peaking in August, and are a short-lived treat. The winters are long here. More than 45 feet of snow falls in a year, and the snow begins by mid-September.

Ravens, jays, and nutcrackers, deer, ground squirrels, and chipmunks are frequently spotted in the park. Although they are rarely seen, elk, black bears, foxes, porcupines, pine martens, chickaree squirrels, and pikas also inhabit the wilderness, as do hawks, owls, juncos, chickadees, coyotes, bald and golden eagles, mule deer, and white-tail deer.

One of the most awe-inspiring qualities of the lake is its remarkably vivid blue color. The actual color of the water is, of course, no more blue than the sky is blue. The scattering of the sun's rays makes the water look this way. The rays are absorbed one color at a time as they pass through clear water. Some of the blue light is scattered back to the lake's surface, giving it that brilliant appearance.

PHOTO BY DAVID LINDQUIST

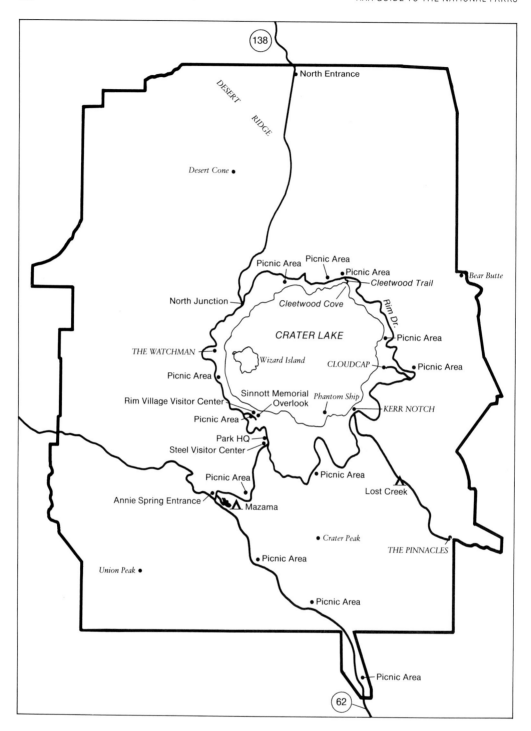

Further Information

Write or call: Superintendent, Crater Lake National Park, P.O. Box 7, Crater Lake, OR 97604; (503) 594-2211

Visitor Information

Park Headquarters/Steel Visitor Center: Three miles south of Rim Village; 18-minute video, displays, information, visitor services.

Rim Village Visitor Center: Information displays. (Closed fall to spring.)

Nuts and Bolts

Entrance Fee: $5/vehicle or $2/person arriving by other means.

Park Open: Highway 62, from the south and west, and Rim Village are open all year. The north entrance and Rim Drive close with the first snowfall (early to mid-October) and open again in mid-June/early July. Visitor facilities closed on December 25.

Permits: Required for backcountry camping.

In Emergency: Call 911.

Acreage: 183,224.05

Practical Advisory

Seasons

Annual precipitation is 67 inches, most of it in the form of snow. Summer: Clear with cool evenings and daytime temperatures usually in the 70s, but sometimes as high as 90°. June is typically warm and sunny but may have occasional storms, and snowpack may linger into July. Water temperature is about 55° in summer. Fall, winter, spring: Snow usually blankets the higher elevations from October to July. Stored heat from the summer sun retards ice formation through the winter, so the lake rarely freezes.

Special Advisories

• Chains or traction devices are often required on snow-covered roadways.

Facilities for Disabled

Most viewpoints are accessible to persons in wheelchairs. Ramps are in place at the Rim Village Visitor Center, the Steel Visitor Center, Mazama Campground, and the Rim Village facilities.

Travel Advisory

Entrances

West: I-5 to Highway 62 at Medford northeast to Annie Spring entrance.

South: U.S. 97 to Highway 62, northwest to the Annie Spring entrance.

North: I-5 to Highway 138 at Roseburg, east and south to north entrance.

Transportation

Airports: At Klamath Falls and Medford.

Train Service: Available in Klamath Falls.

Rental Cars: Available in Klamath Falls and Medford.

Attractions

The large *Crater Lake* is the major feature of the park, although the park does comprise a great deal of the surrounding land. It is possible to drive all around the rim of the lake (weather and conditions permitting) for excellent views. The lake itself is accessible only by one steep trail. In the lake is the small *Wizard Island*. Also of interest are the eroded volcanic spires in the *Pinnacles* area.

Accommodations

Lodges

Mazama Campground Cabins: Open late spring, summer, and early fall. Call Crater Lake Lodge Company at (503) 594-2511.

Crater Lake Lodge: This Rim Village lodge is closed for renovations and is not expected to reopen until 1995.

Campgrounds and Picnic Areas

Campgrounds open when snow melts in early summer and closed by snow in the fall. First-come, first-served; no reservations. Use only dead and downed wood for campfires.

Mazama Campground: Eight miles south of Rim Village; 198 sites; rest rooms, dump station; $10/night.

Lost Creek Campground: On Pinnacles Road; 16 sites, tents only; water, flush toilets; $5/night.

Picnic Areas: 12 areas throughout the park; tables.

Restaurant

Coffee Shop: At Rim Village; snacks, meals.

Activities

Scenic Drives

Rim Drive is a 33-mile roadway, beginning at Rim Village, that circles the caldera rim with pullouts that provide lake views. Some of the more outstanding are the Watchman and Kerr Notch. From Rim Drive a spur road leads to the Pinnacles, an area of eroded volcanic spires. Towed vehicles and trailers are not recommended on East Rim Drive. The north entrance road and Rim Drive are closed from about mid-October to July 1. Highway 62 and the south access road lead to a year-round lake view.

Hiking

There are over 70 miles of trails within the park, ranging from short interpretive walks to 20 miles of the Pacific Crest Trail. A paved footpath near the Rim Village visitor center leads to the Sinnott Memorial, an outdoor area offering history displays and an unobstructed view of the lake. Because of the heavy snows, most trails remain closed until July. Map and trail guides are available. Travel inside the caldera rim to reach the lake is permitted only on the Cleetwood Trail.

Boat Tours

From July through early September, narrated boat tours are offered by the Crater Lake Lodge Company and the National Park Service. The 1¾-hour tour begins at the Cleetwood Cove boat dock. It circles the inside of the caldera and stops at Wizard Island, where you can hike or relax until the midafternoon return trip. You should allow at least one hour to drive from Rim Village to the trailhead and to hike down the one-mile trail. (This very strenuous trail is not recommended for anyone with heart, breathing, or leg problems.) A fee is charged.

Fishing

You may fish in the lake only at Cleetwood Cove and Wizard Island (which you can reach only by tour boat). There is a healthy population of kokanee salmon and rainbow trout.

Skiing and Snowmobiling

Cross-country skiing is permitted on trails and roads that are not plowed during the winter (such as Rim Drive). Skiing is not permitted on the three-mile stretch of road from park headquarters to Rim Village, even if the road is closed. There are no special facilities for skiing. When skiing along the rim, watch for ice and avalanche areas. Skis can be rented at Rim Village. Snowmobiling is permitted on the north entrance road only.

Ranger-Led Programs

Summer campfire programs are presented at the Mazama Campground amphitheater. Hikes and special activities for children are also offered. Park rangers present short geology talks at the Sinnott Memorial. Check the park newspaper for schedules.

Beautiful, unspoiled Alaska is one of the last great frontiers in this country. In Denali National Park you'll find a perfect example of that character; the wildlife are still wild and nature lives by its own rules. This subarctic terrain of forests, tundra, glaciers, and freely roaming animals offers a true wilderness adventure. And looming over it all is the highest peak in North America: Mount McKinley, or Denali ("High One"), as the native Athabaskans call it.

Unlike other mountain slopes covered with deep green forests, the slopes here are covered only in icy white snow. The freezing temperatures on the high peaks of the Alaska Range prevent the vast glaciers from ever melting. Permanent snowfields coat more than half of Mount McKinley. Only plants and animals adapted to living in a harsh environment with long, bitterly cold winters can survive here. Permafrost, earth that has been frozen solid for thousands of years, underlies portions of the park. It usually starts about a foot below the surface and can reach several hundred feet deep. Only a thin layer of topsoil thaws in these areas each summer to support life.

Denali's plant life consists of taiga and tundra. There is not much tree growth in the taiga, and what trees do grow are often stunted, cut down by the fierce winter winds. White and black spruce are the most common; others include quaking aspen, paper birch, and balsam poplar. Shrubs fill

many areas. The tree line is at about 2,700 feet. Above that level, the taiga gives way to a vast tundra full of dwarfed shrubs. In summer, miniaturized wildflowers, adapted to the quick growing season, dot the landscape with beautiful delicacy. They include flowered dryas, moss campion, dwarf rhododendron, and forget-me-not (Alaska's state flower).

One of the most popular features of the park is its numerous species of wildlife. The area is home to grizzly bears, wolves, moose, caribou, and Dall sheep, relatives of the bighorn sheep and the only pure white wild sheep in North America. Smaller mammals include foxes, weasels, lynx, snowshoe hares, red squirrels, porcupines, and beavers. Bird life is varied, with over 150 species recorded including: ravens, gray jays, Lapland longspurs, short-eared owls, marsh hawks, and golden eagles. Most birds migrate long distances between their nesting grounds here and their wintering areas.

In the early part of this century, the rough unexplored territory in this area attracted prospectors, geologists, and adventure seekers. Many brave souls attempted to climb the mountain and failed. Others came just to explore. In 1957, the Denali Highway was completed, providing summer access to the park over a long gravel road. In 1972, the completion of the George Parks Highway offered direct, paved, year-round access. This easy accessibility has meant a continual increase in the number of visitors

NATIONAL PARK SERVICE

to the park each year. In order to preserve the wildlife environment, Park authorities have to limit the number of vehicles on the one road. Although Mount McKinley has been successfully climbed by mountaineers from all over the world, it still remains a challenge because of its harsh and unpredictable weather.

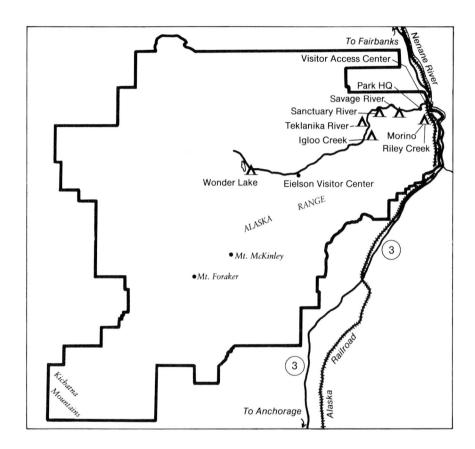

Further Information

Write: Superintendent, Denali National Park, P.O. Box 9, Denali Park, AK 99755; (907) 683-2686

Visitor Information

Bus coupons, general information, backcountry information, books and maps for sale, theater with orientation slide program, and interactive videos are available at all three centers.
Park Headquarers: Park Road.
Visitor Access Center: near park entrance on Park Road.
Eielson Visitor Center: Park Road.

Nuts and Bolts

Entrance Fee: $3/person, good for seven days. Under 17: free.
Park Open: All year.
Permits: Required for campground and backcountry camping.
In Emergency: Inside the park call 683-9100; outside the park, or if no answer, call 911.
Acreage: 4,716,726 (national park); 1,311,365 (national preserve)

Practical Advisory

Seasons

Most visitors come between late May and mid-September. Summer: Cool and wet; snow can occur. Temperatures range from 30° to 90°. Unpredictable weather may delay the opening of or close the road and some facilities. Snowdrifts persist in some protected hollows. Winter: Long and cold; the land is covered with snow from October into May. Mount McKinley: Can be cloud-hidden as much as 75 percent of the summer. Temperatures at the summit are severe even in summer.

Special Advisories

- Some areas may be temporarily closed because of bear or other wildlife activity.
- Avoid encounters with bears and inform yourself of what to do if one occurs.
- Be aware that crossing glacial rivers is treacherous.

Facilities for Disabled

Obtain a copy of "Access Information for the Differently Abled" from the superintendent.

Travel Advisory

Entrance

Highway 3, 240 miles north of Anchorage and 120 miles south of Fairbanks.

Transportation

Airports: The nearest major airports are at Fairbanks and Anchorage. There is a smaller airport at Talkeetna.

Bus Service: Several companies provide service in summer: Denali Express, (800) 327-7651; Alaska Sightseeing Tours, (907) 276-1305; Grey Line of Alaska/Westours, (907) 277-5581.

Train Service: The Alaska Railroad provides daily summer passenger service to the park from Anchorage and Fairbanks. Passenger service is limited in winter. Alaska Railroad Corporation, (800) 544-0552.

Rental Cars: Available in Fairbanks, Anchorage, and Wasilla.

Attractions

The major feature of the park is *Mount McKinley*. It provides a scenic backdrop and can be viewed from many areas of the vast park land. Since private vehicles are restricted beyond the beginning of the park road, the Park Service supplies buses that travel farther into the park for scenic views and for hikes into the surrounding *subarctic terrain* of *forests, tundra, glaciers*, and *wildlife*.

Accommodations

Lodge

Denali National Park Hotel: Near the park entrance; open late spring to early autumn. Reservations: ARA Denali Park Hotel, P.O. Box 87, Denali National Park, AK 99755; (907) 683-2215 (summer) or (907) 276-7234 (winter).

Campgrounds and Picnic Areas

Register for all campsites in person at the Visitor Access Center; 14-day maximum, $12/ night. Campfires are allowed only in certain campgrounds. Trash must be packed out. Food must be stored in the bear-resistant food lockers at each campground or in closed vehicles. Open approximately May through September, except for Riley Creek, which is open all year.

Riley Creek Campground: Accessible by private vehicle. Half a mile west of Highway 3; 102 sites; toilets; water in summer only.

Morino Campground: Accessible without vehicle. Mile 1.5; 15 sites, four persons/site; toilets, water.

Savage River Campground: Accessible by private vehicle. Mile 12; 34 sites; toilets, water.

Sanctuary River Campground: Accessible by bus. Mile 22; seven sites; tents only; pit toilets, water.

Teklanika River Campground: Accessible by private vehicle. Mile 29; 50 sites; pit toilets, water.

Igloo Creek Campground: Accessible by bus. Mile 34; seven sites; tents only; pit toilets, water.

Wonder Lake Campground: Accessible by bus. Mile 85; 28 sites; tents only; toilets, water.

Picnic Area: Near Riley Creek Campground; tables.

Restaurant

Denali National Park Hotel: Near the park entrance; open late spring to early autumn; dining room.

Activities

Scenic Bus Rides

Private vehicles are barred from most of the park road. Buses travel from the Visitor Access Center to Eielson Visitor Center and Wonder Lake. Buses make stops for wildlife viewing and at toilets. You may get on or off the bus anywhere along the park road, except in closed areas. Buses are in heavy demand during July and August; check at the Visitor Access Center for information and schedules. The round trip between the Visitor Access Center and Eielson Visitor Center takes eight hours. The round trip between Eielson Visitor Center and Wonder Lake takes an additional three hours. There is no food service; bring food and drink, warm clothing, and rain gear.

The Denali Wildlife Bus Tour and the Denali Natural History Bus Tour are available through the park concessioner in summer. A guide and food are provided. Contact Denali National Park Hotel for reservations at (907) 683-2215 in summer or (907) 276-7234 in winter. There is a fee.

Hiking

Before setting out, check at Visitor Access Center for backcountry information and to find out which areas are closed to hiking. Denali offers hikes for both novice and experienced hikers. The only established park trails, mostly short loops, are near the hotel. For other hiking, you can be dropped off by the buses anywhere you want to start walking. After your hike, return to the road and flag down another bus; they run frequently.

Mountaineering

All Mount McKinley and Mount Foraker climbers must register with the park superintendent. Groups heading for other peaks are urged to register. For information write: Talkeetna Ranger Station, Box 588, Talkeetna, AK 99676, or call (907) 733-2231.

Air Tours

Aircraft can be chartered for "flightseeing" tours. Arrange with Denali Air (907) 683-2261 or other commercial operators.

Fishing

Most park rivers contain a milky suspension of pulverized silt that fish can't tolerate. Arctic grayling can be caught in a few clear mountain streams. Lake (mackinaw) trout are caught in Wonder Lake. Limits—per person, per day—on take. You may not use live bait or fish eggs.

Bicycling

Bicyclists may travel the park road only. A copy of the rules of the road can be picked up at the Visitor Access Center.

Ranger-Led Programs

Naturalists offer walks, hikes, evening programs, and dogsled demonstrations. Check the Visitor Access Center, hotel, and campground bulletin boards for schedules.

The subtropical world that is the Everglades is a complex mix of plant and animal life unlike any other in the United States. Probably the best-known aspect of the area is the marshland teeming with tall sawgrass. But the park also encompasses several other forest types and a variety of native animal life. The lifeblood of this varied community—in fact, the most important feature to the maintenance of the Everglades' unique character—is its water.

Fresh water from the north flows slowly and gently through the Everglades in a shallow river, 50 miles wide and only six inches deep, that empties into Florida Bay on the Gulf Coast. The tall sawgrass rooted in the river inspired the local Native American name, *Pahayokee*, or "Grassy Water." The level of this water flow changes with the seasons. The wet season begins with the spring rains, which eventually turn into torrential downpours and thunderstorms in the summer. Winter is a much drier time in the park, with the water slowing to a trickle and eventually stopping altogether, leaving only puddles.

The behavior of the park's wildlife fluctuates along with the water flow. Summer's high water allows animals the freedom to roam wherever they choose throughout the land. In the winter, they must congregate around or in the limited water supply, and thus many of the park's inhabitants can be seen from the nature trails. The best-known of these inhabitants are the numerous birds, 400 species in all. One of the most beautiful is the roseate spoonbill, a large bright-pink wading bird often mistaken for the flamingo. Egrets, herons, and ibises are some of the more frequently seen birds, while bald eagles, pelicans, black skimmers, and various shorebirds are also spotted. To maintain the number and variety of birds, most of the small islands in the bay are protected refuges for nesting birds.

Among the other animal life in the park are gray foxes, raccoons, opossums, and more than 20 types of native snakes. The warm waters are home to alligators, various fish, porpoises, and sharks. There are 14 endangered species living within the protection of the park, including the Florida panther, manatee, Everglades mink, green sea turtle, short-tailed hawk, and peregrine falcon. To preserve another endangered species, the crocodile, a sanctuary seasonally closed to visitors is maintained. The number of flying insects in the park intensifies during the hotter and more humid weather of the summer. Most notable are the mosquitoes, which, although irritating beyond endurance to humans, are essential to the area's food chain.

Dominating much of the landscape for miles and miles is the sawgrass that grows in the marshy river; some of it is 10 feet tall. In other areas of the park, clusters of hardwood trees, including mahogany, form islands called hammocks ranging in size from a few feet to hundreds of acres. As the river nears the ocean and fresh water mixes with salt water, the marshy grasses, hammocks, and pine woods give way to dense

thickets of mangroves. Mangroves are important for the food and shelter they offer to both land and sea animals.

The fresh water in the river flowing through the Everglades is essential to the lives of its inhabitants. In recent years, how-ever, the ongoing population growth in southern Florida has created demand for other uses of this water. The Everglades, facing problems in getting sufficient water to maintain life, are struggling to survive.

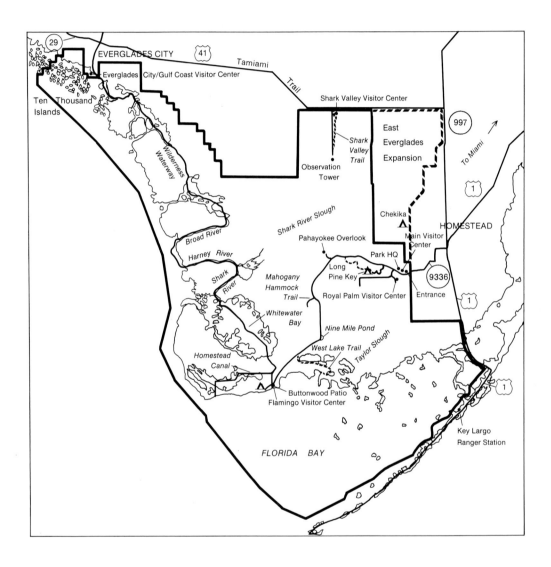

Further Information

Write or call: Information, Everglades National Park, 40001 State Road 9336, Homestead, FL 33034-6733; (305) 242-7700

Visitor Information

Park Headquarters: Near park entrance.
Main Visitor Center: Near park entrance; 15-minute introductory film, displays, information.
Royal Palm Visitor Center: Near park entrance.
Flamingo Visitor Center: Exhibits depicting the flora, fauna, and natural history of the Flamingo area.
Everglades City/Gulf Coast Visitor Center: Displays of typical shore and marine life; information.
Shark Valley Visitor Center: Information, tram-tour tickets.

Please note: The park sustained damage from Hurricane Andrew in 1992. Contact the park before you visit for information on availability of services.

Nuts and Bolts

Entrance Fee: $5/vehicle or $3/person arriving by other means. Under 17 free. Good for seven days; charged only if you enter the park through the main entrance. Shark Valley or Chekika: $3/vehicle or $1/person, good for seven days. (May be applied against the main entrance fee during the applicable seven-day period.)
Park Open: All year.
Permits: Required for backcountry camping. Florida fishing license is required.
In Emergency: Call 242-7700.
Acreage: 1,506,539

Practical Advisory

Seasons

A subtropical climate with average rainfall of 60 inches per year. Winter: Dry and generally clear with moderate temperatures, although a rare cold front can create near-freezing conditions. Average high temperatures are in the 70s to 80s, with lows in the 50s. Summer: Wet with heavy rains falling during torrential downpours, and lightning storms from late May through October, the hurricane season. High temperatures are in the 80s to 90s; lows are in the 60s.

Special Advisories

- Watch for poisonous snakes.
- Be well prepared for mosquitoes, particularly in the warmer, wetter months of summer. Use insect repellent and wear protective clothing.
- Watch your footing when hiking off-trail. Mucky soil, holes, and sharp-edged rocks can make walking tricky.
- Airboats, swamp buggies, and all-terrain vehicles are not allowed in the park.
- Waterskiing and jet-skiing are also barred.
- Swimming is not encouraged: Freshwater ponds have alligators; saltwater areas, shallow with mud bottoms and poor underwater visibility, have sharks and barracudas.

Facilities for Disabled

The Anhinga, Gumbo Limbo, Pineland, Mahogany Hammock, West Lake, Eco Pond, and Shark Valley trails are wheelchair-accessible.

Travel Advisory

Entrances

East: Route 9336 for 10 miles southwest of Homestead to main entrance.

Northwest: Route 29 for 20 miles south of Highway 84 to Everglades City.

North: 35 miles west of downtown Miami on Highway 41 (Tamiami Trail) to Shark Valley.

East: Six miles west of Route 997 on SW 168th Street to Chekika.

Transportation

There is no public transportation to the park.

Airports: Miami International Airport; 50 miles from main entrance.

Rental Cars: At Miami International Airport.

Attractions

The major feature of the park is its diverse *native plant and animal life*. Most notable, and best-known, is the *marshland* with its *sawgrass*. Also of interest are the many waterways including the *rivers*, *bays*, and *ponds* and their inhabitants. *Flamingo* and *Everglades City* are areas of great activity. A park road travels through part of the park and permits good views. Because so much of the park is water, however, it can only be seen by walking on trails and boardwalks or by boating on the waterways.

Accommodations

Lodge

Flamingo Lodge, Marina, and Outpost Resort: At Flamingo, the southern tip of the park. Motel rooms and housekeeping cottages; swimming pool. For reservations: Flamingo Lodge, Marina, and Outpost Resort, Box 428, Flamingo, FL 33030; (305) 253-2241 (this is the phone number for all activities and facilities offered by the lodge/marina). Limited facilities May 1–October 31.

Campgrounds

First-come, first-served; 14-day limit from December 1 to March 31; total of 30 days per year. During winter, campgrounds normally fill every night.

Long Pine Key Campground: 108 sites; water, tables, grills, tent and trailer pads, rest rooms, dump station; $8/night.

Flamingo Campground: 235 drive-in sites at $8/night and 60 walk-in sites (tents only) at $4/night; water, tables, grills, tent and trailer pads, rest rooms, dump station.

Chekika Campground: 20 sites; rest rooms, dump station, water; $8/night.

Backcountry Camping: 48 campsites accessible by boat. Most are chickees, elevated wooden platforms with a roof and chemical toilet. Length of stay and number of people restricted. Use self-contained cooking stoves.

Restaurant

Flamingo Lodge, Marina, and Outpost Resort: At Flamingo; dining room; closed May 1–October 31.

Buttonwood Patio: At Flamingo; dining room for lunch.

Activities

Scenic Drives

The main park road provides the only vehicle access through the park. Beginning at the main visitor center at the park entrance and ending 38 miles later at Flamingo, the southern tip of the park, the drive takes approximately 45 minutes when done nonstop. There are, however, many self-guided trails and points of interest off the road, including Anhinga Trail, Gumbo Limbo Trail, Pahayokee Overlook, and Nine Mile Pond.

Hiking

To fully experience the park, take the time to walk the boardwalks and trails. Trails range from easy walks of less than ¼ mile to more strenuous ones 14 miles long. Cross-country hiking is permitted but difficult.

Fishing

Inland and coastal waters of the Everglades are popular fishing grounds. There is large-mouth-bass fishing in freshwater ponds. The saltwater species most sought after are snapper, redfish, and trout. Both Florida and special federal fishing regulations apply. Obtain a copy of the regulations at the visitor center and find out which areas are closed to fishing. Charter fishing trips are offered at the lodge/marina in Flamingo (see "Accommodations," above).

Boating

The park offers many boating opportunities, including marked canoe trails, rivers, White-water Bay, and Florida Bay. The Flamingo marina can accommodate boats up to 60 feet long with boat-trailer parking and free launch access. Most bay islands are closed to boat landings. The Flamingo lodge/marina rents small powered skiffs, houseboats, patio boats, and canoes. Canoes can also be rented from a concessioner in Everglades City. Navigational charts are strongly suggested. There are many canoe trails in the park, including the Wilderness Waterway, which is the longest (99 miles). Other trails begin near Flamingo. The rivers near Everglades City are also popular for canoeing. Some designated canoe trails have motor-size restrictions; some wilderness trails prohibit motors.

Boat Tours

Concession-operated sightseeing-boat tours leave from Everglades City (contact Sammy Hamilton Boat Tours, [813] 695-2591) and from the lodge/marina at Flamingo. Boat tours from Everglades City go into the Ten Thousand Islands region and the mangrove swamps of the northwestern Everglades. Those at Flamingo explore the Florida Bay and backcountry waters. Fees are charged.

Tram Tours

Guided excursions designed to interpret the plant and animal life of some wilderness areas depart from the Flamingo lodge/marina during the months of November through April. A fee is charged.

Ranger-Led Activities

Naturalists give hikes, talks, canoe trips, tram tours, demonstrations, and campfire programs during the year. Some examples are sunrise bird walks, paddles out into Florida Bay, a cross-country "slough slog," and a moonlight tram tour. Schedules are available at visitor centers.

Shark Valley

Shark Valley is a separate northern section of the park. A two-hour tram ride on the 15-mile loop road to the observation tower leaves several times a day. Contact Shark Valley Tram Tours, (305) 221-8455; a fee is charged. There is also a nature trail; rental bicycles are available. A separate entrance fee is charged.

Chekika

The former Chekika State Recreation Area was added to the park in 1991 as part of the East Everglades Expansion. There are nature trails and a swimming lagoon. A separate entrance fee is charged.

The northernmost of all the national parks is the remote and totally undeveloped Gates of the Arctic. There are no roads, no trails, no services of any kind in the park. There are just miles and miles of vastness, unpeopled and wild, offering properly skilled visitors a true wilderness experience.

The park was given its unusual name by Robert Marshall, who explored the North Fork Koyukuk River in northern Alaska in the 1920s and 1930s. After naming the Frigid Crags and Boreal Mountain on either side of the river, he called these two peaks the "gates" from the Brooks Range into the Arctic. Wide valleys add contrast to the high, ragged peaks of the range, the tallest being Mount Igikpak at over 8,500 feet. Although there are six designated wild rivers, most of the countless rivers and pristine lakes in the park are still unnamed. In fact, most of the landmarks on topographical maps of the area are nameless.

Seasons in this land north of the Arctic Circle are dramatic. Winters are long, dark, and frigid; most activity stops, while sub-zero temperatures prevail. Summers are short, and plant and animal inhabitants must grow and reproduce rapidly to accommodate the limited warmth and sunlight. Wildlife found in the park includes grizzly and black bears, moose, Dall sheep, wolves, and snowshoe hares. Some of the most notable animals being preserved in the park are the vast herds of western Arctic caribou, a major part of whose range is here. In springtime the few resident birds are joined by migratory species. Because the Arctic vegetation is sparse, wildlife is widely dispersed in order for animals to have enough food to sustain themselves.

The southern slopes of the park are taiga, made up of sparse forests of mainly black spruce. Above the tree line, which is at about 2,000 feet, are dwarfed shrub-size birch, alder, and poplar. The higher mountainous areas are alpine tundra. Alder thickets and tussocks are found in valleys and on slopes here. North of the Brooks Range is the treeless Arctic tundra. The entire region rests on a bed of permafrost—permanently frozen ground up to 2,000 feet thick—that usually begins only a few inches below the surface. The most common plants in the tundra are low-growing grasses and sedges dotted with dwarf flowers.

There is evidence that in the past nomadic hunters and gatherers traveled through what is now the park, from the southern slopes of the mountains to the Arctic coast. There are virtually no signs of these travelers to be found in the park today. What can be found are residents who still use the park's resources to support their subsistence way of life. Nunamiut Eskimos in the small village of Anaktuvuk Pass continue to subsist mostly as their ancestors did before them. Athabaskan peoples mostly live in the taiga and foothills. Camps, fishnets, traps, and other equipment found in the park belong to these people and should not be disturbed.

The uncompromising and utterly remote character of the park demands that all visitors be fully self-sufficient and experienced in outdoor survival skills.

NATIONAL PARK SERVICE

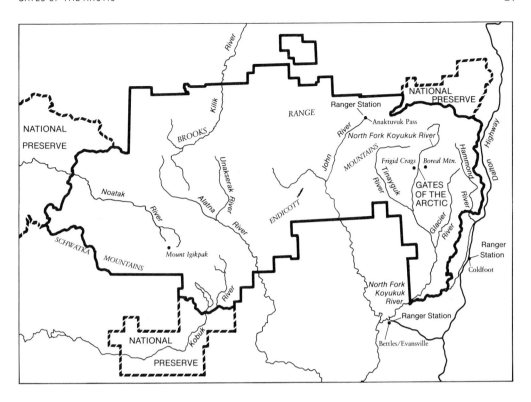

Further Information

Write or call: Superintendent, Gates of the Arctic National Park, P.O. Box 74680, Fairbanks, AK 99707-4680; (907) 456-0281

Visitor Information

Park Headquarters: Located in Fairbanks.
Ranger stations: Located in Bettles, Anaktuvuk Pass, and Coldfoot.

Nuts and Bolts

Entrance Fee: None.
Park Open: All year.
Permits: Alaska fishing license and Alaska hunting license (hunting is allowed only in the adjacent preserve) are required.
In Emergency: Call park headquarters at 456-0281, Bettles at 692-5494, or Anaktuvuk Pass at 661-3520.
Acreage: 7,523,888 (in the national park)

Practical Advisory

Seasons

Rapid, severe changes in the weather are common. Summer: Short and mild. On southern slopes, midsummer temperatures in the lowlands may rise to 80°, with lows near 50°. The highlands are cool, and on northern slopes temperatures range from 70° down to 40°.

Freezing temperatures may occur at any time, but especially from mid-August on. August is usually very rainy. There is continuous daylight from mid-April to mid-August. Winter: Long and cold. Freezing temperatures return in September, and rivers freeze by early October. Temperatures of $-20°$ to $-50°$ from November to March. There is little snow, but what falls stays. Spring: Brief, with thawing beginning in late April and breakup in mid-May.

Special Advisories

- All visitors must be fully self-sufficient and experienced in outdoor survival skills.
- Use safe techniques for crossing streams and rivers, which can be hazardous.
- Avoid encounters with bears; know what to do if one occurs.

- Unstable clumps of tundra grasses can throw you or cause you to twist an ankle.
- Leave an itinerary with friends, stick to it, and notify them when you complete your trip.
- Always allow for extra time and take several extra days' worth of food supplies to cover emergencies and delays caused by weather conditions.
- Clothing should include many layers—even in summer—for warmth in subfreezing temperatures; good rain gear is essential at all times.
- Insect repellent, head nets, and mosquito-proof tents are highly recommended.
- You may carry firearms for protection, but shooting except for protection is prohibited in the park.

Travel Advisory

There are no trails and no designated routes into the park. Scheduled flights serve Bettles/Evansville and Anaktuvuk Pass from Fairbanks. From those points, or from Fairbanks, you can charter small aircraft into the park. Contact park headquarters for a list of licensed air taxis; reservations are recommended.

The park can also be reached from the Dalton Highway, although hiking is a challenge. Drive as far north as Dietrich Camp/Disaster Creek, about 300 miles north of Fairbanks.

Attractions

Frigid Crags and *Boreal Mountain*—the so-called "Gates of the Arctic"—are the best-known features in the park. They lie within a scenic *Arctic landscape* that also includes the other mountains in the *Brooks Range*, six *designated wild rivers*, many other *rivers* and *lakes*, and *native wildlife*. The entire park is wild, without trails or roads, so you are on your own in exploring it.

Accommodations

There are no developed facilities, not even campgrounds, in the park. Camp only on gravel bars or areas of hardy heath or moss.

Activities

Hiking

There are no roads or trails in the park. Obtain U.S. Geological Survey topographical maps and study them before arrival. Both small and large tracts of privately owned lands are located in and next to parklands. These are not open for public use or travel without the owner's permission. There are free public-access hiking routes across private lands; ask a ranger for route directions.

Fishing

Grayling are found in clear streams and lakes, lake trout in deep lakes, char in north slope streams and some lakes, and sheefish and chum salmon in the Kobuk and Alatna Rivers. Catch-and-release fishing is encouraged due to limited reproduction in these cold waters and short seasons. To prevent bear problems, avoid getting fish odors on clothing and equipment.

Hunting

Sport hunting is prohibited in the park, but permitted in the preserve in season.

Guides

Guides can be hired for many kinds of trips into the park, including backpacking and hiking, hunting, lake touring, mountaineering, photography, river trips, sport fishing, winter backcountry (skiing, snowshoeing, etc.), dog-sled tours, and "flightseeing." Backpacking and river trips are the predominant activities. The period from mid-June to September is best for hiking. July and August are the best time to take float trips. March and April are the best months for skiing.

Glacier National Park offers an abundance of spectacular natural scenery. Jagged mountain peaks, deep-green forests, and wildflower-strewn meadows are sprinkled with pristine lakes and sparkling streams. In fact, few places in the park are out of sight or sound of water. There are over 200 bodies of water, from Lake McDonald—the largest lake with a cascading waterfall—to the small lakes, called tarns, on the slopes of the mountains.

The northern border of the park adjoins Canada's Waterton Lakes National Park. In 1932, the two parks united to become the Waterton-Glacier International Peace Park, the first of its kind. The establishment of this joint park recognizes that the park land in both countries has many of the same resources and is the shared territory of gray wolves, grizzly bears, bald eagles, and other species. It is possible to go back and forth over the international boundary at certain border crossings.

Although there are more than 50 glaciers here, the park was not named for them. Its name pays homage to the vast glaciers of the last ice age, which dramatically carved today's outstanding landscape. For 3 million years, this land was being made and remade by ice. At least four times, glaciers covered the land and then retreated, changing the shape of the terrain each time.

Narrow glens were widened into U-shaped valleys, long deep basins were carved out of the sides of the mountains, and round peaks were cut into sharp ridges.

When the glaciers retreated, they occasionally left debris at the end of a stream of meltwater. The water flow, blocked by the debris, would eventually form the beautiful lakes and other bodies of water in the park. The glaciers in the park today are a mere 4,000 years old and are moving much more slowly than their predecessors. Sperry Glacier, the largest, moves only about 30 feet per year, which is considered a snail's pace in comparison to the former glaciers.

The park straddles the Continental Divide. The eastern and western areas of the park are separated by the Rocky Mountains and can be as different as night and day in climate. The moister western side produces deep forests of ponderosa pine, Douglas fir, larch, hemlock, and even red cedar trees, some of which are over 500 years old. The drier eastern side has shorter trees, including Engelmann spruce, subalpine fir, and lodgepole pine. During a brief but brilliant blooming season, the meadows are blanketed with wildflowers, including gentians, asters, monkeyflowers, and bear grass, the official park flower. Actually a misnamed member of the lily family, bear grass has stiff, grasslike leaves and is topped with spikes of small white flowers.

An interesting seasonal event takes place near the southern boundary of the park: Each spring, mountain goats come to lick an exposed riverbank cliff. The cliff contains mineral salts, which the goats use to satisfy their need for sodium. Usually one to 12 goats can be seen at a time. Other ani-

GLACIER NATIONAL PARK

mals making their home in the park include two groups of wolves called the North and South Camas Pack (they are being tracked by park rangers), grizzlies, ptarmigan, bighorn sheep, golden eagles, and moose.

Many parts of the park landscape have interesting and colorful-sounding names, such as Two Medicine Lake, Scalplock Mountain, and Going-to-the-Sun Road. Many of these names are from the days

when the Blackfoot tribe of Native Americans lived here. The eastern part of the park was part of their reservation until they sold it in 1896. Many areas were used by tribal elders as vision quest sites, where they underwent four days of fasting for the benefit of the tribe. Presently, their home adjoins Glacier's eastern border. However, the land in the park is still sacred to them.

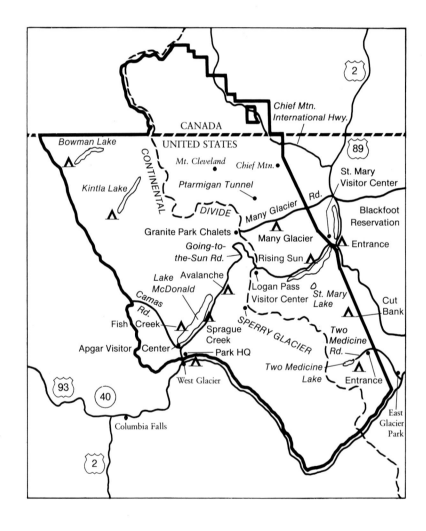

Further Information

Write or call: Superintendent, Glacier National Park, West Glacier, MT 59936; (406) 888-5441

Visitor Information

Glacier Park Headquarters: Just inside the park at the west entrance.
Apgar Visitor Center: In Apgar Village. (Closed mid-December to mid-May.)
St. Mary Visitor Center: At east entrance of the park. (Closed mid-October to mid-May.)

Logan Pass Visitor Center: At the summit of Going-to-the-Sun Road. (Closed from mid-September to mid-June.)

Nuts and Bolts

Entrance Fee: $5/vehicle for seven days, $3/person arriving by other means.
Park Open: All year, but most roads are closed in winter.
Permits: Required for backcountry camping.
In Emergency: Contact a park ranger.
Acreage: 1,013,572.43

Practical Advisory

Seasons

Weather is unpredictable; sudden rain, hail, or snow may occur at any time of year. Summer evenings are cool. At high elevations, you can experience freezing temperatures even in midsummer. High temperatures in the summer are in the upper 70s; lows are in the 40s. Winter highs are in the low 30s, and lows are in the teens.

Special Advisories

- Avoid encounters with bears and know what to do if one occurs.
- Carry and use insect repellent.

Facilities for Disabled

The Apgar and St. Mary visitor centers, the Trail of the Cedars, the evening slide and campfire programs in campgrounds, and the Apgar bike path (made of asphalt) are wheelchair-accessible. For the hearing-impaired, some texts and written descriptions of talks and walks are available, and limited sign-language interpretation is available on request. Also, some tactile exhibits at the visitor centers and some interpretive programs are available. For the visually impaired, a tape recording of the park brochure is available on request, as are small-scale relief maps of Apgar and St. Mary visitor centers.

Travel Advisory

Entrances

West: U.S. 2 from Columbia Falls.

East: U.S. 89 from Great Falls.

Transportation

Airports: Glacier Park International Airport in Kalispell, Montana.

Bus Service: There is a regularly scheduled commercial bus from Glacier Park International Airport to West Glacier. Call (406) 752-4022.

Train Service: Amtrak stops at both East Glacier (Glacier Park Station) and West Glacier (Belton Station). Visitors arriving by train and staying in concessioner-operated lodges can make arrangements to be picked up.

Rental Cars: Available in both East and West Glacier, at Glacier Park International Airport, and in Lethbridge and Calgary, Alberta.

In-Park Transportation: Scheduled bus transportation is available between in-park lodges, hotels, and motor inns. There is also transportation to other areas. Schedules are available at all Glacier Park, Inc.–operated locations. For reservations, contact Glacier Park, Inc. (See "Accommodations," below.)

Attractions

The park is most known for the natural beauty of its *mountains, lakes, glaciers,* and *forests.* Many scenic views can be enjoyed from the park roads, especially the *Going-to-the-Sun Road,* which crosses the park. The many lakes, most notably *Lake McDonald, St. Mary Lake, Two Medicine Lake,* and *Swiftcurrent Lake,* are popular for boating. Other scenic features of the park include *Mount Cleveland* and *Sprague Creek.*

Accommodations

Lodges

Village Inn Motel: In Apgar; open May through September. For reservations contact Glacier Park, Inc., in summer at Glacier Park Lodge, P.O. Box 147, East Glacier, MT 59434, (406) 226-5551; in winter at Greyhound Tower, MS 1210, Phoenix, AZ 85077, (602) 248-6000.

Apgar Village Lodge: In Apgar; open May through September. For reservations call (406) 888-5484.

Lake McDonald Lodge: Lodge, cabins, and motel at Lake McDonald; open June through Setpember. For reservations contact Glacier Park, Inc. (See Village Inn Motel listing.)

Rising Sun Motor Inn: Motel and cabins at St. Mary; open June through September. For reservations contact Glacier Park, Inc. (See Village Inn Motel listing.)

Many Glacier Hotel: At St. Mary; open June through early September. For reservations contact Glacier Park, Inc. (See Village Inn Motel listing.)

Swiftcurrent Motor Inn: Motel and cabins; open from June through September. For reservations contact Glacier Park, Inc. (See Village Inn Motel listing.)

Granite Park and Sperry Chalets: Backcountry chalets. Open July through early September. For reservations contact Belton Chalets, Inc., P.O. Box 188, West Glacier, MT 59936, (406) 888-5511.

Campgrounds and Picnic Areas

First-come, first-served. Most campgrounds are open approximately June through September; check with the park authorities for exact dates. Apgar, Bowman Lake, Cut Bank, Kintla Lake, St. Mary, and Two Medicine are open for primitive camping in winter (some until closed by snow).

Apgar Campground: 196 sites; toilets, water, dump station, picnic area; $8/night.

Avalanche Campground: 87 sites; toilets, water, dump station, picnic area; $8/night.

Bowman Lake Campground: 48 sites; reachable by unimproved access road; water, picnic area; $6/night.

Cut Bank Campground: 19 sites; reachable by unimproved access road; water; $6/night.

Fish Creek Campground: 180 sites; toilets, water, dump station, picnic area; $8/night.

Kintla Lake Campground: 13 sites; reachable by unimproved access road; water; $6/night.

Many Glacier Campground: 117 sites; toilets, water, dump station, picnic area; $8/night.

Rising Sun Campground: 83 sites; toilets, water, dump station, picnic area; $8/night.

Sprague Creek Campground: 25 sites; toilets, water, picnic area; no towed units; $8/night. Two campsites are designated for bicyclists' use and held for this purpose until seven P.M. Each site can be used by six bicyclists. Cost is $2/person.

St. Mary Campground: 156 sites; toilets, water, dump station; $8/night.

Two Medicine Campground: 99 sites; toilets, water, dump station, picnic area; $8/night.

Backcountry Camping: Backcountry campsites available.

Picnic Areas: Several, off the main roads.

Restaurants

Eddie's Restaurant: In Apgar; dining room; open May through September.

The Cedar Tree Deli: In Apgar; open June through September.

Lake McDonald Lodge: Dining room; breakfast, lunch, and dinner. Also coffee shop and snack bar; breakfast.

Stockade Lounge: In the Lake McDonald Lodge; cocktail lounge.

Rising Sun Motor Inn: At St. Mary; coffee shop and snack bar.

Many Glacier Hotel: Dining room; breakfast, lunch, and dinner.

Heidi's Snackbar: In Many Glacier Hotel; breakfast.

Swiss Lounge and St. Moritz: In Many Glacier Hotel; cocktail lounges.

Swiftcurrent Motor Inn: Coffee shop; breakfast, lunch, and dinner.

Activities

Scenic Drives

The 50-mile Going-to-the-Sun Road, one of the most spectacular in the country, is the only road that crosses the park, traveling from St. Mary at one end across the Continental Divide to West Glacier at the other. The high point—6,680 feet—is at Logan Pass. Because of the mountainous terrain, the narrowness of the road, and the scenery along the way, plan to take 1½ to three hours or more to travel from one side to the other. There are vehicle length restrictions—check with the superintendent for current regulations. The road is closed in winter. There are several other beautiful roads: Camas Creek Road, running 10 miles through forests of different ages, which offers roadside exhibits; Chief Mountain International Highway, which takes you to Waterton Lakes National Park in Canada and offers a clear view of Chief Mountain; Two Medicine Road; and Many Glacier Road.

Hiking

There are more than 700 miles of trails, at various difficulty levels, throughout the park. They include a self-guided trail through alpine meadows, beginning behind the Logan Pass Visitor Center and ending at Hidden Lake Overlook; the one-mile Sun Point Nature Trail, which begins at the Sun Point Picnic Area and acquaints you with the balance among the geology, plants, and animals of Glacier; the ½-mile boardwalk Trail of the Cedars through a cedar-and-hemlock forest, starting near the entrance to Avalanche Campground; and the trails leading from the vicinity of Many Glacier Hotel to the glaciers, lakes, peaks, and lookouts, and the famous Ptarmigan tunnel. Information and maps are at the visitor centers. Guided one- to seven-day backcountry hikes are offered by Glacier Wilderness Guides. In summer call (406) 888-5466, in winter (406) 862-4802.

Boat Tours

From June through September, the Glacier Park Boat Co., (406) 732-4480, offers nar-rated boat tours of Lake McDonald (departing from the Lake McDonald Lodge boat dock, lake side), St. Mary Lake (departing from the Rising Sun boat dock), Swiftcurrent and Josephine lakes (departing from the Many Glacier Hotel dock, lake side of hotel), and Two Medicine Lake (departing from the Two Medicine Lake boat dock). Fees are charged.

Boating

Rowboats, canoes, and motor boats can be rented at Two Medicine Lake boat dock and the Many Glacier Hotel dock from the Glacier Park Boat Co. (see "Boat Tours," above) or at Lake McDonald from the Lake McDonald Boat Co. (in summer, [406] 888-5227; in winter, [406] 837-4466).

Horseback Riding

Saddle-horse rides are available to scenic points in the park. Trips range from hour-long to day-long and are accompanied by guides who can tell you about the area. Glacier Park Outfitters—in summer, (406) 732-5597—offers trips from June through September, starting at the Apgar Corral, the Lake McDonald Corral, and the Many Glacier Corral. Fees are charged.

Swimming

The water in the park is cold. Suddenly plunging in and staying in for long periods can cause hypothermia. Children can become chilled just by playing in the water. Never swim alone; there are dangerous swift-flowing streams and slippery rocks and logs.

Fishing

Pick up a copy of the fishing regulations before you begin. Some waters are restricted to certain angling techniques or are closed for spawning purposes. You can rent fishing equipment at the Lake McDonald Boat Co. (see "Boating," above) in Apgar from May through September.

Bicycling

Bicycles are restricted to established roadways. They are not allowed on backcountry or nature trails. They are barred from Going-to-the-Sun Road at certain times of the day because of heavy traffic. It takes about three hours to ride from Logan Creek to Logan Pass. You can rent bicycles at the Village Inn Motel (see "Accommodations," above) in Apgar from May through September.

Mountaineering

Climbers are requested to register with a ranger before starting. Climbing the peaks is dangerous due to loose, crumbly sedimentary rocks that provide unstable handholds and footing.

Native American Programs

Speakers from the Blackfoot tribe lecture on their tribal history, culture, and legends at Rising Sun Campfire Circle, Two Medicine, and Many Glacier campgrounds. Check with the visitor centers for schedules.

Winter Sports

Cross-country skiing and snowshoeing are permitted in the park in winter. Trails are available.

Naturalist Programs

Park naturalists offer evening slide and campfire programs in the campgrounds. Check at the visitor centers for schedules. The Glacier Institute offers one- to seven-day outdoor classes about the wildlife, flowers, history, and geology of the park. Call for information: (406) 756-3911.

Visiting Glacier Bay National Park is much like going back in time to the days when the earth was emerging from the last ice age. Retreating glaciers and the land they have recently uncovered can be seen, as can newly calved icebergs floating in the frigid waters of the bay and the fjords. The park presents a vivid lesson in how our earth changes and adapts over time.

The glaciers in Glacier Bay are formed from snow on the peaks of the Fairweather Range. Without enough warmth to melt the snow fully, layers pile upon layers until eventually the snow becomes a thick mass of ice. Gravity causes the ice mass to stretch or move slowly down the side of the slopes in the form of a glacier. Those that reach the water are called tidewater glaciers. There are 16 tidewater glaciers in the park. At some points, huge blocks of ice up to 200 feet high break off, or "calve," and crash into the water, creating waves up to 35 feet high. These blocks form icebergs that eventually melt into the water. Larger ones can last a week or more before melting, however. Often the ice will take underlying pieces of the mountain's surface with it, eroding the land. This is how the fjords were formed.

When Captain George Vancouver was exploring this part of southeastern Alaska's coast in 1794, there was no bay, only a sheet of ice more than 4,000 feet thick. By 1879, naturalist John Muir found that the ice had retreated 48 miles up the bay. By 1916 the ice was 65 miles from the mouth of the bay. The glaciers in the park are in retreat. They are covering less and less of the land with the passage of time. No glaciers anywhere else have been seen to retreat as rapidly as these.

Scientists in the park have also been able not only to make glacier observations, but also to see how nature responds when given the chance to start over from scratch. Once the glaciers have retreated, the newly bared land is barren. Plants and animals must find their way here to reinhabit it. In the park, the first plant to begin to grow after moss is dryas, important to the process of building the soil. Alder shrubs then move in and crowd out the dryas. Finally, forests of spruce and hemlock overtake the area. Each successive plant community creates new conditions that lead to its replacement. You can actually see this process in the park: The area far inland is barren; farther out is sparse but growing vegetation; and finally, there is a lush, well-developed rain forest near Bartlett Cove at the mouth of the bay.

For animals, reinhabitation is not as simple as it is for plants: Animals must either walk or swim, and do not hitch rides, as plants often do, in the air. Many have managed to find their way here, however. The animals in the park today include otters, coyotes, moose, foxes, black, brown, and grizzly bears, and mountain goats. In spring and fall the park is full of thousands of migratory ducks and geese, among them mallards and Canada geese. There are puffins, loons, herons, and various shorebirds. Dall

NATIONAL PARK SERVICE

porpoises and harbor porpoises swim in the icy waters of Glacier Bay, as do two great whales—the minke and humpback—and one smaller, the orca. The park residents also include one of the largest populations of harbor seals along the Pacific coast. They can be seen swimming or basking on rocks and icebergs.

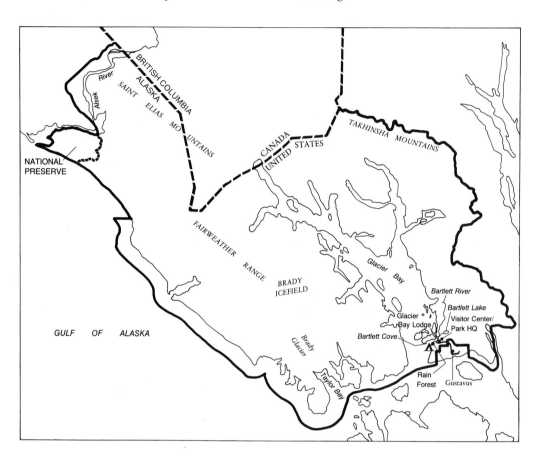

Further Information

Write or call: Superintendent, Glacier Bay National Park, Gustavus, AK 99826; (907) 697-2230

Visitor Information

Park Headquarters/Visitor Center: Upstairs in the lodge at Bartlett Cove; information, auditorium for talks, nature and history exhibits, films, slide presentations.

Nuts and Bolts

Entrance Fee: None
Park Open: All year, but visitor services are limited mid-September to late May.
Permits: Required for backcountry camping. Vessel permits are required to enter Glacier Bay from June 1 to August 31. An Alaska fishing license is required.
In Emergency: Call 697-2229. Summertime, for all backcountry and boat-related questions, call 697-2268 (daytime).
Acreage: 3,225,284 (in national park)

Practical Advisory

Seasons

Long periods of rainy, overcast, and cool weather are normal. In summer, daytime temperatures are usually 45° to 65° (55° to 75° at Bartlett Cove), with an average of 50°, but nights may cool to near freezing. Rain is the norm.

Special Advisories

- A hat, gloves, and rain gear are essential. Waterproof footgear is desirable.
- Avoid encounters with bears and know what to do if one occurs.
- Mosquitoes and biting flies may make repellent necessary in some areas.
- Before heading out, check at the visitor center on temporary closures of some areas.

Facilities for Disabled

Rest rooms, the visitor center, and two cabins at Glacier Bay Lodge are wheelchair-accessible. One section of the forest trail is accessible via a boardwalk.

Travel Advisory

Bay can be reached only by boat or plane. Travel options from mid-May through September include scheduled and charter air services, cruise ships, and charter boats. Write to the park superintendent for a complete list of companies that provide transportation to the park. Flights from Juneau land in Gustavus airfield, and buses or taxis are available to the park.

Attractions

The 16 *tidewater glaciers* are the major features of the park, along with *Glacier Bay* itself. Approaching the glaciers by boat affords the most scenic views, although it is also possible to hike the backcountry. Also of interest is the *rain forest* near Bartlett Cove.

Accommodations

Lodge

Glacier Bay Lodge: At Bartlett Cove; lodge rooms and less expensive dormitory rooms. For reservations: 520 Pike St., Suite 1610, Seattle, WA 98101; (800) 451-5952. Open May to September.

Campgrounds

Campers should attend an orientation given twice daily at the lodge.

Bartlett Cove Campground: 14-day limit; no reservations; firewood, warming hut, bear-resistant food caches; free.

Backcountry Camping: Before heading out, obtain up-to-date information on bear ac-

tivity, camping and food-storage recommendations and requirements, and more. Cookstoves are necessary: Wood is scarce and often wet. You may be dropped off by concession tour vessels originating in Bartlett Cove or Juneau; reservations are suggested.

Restaurant

Glacier Bay Lodge: At Bartlett Cove; dining room; open May to September.

Activities

Hiking

Three miles of maintained trails wind through the rain forest near Bartlett Cove. Access to the backcountry requires a dropoff by tour boat or floatplane. There are no backcountry trails, but beaches, recently deglaciated areas, and alpine meadows offer excellent hiking. Backcountry users should be self-sufficient and fully equipped and provisioned. Avoid glaciers unless you are experienced and properly equipped.

Boating and Boat Tours

Many of Glacier Bay's features of interest are easily reached by boat. Day and overnight tour boats to tidewater glaciers are available at Glacier Bay Lodge, as are charter boats. Vessels based outside the park—including cruise ships, smaller tour vessels, and charter boats—also tour Glacier Bay. Check with a travel agency. Kayaking is popular. Kayak rentals are available from Glacier Bay Sea Kayaks at (907) 697-2257. Tour boats will drop off backcountry users and their kayaks.

Private boaters planning to visit between June 1 and August 31 must contact the park

well in advance. The number of vessels is limited. Special care is essential when navigating near tidewater glaciers and icebergs.

Fishing

Fishing here is good for halibut, salmon, Dolly Varden trout, and cutthroat trout. Charter boats are available at the lodge.

Guides

Guides are available for a number of types of trips, including kayaking, backpacking, rafting down the Alsek River, hunting, and fishing.

"Flightseeing" Tours

Local "flightseeing" tours are available from Glacier Bay Airways, (907) 697-2249, or Air Excursions, (907) 697-2375.

Naturalist Programs

Park naturalists present evening programs and films daily in the auditorium, and conduct hikes and nature walks that begin at the lodge.

To visit the Grand Canyon is an experience unlike any other on earth. This enormous geological wonder is awesome, its grandeur unsurpassed. The approach to the canyon rim gives no indication of what is to come. Suddenly, the solid earth falls away, and a panorama of incredible multicolored canyon cliffs is revealed, stretching as far as the eye can see.

Looking down from the rim, you can barely see the red ribbon of the meandering Colorado River on the canyon floor. Up close, at the bottom of the canyon, it becomes more obvious what a mighty force the river is. It enters the Grand Canyon from the north between walls of limestone and sandstone. Over the next 61 miles, it flows steadily southward, at times becoming sudden, sharp rapids. The river is gritty with the sand, gravel, and rock stripped from the places it has been, including Colorado, Utah, New Mexico, and Arizona. The debris in the water helps it erode the sides of the canyon, crumbling and gouging it as it travels along.

The driving power of this mighty river is responsible for the beautiful canyon of today. For 6 to 25 million years it has been slicing away at the rock here, which originally was a level plain. The rock at the base of the cliffs is 2 billion years old. The different types of rock layers in the canyon walls respond to erosion in different ways. Some form slopes, some form cliffs, and some erode more quickly than others. This has caused the distinctive shapes of the canyon

of today. The vivid colors of many of these rock layers are due mainly to trace amounts of certain minerals, which give the canyon walls their subtle shades of red, yellow, or green.

There are several theories as to how and why the Colorado River began its mighty carving of the land to create this remarkable canyon. Scientists do not agree on any one theory. But all agree that the power of the river will continue to cut away at the Grand Canyon of today as long as the Colorado River continues to flow. It is a slow but continuous process of natural sculpture.

There are three very distinct sections of the park: the South Rim, the North Rim, and the inner canyon. Each section has a very different climate. The North Rim is the coldest and the wettest. It gets up to 26 inches of precipitation a year, compared to the South Rim's 16 inches. The South Rim, the easiest area to reach, is the most visited section of the park. The width of the canyon between the North and South rims ranges from 18 miles to less than ½ mile. The canyon ranges in width from one-tenth of a mile to 18 miles. The deeper you go into the inner canyon, the hotter and drier it gets. The floor of the canyon, on average a mile below the rims, is up to 35° hotter than the North Rim. Much of the rain that falls into the canyon evaporates before it hits the ground.

Vegetation in the three sections also varies. The North Rim contains blue spruce and fir forests not found on the other side.

PHOTO BY WOODBRIDGE WILLIAMS, NATIONAL PARK SERVICE

Ponderosa pines and oaks can also be seen. Two of the most famous inhabitants of the park are the Abert squirrel, found only on the South Rim, and the Kaibab squirrel, found only on the North. Both are descendants of the same species, the tassel-eared squirrel. But separation by the canyon for so many years has left the Abert and the

Kaibab to evolve separately until they are now considered different species.

Farther down in the canyon, the vegetation grows sparser and shorter. Piñons and junipers along the cliffs give way to dry desert scrub at the bottom, where the river is the only water source.

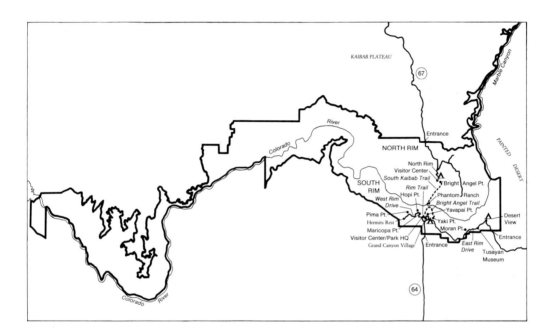

Further Information

Write or call: Superintendent, Grand Canyon National Park, P.O. Box 129, Grand Canyon, AZ 86023; (602) 638-7888

Visitor Information

Park Headquarters: South Rim at the east end of Grand Canyon Village; orientation slide program, exhibits, book sales, information.
Visitor Center: North Rim; information desk in the lobby of Grand Canyon Lodge.

Nuts and Bolts

Entrance Fee: $10/car or $4/person arriving by other means.
Park Open: South Rim open all year, North Rim open from mid-May through late October.
Permits: Required for backcountry camping; must be applied for well in advance (up to a year). Arizona fishing license is required.
In Emergency: Call 911.
Acreage: 1,218,375

Practical Advisory

Seasons

Summer: Temperatures on the South Rim are relatively pleasant—50°–80°—but thunderstorms may be a daily occurrence. Inner canyon temperatures are extreme; daytime highs at the river often exceed 100°. North Rim temperatures are 5°–10° cooler than those on the South Rim. Winter: The South Rim can have extreme weather; expect snow, icy roads, and possible road closures. Canyon views may be temporarily obscured during winter storms with heavy snow and fog; these can strike from September through May. Spring and fall: Weather is extremely unpredictable.

Special Advisories

- Use caution near the edge, guardrails exist only on portions of the rim.
- The park averages 7-8,000 feet above sea level. Walking at this elevation can be strenuous.
- Temperatures can be extreme in the inner canyon, be prepared.

Facilities for Disabled

A park "Accessibility Guide" is available at the visitor center. Or write to the park to request one.

Travel Advisory

Entrances

South Rim: Highway 64 for 60 miles north of Williams or 57 miles west of Cameron.

North Rim: Highway 67 for 45 miles south of Jacob Lake.

Transportation

Airports: Commercial airlines serve Phoenix, Flagstaff, and Las Vegas. There is limited air service into Grand Canyon airport from Las Vegas and elsewhere.

Bus Service: Greyhound provides bus service to Flagstaff. Nava-Hopi Bus Lines offers transportation between Flagstaff and the South Rim; call (602) 774-5003.

Train Service: Amtrak service is available to Flagstaff, with connecting bus service to the canyon. Grand Canyon Railway offers daily train service from Williams, Arizona, to Grand Canyon Village.

Rental Cars: Available at all airports.

In-Park Transportation: Van shuttle service is available for rim-to-rim hikers and others who need transportation to or from the North or South rim. Contact Trans Canyon Van Service, (602) 638-2820. A hikers' shuttle is available to the South Kaibab Trailhead from the Backcountry Reservations Office and Bright Angel Lodge.

Attractions

The park comprises the spectacular *Grand Canyon* itself. The multicolored cliffs of the canyon, as well as the *Colorado River* winding along its floor, can be visited and viewed in many different ways and from many different vantage points. Scenic overlooks can be reached from the paved road along the South Rim. (During the summer months, shuttle buses replace private vehicles on part of the road.) It is also possible to hike or take a mule trip either partway or all the way down into the canyon.

Other Points of Interest (Museums, Historic Sites, etc.)

The *Yavapai Museum,* ¾ mile east of the visitor center, features exhibits about the geological history of the Grand Canyon. A panorama of the canyon is visible through the museum's large windows. The *Tusayan Museum,* three miles west of Desert View, provides a glimpse of Anasazi life at Grand Canyon some 800 years ago. A self-guiding trail leads through the adjacent ruin.

Accommodations

Note: Reservations for all accommodations should be made well in advance.

Lodges

SOUTH RIM

For reservations at any of the lodges on the South Rim, contact Grand Canyon National Park Lodges, P.O. Box 699, Grand Canyon, AZ 86023, (602) 638-2401. All are in the vicinity known as Grand Canyon Village, which also contains shops and services.

Bright Angel Lodge: On the rim.

El Tovar Hotel: On the rim.

Kachina Lodge: On the rim.

Thunderbird Lodge: On the rim.

Maswik Lodge: At the west end of the Village.

Yavapai Lodge: Near Mather Center.

NORTH RIM

Grand Canyon Lodge: Open from mid-May through mid-October. For reservations: TW Recreational Services, Box 400, Cedar City, UT 84720; (801) 586-7686.

CANYON BOTTOM

Phantom Ranch: Accessible only on foot or by mule. Overnight dormitory and cabin space, breakast, lunch, and dinner served. For reservations: Grand Canyon National Park Lodges (see above).

Campgrounds and Picnic Areas

Camp only in established campgrounds in developed areas. Dump station, in summer, adjacent to Mather and Trailer Village.

SOUTH RIM

Mather Campground: At Grand Canyon Village. For reservations: MISTIX, P.O. Box 85705, San Diego, CA 92138-5705; (800) 365-2267. December 1–March 1; first-come, first-served; no reservations; $10/night.

Trailer Village: At Grand Canyon Village; RV sites with hookups. For reservations: Grand Canyon National Park Lodges (see above); $16/night.

Desert View Campground: 26 miles east of Grand Canyon Village; open mid-May through mid-October; first-come, first-served; $10/night.

Picnic Areas: Five off main park roads.

NORTH RIM

North Rim Campground: ½ mile north of the rim, open in summer. Reservations: MISTIX (see above).

Picnic Areas: Six off main park roads.

BACKCOUNTRY

Camping below the rim or in undeveloped areas on the rim requires a permit from the Backcountry Reservations Office (as much as a year in advance). Write to them at the park address.

Restaurants

SOUTH RIM

Babbitt's Delicatessen: Across from visitor center; open 8 A.M–6 P.M.

Bright Angel Restaurant: Open 6:30 A.M.– 10 P.M.; lounge open 11 A.M.–12:30 A.M.

Arizona Steakhouse: On the rim near Bright Angel Lodge; open 5 P.M.–10 P.M.; cocktails.

El Tovar Dining Room: View of the canyon; breakfast, lunch, dinner, and lounge.

Hermit's Rest Fountain: End of the West Rim Drive; open 9 A.M.–4:30 P.M.

Maswik Cafeteria: Open 6 A.M.–10 P.M.; lounge open 11 A.M.–1 A.M.

Yavapai Cafeteria: Across from visitor center; open 6 A.M–10 P.M.; dancing 9:30 P.M.– 12:30 A.M.; cocktails.

NORTH RIM

Grand Canyon Lodge: Open from mid-May through mid-October; dining room and cafeteria.

Activities

Scenic Drives

There are many overlooks, accessible by car, which offer spectacular views of the canyon. The Coloraro River is visible only from certain viewpoints. On the South Rim: The East Rim Drive (Highway 64) follows the canyon rim for 26 miles east of Grand Canyon Village to Desert View. The East Rim Drive is open to private vehicles throughout the year. The West Rim Drive follows the rim for eight miles west from Grand Canyon Village to Hermits Rest. The West Rim Drive is closed to private automobiles from late May through September, but the park provides free shuttle buses that stop at the overlook points during that time. You can get on and off the buses as you like.

Hiking

A hiking trail follows the rim from Yavapai Point to Hermits Rest. The Rim Trail is paved from Yavapai Point west only as far as Maricopa Point. Unpaved portions of the trail are narrow and close to the edge. It is a two-day (round-trip) hike to the river from the South Rim for most people. It is a longer trip from the North Rim. The inner canyon trails are steep and precipitous. Extreme temperatures can be life-threatening. Day hikers may wish to hike a portion of either the Bright Angel Trail or the South Kaibab Trail, both of which travel into the canyon. Check for trail conditions first.

Mule Trips

Mule trips from the South Rim into the canyon are available all year through Grand Canyon National Park Lodges; call (602) 638-2401. It is a two-day round trip to the Colorado River at the canyon bottom. A one-day trip is also offered, which goes partway to the river. Overnight riders stay and eat at Phantom Ranch. Mule trips are often booked a year in advance. There are size and weight restrictions on riders. Contact park superintendent for information. In the summer, one-day and half-day trips from the North Rim are offered; they do not go all the way to the river. Call (602) 638-2292 in summer, (801) 679-8665 rest of year.

Colorado River Trips

Commercial whitewater trips through Grand Canyon begin at Lees Ferry (six miles from Marble Canyon, Arizona) and vary from three days to 18 days in length. You must make reservations well in advance. Trips are available March through November. Call (602) 638-7888 from a touch-tone phone and press 1-3-7-1 to be mailed a list of commercial operators, or write to the River Permits Office, Grand Canyon National Park, P.O. Box 129, Grand Canyon, AZ 86023.

Bus Tours

Scenic bus tours of the South Rim are available through Grand Canyon National Park Lodges; call (602) 638-2401. Visitors arriving in the park should proceed to the Bright Angel Lodge transportation desk to make arrangements. A variety of different tours is available throughout the year.

Air Tours

Air tours are operated from Tusayan, Grand Canyon airport, Las Vegas, and elsewhere. Contact a travel agent or, for a list of air tour operators, write Grand Canyon Chamber of Commerce, P.O. Box 3007, Grand Canyon, AZ 86023.

Bicycling

Bicycles are not available for rent at the park. If you plan to bring one, remember that they are subject to the same traffic rules as automobiles. The West Rim Drive is open to bicycles throughout the year, but during the summer, there is heavy bus traffic. Bicycles are not allowed on park trails.

Fishing

Details on fishing regulations are available at the Backcountry Reservations Office.

Ranger-Led Programs

Park rangers offer a wide variety of interpretive programs throughout the year on the South Rim and in May through October on the North Rim. Detailed information is listed in *The Guide* or may be obtained by calling (602) 638-7888 from a touch-tone phone and pressing 1-3-2-3.

The Teton Range is one of the most majestic mountain ranges in the country. It is not the height of the mountains that draws such praise. The Tetons' highest peak is 13,766 feet; there are many taller mountains elsewhere. The most spectacular thing about the Tetons is that there are no foothills; there is no gradual ascent into the sky. The mountains just suddenly rise out of the valley floor in dramatic sharp-walled grandeur. And on clear days, the water in the park's lakes and the winding Snake River can reflect the Tetons in a way that makes them appear to double in size and breathtaking splendor.

Early trappers and settlers called the Snake River the Mad River because of the way it swells with meltwater, making crossing a formidable challenge. But the many aquatic animals and plants that make the river home find it suits them just fine. Bald eagles and ospreys nest along the riverbanks, where otters are at play. Beaver dams create small ponds that are inhabited by Canada geese, mallards, and many other migratory waterfowl. Each spring great blue herons return to their rookery at the Oxbow Bend, while the summer brings scores of woodland birds to dive and wade. Trumpeter swans, the largest North American waterfowl, are protected here. Along the stream and riverbanks grow tall cottonwoods, spruce, and aspens, while the low-growing willows make meals for moose.

As part of the Greater Yellowstone Ecosystem, the park boasts a remarkable diversity of wildlife. The area supports the largest elk herd remaining in the world, many of which summer in the park. A small herd of bison also summers in the park. Pronghorn travel in the sagebrush flats of Jackson Hole, while mule deer prefer lodgepole-pine forests for their home. Seldom-seen black bears, and an occasional grizzly north of Mount Moran, forage in canyons and woodlands.

An amazing variety of wildflowers blooms on the valley floor, beginning in early spring and continuing through the warm months, until the first frosts of autumn. Sagebrush buttercups follow behind the receding snowbanks, followed closely by spring beauties, yellowbells, and steer's head. A profusion of brilliant colors are at their peak in late June with meadows of scarlet gilia, balsamroot, lupine, larkspur, and the official flower of the park, the alpine forget-me-not.

Less than 9 million years old, the Tetons is actually the youngest range in the Rocky Mountain system. Before the mountains were here, there was a fault, or break, in the earth's crust. The blocks of earth on either side of the fault moved, and the west block swung skyward, forming the Teton range. The east block dropped downward, much like a trapdoor, forming the valley called Jackson Hole. Although miles and miles of earth were pushed upward to form the mountains, the forces of erosion and glacial activity over millions of years have worn and carved away the earth to create

NATIONAL PARK SERVICE, GRAND TETON NATIONAL PARK

the jagged peaks and broad canyons of today.

The Blackfoot, Crow, Gros Ventre, Shoshone and other Native Americans lived in areas surrounding what is now the park for many years; Jackson Hole was a neutral ground that all used. John Colter, of the Lewis and Clark expedition, is credited with having been the first white person on the land, in 1807. French-Canadian trappers saw the peaks from the west in 1819 and

called them *Les Trois Tetons*, "The Three Breasts." Following them were scores of "mountain men," trappers in search of beaver, many of whom have become legendary for their adventures in the wilderness. Eventually, about 1840, the beaver population was so diminished that the mountain men stopped coming. After 1900 some settlers started dude ranches; there is still one operating in the park today.

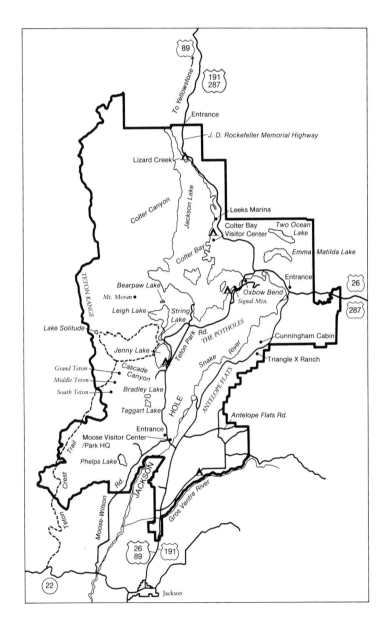

Further Information

Write or call: Superintendent, Grand Teton National Park, P.O. Drawer 170, Moose, WY 83012; (307) 733-2880

Visitor Information

Park Headquarters/Moose Visitor Center: Wildlife exhibits, geology exhibits, vertical relief map of the park; displays of original oils by area artists.
Colter Bay Visitor Center: Native American Arts Museum, audiovisual programs. (Closed October to mid-May.)

Nuts and Bolts

Entrance Fee: $10/vehicle or $4/person arriving by other means. Good for seven days; includes entrance to Yellowstone National Park.
Park Open: All year. Moose Visitor Center closed December 25; the main park road is the only one open in winter.
Permits: Required for backcountry camping and for all boats, rafts, and snowmobiles. A Wyoming fishing license is required.
In Emergency: Call Park Dispatch at 733-2880 or 543-2851.
Acreage: 310,521

Practical Advisory

Seasons

Spring, summer, and fall: In spring, rain is frequent and temperatures are cool, ranging from below 0° to 70°, with snow possible even in May and June. July and August days are generally warm and occasionally hot. Afternoon thunder showers are possible, with daytime temperatures averaging near 80° and dropping to 40° at night. Days are cool and clear during September and October, with frosty nights, warming to about 65° during the day. Winter: Cold weather lasts for more than half the year, from November through April, with an average 16 feet of snowfall; ground accumulation averages three to five feet of snow. Blizzards may last for several days. Cold, clear air permits unsurpassed views.

Facilities for Disabled

Contact the park for a copy of the "Handicapped Access" handout.

Travel Advisory

Entrances

South: Routes 26–89–191 north from Jackson.

East: Routes 26–287 west from Dubois.

North: Two miles south of south entrance to Yellowstone National Park.

Transportation

Airports: Airlines serve Jackson Hole airport.

Bus Service: Grand Teton Lodge Company provides bus service from the airport from early June through mid-September; call (307)

543-2811, (307) 543-2855, or (307) 733-2811.

Train Service: Not available.

Rental Cars: Available in Jackson and at Jackson Hole Airport.

Attractions

The *Teton Range* is the major feature of the park. Most park activity takes place in and around the lakes—especially *Jackson Lake* and *Jenny Lake*—and the *Snake River*. All these areas are easily reached by car on the scenic park roads.

Other Points of Interest (Museums, Historic Sites, etc.)

Cunningham Cabin was the home of rancher Pierce Cunningham in 1889. A half-mile self-guiding trail explores the site. The *Native American Arts Museum* houses an extensive collection of Native American art, especially of the Plains tribe, in the Colter Bay Visitor Center.

Accommodations

Lodges

Signal Mountain Lodge: Log cabins (some with fireplaces), motel units, and lakefront apartments on Jackson Lake; European plan; open May through October. For reservations: Signal Mountain Lodge, Box 50, Moran, WY 83013; (307) 543-2831 or (307) 733-5470.

Colter Bay Cabins: Near Jackson Lake; cabins; European plan; open May through September. For reservations: Grand Teton Lodge Co., Box 250, Moran, WY 83013; (307) 733-2811, (307) 543-2811 or (307) 543-2855.

Jackson Lake Lodge: Lodge and motel rooms; European plan; swimming pool; open June through September. For reservations: Grant Teton Lodge Co. (see above).

Jenny Lake Lodge: Cabins; guest-ranch style; modified American plan; open June through September. For reservations: Grand Teton Lodge Co. (see above).

Triangle X Ranch, Dude Ranch: 13 miles north of Moose; all Western ranch activities for weekly guests; open all year. For reservations: Box 120T, Moose, WY 83012; (307) 733-2183.

Campgrounds and Picnic Areas

First-come, first-served (except at two concession-operated campgrounds); 14-day maximum (seven days at Jenny Lake); campfires prohibited except at designated campsites; all have modern toilets; $8/night. All campsites close in September.

Gros Ventre Campground: 360 sites; dump station; opens early May.

Jenny Lake Campground: 49 sites; tents and small camping vehicles only (no trailers); opens late May.

Signal Mountain Campground: 86 sites; dump station; opens mid-May.

Colter Bay Campground: 310 sites; dump station; opens mid-May.

Lizard Creek Campground: 60 sites; opens mid-June.

Colter Bay Village Trailer Park: 112 sites; full hookups; open May through September. Reservations suggested, through Grand Teton Lodge Co. (see "Lodges," above).

Colter Bay Tent Village: Canvas units; European plan; open June through September. Reservations suggested, through Grand Teton Lodge Co. (see "Lodges," above).

Picnic Areas: 11, off the roads in the park.

Restaurants

Colter Bay Chuckwagon Restaurant: Breakfast, lunch, and dinner; open May through September.

Leek's Restaurant/Marina: Light meals and snacks; open June through early September.

Signal Mountain Lodge (Aspens Dining Room and Coffee Shop): Open May through October; breakfast, lunch, and dinner; cocktail lounge.

Colter Bay Grill: Breakfast, lunch, and dinner; open June through early September.

John Colter Bar at Colter Bay: Cocktail lounge; open May through September.

Moose Snack Bar: Open June through early September.

Colter Bay Snack Bar: Near general store; open May through September.

Jackson Lake Lodge (Mural Room, Pioneer Room, and Blue Heron Lodge): Breakfast, lunch, and dinner; June through September; cocktail lounge has entertainment.

Jenny Lake Lodge Dining Room: Lunch and dinner; reservations suggested for dinner; call (307) 733-4647; open June through September.

Dornans' Chuckwagon at Moose: Breakfast, lunch, and dinner; open June through early September.

Dornans' Moose Bar: Cocktail lounge and view deck; open all year.

Activities

Scenic Drives

Two main park roads offer excellent opportunities to view and photograph the mountain scene. Teton Park Road skirts the eastern shore of Jackson and Jenny lakes at the very foot of the peaks, which are reflected in the waters, while Rockefeller Memorial Parkway follows the Snake River and affords a better opportunity to view the range as a whole. Wayside exhibits at many turnouts along the roads identify major peaks and explain natural features. Signal Mountain Overlook, a five-mile side trip, offers one of the favorite views.

Hiking

The park includes more than 200 miles of trails ranging from easy to strenuous and requiring from a few minutes to several days to complete. They provide access to backcountry lakes, streams, canyons, and camping zones. You can pick up trail brochures at visitor centers and at the trailheads. The Cascade Canyon Trail, one of the most popular, begins at the south end of Jenny Lake and explores natural features up to Lake Solitude. Other trails include the two-mile Colter Bay Nature Trail and the half-mile Menor's Ferry. The Teton Crest Trail runs from the south boundary of the park to Cascade Canyon and offers extensive views of the range. You can buy topographical maps and trail brochures at visitor centers.

Boat Trips

Scenic cruises are offered by Teton Boating Co. on Jenny Lake—call (307) 733-2703—and by Colter Bay Marina on Jackson Lake—call (307) 543-2811. Fees are charged. Contact the park for a list of concessioners offering interpretive Snake River float trips between mid-May and mid-September.

Boating

Signal Mountain Marina on Jackson Lake offers pontoon, paddleboat, canoe, and water-ski boat rentals, (307) 543-2831. Canoe rentals are available at Dornans' Grocery Store.

For those with their own boats, motorboats are permitted on Jackson, Jenny (7½-horsepower maximum), and Phelps lakes. Hand-propelled craft are permitted on Jackson, Jenny, Phelps, Emma Matilda, Two Ocean, Taggart, Bradley, Bearpaw, Leigh, and String lakes. Sailing, windsurfing, jet skiing, and waterskiing are allowed only on Jackson Lake. You can dock at Leek's Marina, Signal Mountain Marina, or Colter Bay Marina, all on Jackson Lake. Floating the Snake River within the park is allowed only in hand-propelled boats and rafts, not in inner tubes. Although the Snake may not seem powerful on the surface, only experienced floaters should attempt this swift, cold river.

Bicycling

Ride bicycles only where cars can legally go. Don't ride in the backcountry, on-trail or off-trail. Bicycles can be rented and repaired at Dornans' in Moose by Mountain Bike Outfitters, Inc., from mid-May to mid-September. Call (307) 733-3314.

Horseback Riding

Trail rides of various lengths are available at Colter Bay Village Corral, mid-May through September, (307) 543-2811; at Jackson Lake Lodge Corral, June through mid-September, (307) 543-2811; at Teton Trail Rides, Inc.,

on Jenny Lake, June through September, (307) 733-2108. Fees are charged.

Swimming

Swimming in park waters is generally a cold experience. Shallow areas of Jackson, String, and Leigh lakes have reasonable water temperatures during July and August, but there are no swimming areas with lifeguards. Swimming in the Snake River is not recommended.

Fishing

Fishing is allowed in most park lakes and streams. Check at visitor centers for special regulations. Catch whitefish and cutthroat, lake, and brown trout in lakes and rivers. Teton Boating Co., on Jenny Lake, offers fishing-boat rentals from June through September; call (307) 733-2703. Signal Mountain Marina on Jackson Lake offers fishing-boat rentals and guided fishing trips from May through September; call (307) 543-2831. Moose Village Store offers guided fishing trips; call (307) 733-3471. Colter Bay Marina offers guided fishing trips; call (307) 543-2811.

Mountaineering

There are 16 routes leading to the summit of Grand Teton. Climbing mountains is a technical sport requiring proper knowledge, experience, physical condition, and equipment. Climbers must sign in before and immediately after each climb at the Jenny Lake Ranger Station. Exum Mountain Guides and School of American Mountaineering, (307) 733-2297, offers basic and intermediate classes and guided ascents of all peaks, as does Jackson Hole Mountain Guides and Climbing School, (307) 733-4979.

Skiing and Snowmobiling

Cross-country skiing and snowshoeing are permitted, and snowmobiles are permitted on the park's unplowed roads and in the Potholes area when snow conditions permit. Moose Vistor Center distributes a map of park ski trails and permitted snowmobile routes and other information. Snowmobiles can be rented outside the park.

Bus Tours

Bus tours of the park are available from June through mid-September; call (307) 733-2811. Fees are charged.

Ranger-Led Activities

Rangers lead talks, walks, and hikes, and provide demonstrations and other programs from mid-June through September. Slide-illustrated campfire programs, at Gros Ventre, Signal Mountain, and Colter Bay amphitheaters, cover a wide range of topics. Check at visitor centers for schedules.

Native American Dances

Native American dances are performed at Jackson Lake Lodge during July and August; check at the lodge for schedules. Admission charged.

Teton Science School

A wide variety of in-depth natural-science courses is offered at the Teton Science School. Classes for all ages include field study supplemented by informal lectures. For information: Director, Teton Science School, Box 68P, Kelly, WY 83011; (307) 733-4765.

One of the newest national parks in the system and the only one in Nevada, Great Basin National Park was established in 1986 by combining the former Wheeler Peak Scenic Area, the former Lehman Caves National Monument, and lands formerly part of Humboldt National Forest. The park's landscape is part of the Great Basin territory. Stretching from the Wasatch Mountains in Utah to the Sierra Nevada in California, the Great Basin is an area of sagebrush-covered valleys and narrow mountain ranges. The name comes from the fact that there is no outlet to the sea for rivers and streams, so water must collect and then evaporate. There are actually many basins in the Great Basin, and each is separated by north–south mountain ranges.

The park includes the southern Snake Range, a mountain island in the sagebrush-covered desert. Thirteen of the peaks here are over 10,000 feet high; Wheeler Peak, is the highest peak in the park, with a summit at 13,065 feet. There are also streams, lakes, alpine tundra, wildflower-strewn meadows, abundant wildlife, and groves of spruce, aspen, and pines.

One of the more unusual plants in the park is the bristlecone pine. These interesting trees, especially those growing at the highest levels, live extraordinarily long lives that are measured not in hundreds, but in thousands of years. One tree in the park has been determined to be 4,950 years old; it is the oldest living thing in the world. Even after death, these wonders remain durable.

Because of the high resin content of their wood, the trees do not rot; rather, they erode, much as rock does. Scientists have found a piece of bristlecone wood that is 9,000 years old.

This desert area was formed about 10,000 years ago when the climate here turned warmer. The lakes dried up; the alpine glaciers at the tops of the mountains melted; and what was left was the desert country you see now. The native Fremont peoples hunted and farmed here around A.D. 1100 to A.D. 1300, and some of their rock art can be seen throughout the park. Following them came the Shoshone and Paiute peoples, who settled near streams and other water sources. Hunters and gatherers, they relied heavily on the local piñon nut for survival. Some of their descendants still live in the area today.

There are a number of limestone caverns in the park, including the well-known Lehman Caves. Actually a single cavern, Lehman extends a quarter-mile into the limestone and low-grade marble at the base of the Snake Range. Discovered about 1885 by Absalom Lehman, a rancher and miner, this cavern is one of the most richly decorated caves in the country.

Lehman contains structures such as stalactites, stalagmites, columns, draperies, and flowstone. The delicate formations are the result of rainwater finding its way below the surface of the earth to the limestone, first dissolving what was there and then building it again, drop by drop, in fabulous designs.

NATIONAL PARK SERVICE

But Lehman is most famous for the rare and mysterious structures called shields. Shields consist of two roughly circular halves, al- most like flattened clamshells. How they are formed remains a subject of controversy.

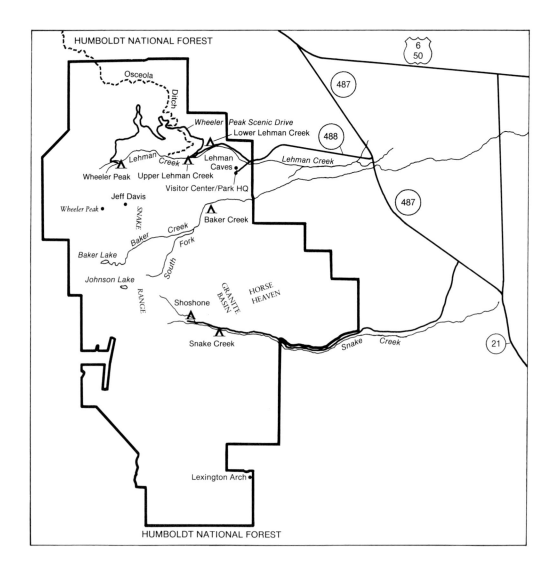

Further Information

Write or call: Superintendent, Great Basin National Park, Baker, NV 89311-9701; (702) 234-7331

Visitor Information

Park Headquarters/Visitor Center: Near park entrance; exhibits, slide show, maps, information.

Nuts and Bolts

Entrance Fee: None.
Park Open: All year. Visitor center is closed Thanksgiving, December 25, and January 1.
Permits: Nevada fishing license is required. If you are hiking or camping in the back-country, registration, though voluntary, is strongly recommended.
In Emergency: Call 234-7331 (daytime) or sheriff's office, 1-289-8808 (after hours).
Acreage: 77,109.15

Practical Advisory

Seasons

Summer: Average daytime temperatures are 85°–95°. Nighttime temperatures average in the mid-40s. Winter: Average daytime temperatures are 25°–30°. Nighttime temperatures average 5°–10°. At higher elevations, temperatures can be as much as 10°–20° colder all year.

Special Advisories

• Be aware that, since the park is still new, services continue to change.

• While in Lehman Caves, stay on the trail and with the ranger at all times.
• Many park trails reach elevations above 10,000 feet; avoid overexertion.
• Do not enter mine shafts and tunnels; they are dangerous.

Facilities for Disabled

The visitor center and the first room of the cave are wheelchair-accessible. There are also accessible camping facilities.

Travel Advisory

Entrance

Highways 487 and 488 for 10 miles from U.S. 6-50.

Transportation

Airports: Reno (385 miles from the park), Las Vegas (286 miles from the park), and Salt Lake City (230 miles from the park) have major airports. A small airport in Ely (70 miles from the park) is closest.

Bus Service: A bus passes through Ely, 70 miles from the park, from Reno once a week.

Train Service: Trains serve Reno, Las Vegas, and Salt Lake City.

Rental Cars: In Reno, Las Vegas, and Salt Lake City.

Attractions

The peaks of the *Snake Range,* especially the highest point—*Wheeler Peak*—as well as *Lehman Creek* and the other *creeks* and *small lakes* are the major features of the park. It is possible to drive part of the way up Wheeler Peak, and to hike to the summit. Also of interest are the *Lehman Caves,* which can be toured. The *bristlecone pine* trees growing throughout the park are remarkable.

Other Points of Interest (Museums, Historic Sites, etc.)

The *Rhodes log cabin* was used in the early part of the century by cave visitors staying overnight. It now houses exhibits concerning early pioneer life. Portions of the *Osceola Ditch,* which was built to bring water to the gold miners in Osceola, can still be seen in the park.

Accommodations

There are no lodges in the park.

Campgrounds and Picnic Areas

Campfires are permitted in campgrounds and picnic areas in designated fireplaces only. First-come, first-served; no reservations. Dump station near visitor center.

Lower Lehman Creek Campground: 11 sites; water, toilets, fire rings, tables, tent pads; open all year; $5/night.

Wheeler Peak Campground; 37 sites; toilets, fire rings, tables, tent pads; open only in summer; free.

Upper Lehman Creek Campground: 24 sites; water, toilets, fire rings, tables, tent pads; open only in summer; $5/night.

Baker Creek Campground: 32 sites; toilets, fire rings, tables, tent pads; open only in summer; free.

Backcountry Campgrounds: At Shoshone and Snake Creek; primitive; tables, tent sites, pit toilets; free.

Picnic Areas: Two, off the main road.

Restaurant

Lehman Caves Cafe: At the visitor center; breakfast, lunch, and snacks; open April to October.

Activities

Scenic Drives

Wheeler Peak Scenic Drive provides good views of the Snake Range at overlooks all along the road. Beginning near the park entrance, the drive leaves Lehman Creek to climb across a dry shoulder of the mountain; in 12 miles it gains 3,400 feet in elevation and passes through a variety of habitats. Because of snow, the road is closed above the 7,500-foot level from approximately October to May. All other park roads are unpaved and infrequently traveled.

Hiking

Hiking opportunities abound, with easy to moderate trails. The visitor center Nature Trail, for example, is a short, leisurely quarter-mile trail north of the visitor center; the Baker Creek Trail runs five miles from the Baker Creek Campground to Baker Lake. A more strenuous hike is a climb up Wheeler Peak, the park's highest point. Trail guides are available at the visitor center. There are few maintained trails in the backcountry. Routes generally follow ridge lines or valley bottoms. Get topographical maps and information at visitor center.

Cave Tours

Rangers lead a half-mile tour of Lehman Caverns on a paved trail with stairways and indirect lighting. It takes about 1½ hours. Wear warm clothing; the cave temperature is 50° year-round. The tours are limited to 30 people and are filled on a first-come, first-served basis. A fee is charged. More adventuresome visitors can join a ranger on a spelunking expedition to an undeveloped cave on summer weekends; check at the visitor center for information.

Fishing

Lahonton cutthroat trout are in Baker Lake; Johnson Lake has brook trout; Snake and Lehman creeks have rainbow trout; and Baker Creek has both rainbow and brown trout. State regulations apply.

Ranger-Led Programs

Rangers lead guided nature walks and present evening campfire programs. Check at the visitor center for schedules.

Along the shared border of North Carolina and Tennessee lies a beautiful stretch of the Appalachian highlands known as the Great Smoky Mountains. The "Smoky" in the name comes from the ever-present smoke-like haze that hovers around the peaks, creating a climate and a mood unlike any other in this part of the South.

The vegetation here is also unlike any other in this area. Because of the constant dampness, the abundant rainfall, and the fertile soil, the area is blanketed in rich forests of evergreens. In fact, the park is home to the world's finest example of temperate deciduous forest, with more kinds of trees than are found in all of Europe. During the last ice age, these cold-weather-loving trees extended their range farther and farther south to escape the ice. Even after the glaciers retreated and the weather grew warmer, the evergreens remained on the cooler slopes of the mountains and still thrive today. Broadleaf trees predominate in the valleys and lower elevations. These areas with rich soil, plenty of sunshine, and the right amount of rain are called coves. Above 6,000 feet are conifer forests like those you'll find in central Canada.

The park is known not only for its remarkable forests but also for its other plant life. The variety is outstanding, from the profusion of wildflowers that bloom in the early spring to the more than 600 types of flowering plants. One of the most impressive of these is the rhododendron, which blooms in June and July. The spectacle of these beautiful flowers attracts hikers who are drawn here with the desire to wander among them. But the bushes grow from two to 20 feet high, in thickets so dense that they are all but impenetrable.

The Great Smoky Range has some of the oldest mountains on earth. They were formed some 200 million years ago during a long period known as the Appalachian Revolution. The tallest in the range is Clingmans Dome, near the center of the park, at 6,642 feet. The Cherokee tribe lived and reigned in these mountains for hundreds of years. They were squeezed out about 200 years ago by white settlers who were moving south and west. Today there is a small Cherokee reservation bordering the park's southeast side.

John Jacob Mingus, probably the first white man to live in what is now the park, settled in the Oconaluftee Valley in 1792. Others followed in the 1880s, staking out difficult lives of complete self-sufficiency in this rugged mountain territory. One of the more interesting aspects of the park is the earlier settlers' log cabins and barns, which are scattered throughout the area. Now restored, they stand as living museums of pioneer life.

Eventually this forested land was taken over by logging and pulpwood companies. These companies remained the owners of the land until the federal government decided to turn the area into a national park. Although some areas—for example, Mount LeConte—were relatively untouched, the other heavily logged areas have been and continue to be restored fully.

NATIONAL PARK SERVICE

Further Information

Write or call: Superintendent, Great Smoky Mountains National Park, Gatlinburg, TN 37738; (615) 436-1200

Visitor Information

Park Headquarters/Sugarlands Visitor Center: Near Gatlinburg, Tennessee; natural history exhibits; mounted specimens of plants and animals found in the Smokies; orientation film, shown during the off season; slide presentation from spring through fall; books and maps for sale.

Oconaluftee Visitor Center: At main southern entrance; exhibits about pioneer life; information; book and map sales.

Cades Cove Visitor Center: On Cades Cove Loop Road; exhibits about the cultural history of the Smokies; information; book and map sales. (Closed January to mid-March.)

Nuts and Bolts

Entrance Fee: None.

Park Open: All year. Visitor centers closed December 25.

Permits: Required for backcountry camping. Tennessee or North Carolina fishing license is required.

In Emergency: Call Ranger Communications Division, (615) 436-1230, or 911.

Acreage: 520,269.44

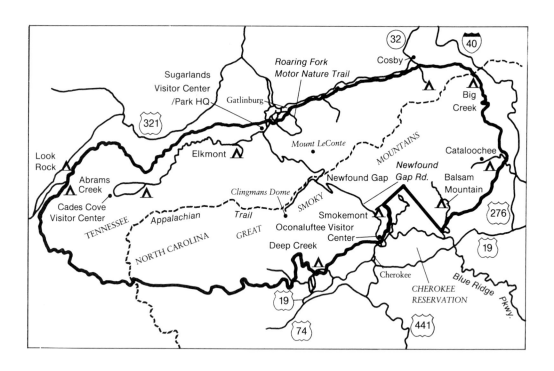

Practical Advisory

Seasons

There may be rapid and severe changes in weather conditions in the spring and winter. Always be prepared for rain during any season. Generally, precipitation and clouds increase and temperature decreases with the rise in elevation. Summer: Warm and humid with frequent showers. Highs are in the 90s and lows in the 60s and 70s. Late spring and early fall: Mostly pleasant with warm days and cool nights. Highs are in the 70s and 80s and lows in the 40s and 50s. Winter: Moderately cold, with occasional snow, especially at the higher elevations. Highs are in the 50s and lows in the 20s and 30s.

Special Advisories

- Avoid contact with bears, and know what to do if you do encounter a bear.
- Stay off cliff faces.
- In the summer, ticks are fairly common; check yourself after hiking.
- Because of flash floods, rapids, and submerged debris, most park streams are not suitable for swimming or other water sports.

Facilities for Disabled

Write to the park for a copy of "Guide to Accessibility for the Disabled."

Travel Advisory

Entrances

North: U.S. 441 for two miles south of Gatlinburg, Tennessee.

South: U.S. 441 for two miles north of Cherokee, North Carolina.

Transportation

Airports: Major airports are located in Knoxville, Tennessee, and Asheville, North Carolina.

Bus and Train Service: There is no public transportation to the park.

Rental Cars: At the airports; there are small car-rental establishments in Sevierville and Gatlinburg, Tennessee.

Attractions

The *Great Smoky Mountains* are the major natural feature in the park. The tallest of the peaks in the park is *Clingmans Dome*. The rich ever-*green forests* offer much scenic beauty throughout the park. The *Newfound Gap Road*, which crosses the park, offers superb views.

Other Points of Interest
(Museums, Historic Sites, etc.)

There are several remnants of the early-19th-century pioneer residents of the area. The *Pioneer Farmstead* is a collection of authentic structures and artifacts from throughout the park, including a house, woodshed, meat house, and blacksmith's shop. The *Mingus Mill*, a large water-powered mill for grinding corn, can be seen in operation from mid-April through October. *Noah "Bud" Ogle's Place* is a former farm. The remains of the community of *Cataloochee,* the biggest settlement in the Smokies, include a barn, a chapel, a school, and houses. At *Cades Cove* there is an 11-mile loop road past fields, barns, churches, and homes.

Lodges

LeConte Lodge: On Mount LeConte. Accessible only by trail; allow a half-day for hiking up one of the five mountain trails that reach this secluded retreat. Open mid-March to mid-November. For reservations: LeConte Lodge, Gatlinburg, TN 37738; (615) 436-4473.

Wonderland Hotel: At Elkmont; rustic hotel accommodations; May to October. For reservations: Wonderland Hotel, Route 2, Gatlinburg, TN 37738; (615) 436-5490.

Campgrounds and Picnic Areas

Reservations are recommended at Cades Cove, Elkmont, and Smokemont from May 15 to October 31. To make reservations, call (800) 365-CAMP. Other campgrounds are first-come first-served. Seven-day limit between May and October; fourteen days between November and April. All campgrounds have water, fire grills, tables, and flush toilets.

Abrams Creek Campground: 16 sites; tents and trailers to 16 feet; $6/night.

Balsam Mountain Campground: 46 sites; RVs and tents; $8/night.

Big Creek Campground: 12 sites; tents; $6/night.

Cades Cove Campground: 161 sites; RVs and tents; dump station; open all year; $11/night from mid-May through October; $8/night from November through mid-May.

Cataloochee Campground: 27 sites; tents and trailers up to 16 feet; $6/night.

Cosby Campground: 175 sites; RVs and tents; dump station; $8/night.

Deep Creek Campground: 119 sites; RVs and tents; dump station; $8/night.

Elkmont Campground: 220 sites; RVs and tents; dump station; open all year; $11/night from mid-May through October; $8/night from November through mid-May.

Look Rock Campground: 92 sites; RVs and tents; $8/night.

Smokemont Campground: 140 sites; RVs and tents; dump station; open all year; $11/night from mid-May through October; $8/night from November through mid-May.

Backcountry Camping: 18 shelters and some 80 sites are available; some use is rationed. Contact the Backcountry Office, (615) 436-1231.

Picnic Areas: 10 areas, off park roads; tables.

Restaurant

Wonderland Hotel: At Elkmont; June–October; dining room.

Activities

Scenic Drives

Newfound Gap Road is a scenic, high mountain road that winds across the crest of the Smokies and connects the Sugarlands and Oconaluftee visitor centers. Along the road are superb views with numerous scenic pullouts. One is at the crest at Newfound Gap, where the Appalachian Trail crosses the road. There is a seven-mile spur road here, leading out to Clingmans Dome, the highest point in the park, and its observation tower. The tower can be reached via a strenuous half-mile hike from the parking lot. The views from the tower are beautifully panoramic.

Hiking

There are some 900 miles of hiking trails throughout the Smokies, traveling past waterfalls, coves, and rushing streams. There are short, self-guiding nature trails, with leaflets to be picked up at the start of each one. There are also more strenuous hikes. The Appalachian Trail runs through the park for 71 miles. You can sample part of it starting from Newfound Gap. A trail map may be purchased at visitor centers.

Bicycling

Bicycles may be ridden only on roads that are open to motor vehicles; they are not permitted on trails. Park terrain is generally not well suited for bicycles because of its steepness. The 11-mile loop through Cades Cove is a favored spot, but caution is advised because of steep grades and heavy traffic. Bicycles can be rented at the Cades Cove Campground Store.

Fishing

Many park streams provide fishing for rainbow and brown trout all year long. Check park regulations at a ranger station or visitor center before you fish. Possession of any brook trout is prohibited.

Horseback Riding

Saddle horses are available from April to October at Cades Cove, at Smokemont, at Cosby, near Greenbrier on U.S. 321, and near park headquarters.

Naturalist Activities

From mid-May through August, evening programs and nature walks are offered at most developed campgrounds. Spring and fall activities are limited. Check schedules at a visitor center or in the park's free newspaper.

In a part of western Texas near the northern border with New Mexico lies a rugged piece of the Old West known as Guadalupe Mountains National Park. Towering high over the surrounding Chihuahuan desert is the centerpiece of the park, the Guadalupe Mountains, including Guadalupe Peak, at 8,751 feet the tallest in Texas. These mountains have more than just their beauty to offer, however. As part of one of the most extensive ancient marine fossil reefs on earth, they have scientific significance as well.

About 250 million years ago, an enormous sea filled with various forms of ocean life covered the land in this area. Lime-producing marine organisms combined with lime in the seawater to slowly build up a 400-mile-long horseshoe-shaped limestone reef, now known as the Capitan Reef. Eventually the climate grew warmer and drier, the water in the sea evaporated, and the reef was completely covered with sediment.

Millions of years later, when an uplift took place and the Guadalupe Mountains were formed, part of the reef was raised and exposed. Scientists have found fossils embedded in the reef that have helped them learn about life 250 million years ago. Most of the reef still remains buried thousands of feet underground, although some is also exposed in the Apache and Glass mountains.

Aside from the reef, the land in the park is an interesting mix of desert, canyon, and mountain highland. Not much of the Chihuahuan desert actually lies within the park

boundary, but it dominates the views from the peaks. The many deep canyons in the park contain a diversity of life forms. One of the best examples is McKittrick Canyon, nearly five miles long and several thousand feet deep. It was named for the outlaw Kid McKittrick, who, according to one of many legends in the park's Wild West history, hid out here after robbing banks in New Mexico. A walk through McKittrick Canyon starts with desert shrubs and animals near the mouth. But farther along McKittrick Creek, the area becomes more lush, with deciduous trees, wildflowers, and ferns. Finally, near the top of the canyon, the habitat begins to resemble that of the high mountains.

A dense forest of ponderosa pine, southwestern pine, Douglas fir, and aspen covers most of the high country. The forest is especially lush in the Bowl, a two-mile-wide depression at the top of the mountains. These evergreens are remnants of the days when the temperature here was much cooler. Although the climate warmed, the conifers at higher and cooler elevations remained. Throughout the mountains roam elk, mule deer, wild turkeys, and black bears. The ruler in the animal world here is the sleek mountain lion, also known as a cougar or panther. Although these animals are frightening to imagine, spotting one or even just hearing its call is a rare event.

The Apaches dominated this land until about the mid-1800s, when white settlers were drawn here by its sheltering peaks and

PHOTO BY RUSS FINLEY, NATIONAL PARK SERVICE

its water sources. Clashes between the groups eventually brought in the U.S. Army, which continued to fight the Apaches for 30 years until the Native Americans were eliminated from the area by 1880.

Around the same time, a different kind of history was being made. John Butterfield's stagecoaches were beginning to travel across the country on the first transcontinental mail route. In what is now the park,

he built the Pinery stagecoach station, where the driver could stop on his way to meet the coach coming from the west. Eventually, Butterfield found an easier route south of here and abandoned the Pinery stagecoach station. But part of it is still standing today and can be visited, as can several 19th-century ranches that give a real sense of the history of the West.

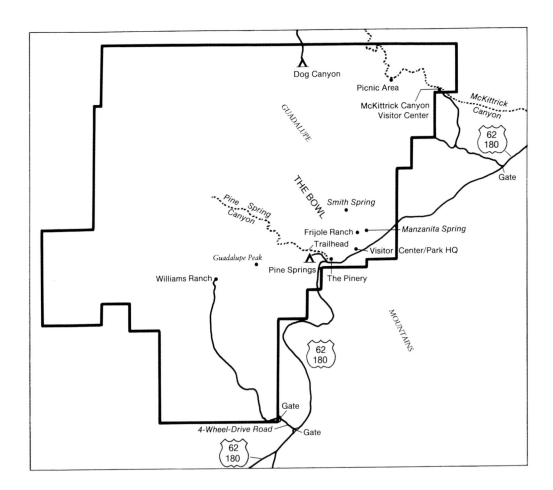

Further Information

Write or call: Superintendent, Guadalupe Mountains National Park, HC 60, Box 400, Salt Flat, TX 79847-9400; (915) 828-3251

Visitor Information

Park Headquarters and Visitor Center: Information, flora and fauna exhibit, other exhibits, 13-minute orientation slide show; books and maps for sale. Keys available for Williams Ranch.
McKittrick Canyon Visitor Center: Information, 10-minute slide show focusing on the canyon. (Closed at times in winter.)

Nuts and Bolts

Entrance Fee: None.
Park Open: All year. Visitor centers closed December 25. The road to McKittrick Canyon is closed at the entrance from U.S. 62-180 each night.
Permits: Required for backcountry camping.
In Emergency: Contact a park ranger; after hours call emergency number posted near the telephones.
Acreage: 86,416.01

Practical Advisory

Seasons

Sudden changes in the weather are common. High winds up to 60 or 80 miles per hour—and higher—can occur and can be dangerous at times. They are particularly prevalent in the spring. Summer: Extreme temperatures, with thunderstorms and the danger of lightning in late summer. Moderate to warm temperatures; high of 80s and low of 60s. Winter: Some snow, rainfall, and cold temperatures. But mild, cool days are the norm: High 50s, low 30s.

Special Advisories

- Climbing cliffs is dangerous; the rock is unstable and considered unsafe even for technical climbers.
- Beware of cacti, rattlesnakes, scorpions, and desert centipedes.

Facilities for Disabled

Wheelchair-accessible rest room and fully accessible site at Pine Springs Campground.

Travel Advisory

Entrances

Northeast: Highway 62-180 for 55 miles southwest of Carlsbad, New Mexico.
Note: Roads into the park are severely limited; most of the park can be seen only from the trails.

Transportation

Airports: Commercial airlines serve Carlsbad, New Mexico (55 miles), El Paso (115 miles), and Midland-Odessa (170 miles), Texas.

Bus Service: Available from TNM&O Bus Lines, (806) 765-6641. Arrange with the driver to be let off at Pine Springs, Texas.

Train Service: Trains serve El Paso, Texas.

Rental Cars: Available at Carlsbad, New Mexico, and at El Paso and Midland-Odessa, Texas.

Attractions

The *Guadalupe Mountains* and their highest member, *Guadalupe Peak*, are the major natural features in the park, along with the *canyons*, especially *McKittrick Canyon*. Most of the park can only be seen by using the hiking trails throughout the mountains and the park.

Other Points of Interest
(Museums, Historic Sites, etc.)

The ruins of a mid-1800s stagecoach station, called *The Pinery*, which was part of the na-

tion's first transcontinental mail route. The trail is less than 100 yards round-trip from the main park road. The *Williams Ranch* is a historic site on the remote west side of the Guadalupes. It is reachable by a four-wheel-drive road (you need a key from the park headquarters to open the entrance gate) or an 18-mile round-trip trail. The *Frijole Ranch* is a typical 19th-century West Texas cattle ranch.

Accommodations

The park has no lodging or food.

Campgrounds and Picnic Areas

All are first-come, first-served, and have a 14-day limit.

Pine Springs Campground: 20 tent sites and 18 RV sites; water, rest rooms, tables; only camp stoves allowed for cooking; $6/night.

Dog Canyon Campground: Nine tent sites and five RV sites; water, rest rooms, tables; $6/night.

Backcountry Camping: Allowed only in 10 backcountry campsites. Cook only on camp stoves.

Picnic Areas: Two, in McKittrick Canyon area; tables.

Activities

Hiking

The park's more than 80 miles of trails offer a wide range of opportunities for exploring the desert, canyons, and highlands. Trails vary in length and difficulty: There are short nature trails, trails for all-day hikes, and longer trails, or series of trails, that take several days. The park's major trailhead is located at the Pine Spring Campground; there is easy access to most trails from there. Many trails, especially those leading to the high country, are steep and rough; the ascent may be as much as 3,000 feet. Trails in canyons and other lowlands are less strenuous. McKittrick Canyon is a popular spot for hiking—daytime use only—with trails ranging up to seven miles round-trip. There is a 2⅓-mile round-trip trail around the Smith and Manzanita springs, two small oases with freshwater springs that attract wildlife. Trails to the Bowl, 2,500 feet above the desert, are 11 miles and longer round-trip. A topographical map, essential for longer trips, is available at visitor centers.

Horseback Riding

Horses are allowed on most trails, but there is no place to rent horses nearby.

Ranger-Led Activities

Rangers guide walks, talks, and other park activities. There are programs at the Pine Springs Campground amphitheater every evening from late spring through early fall. See schedules in visitor centers.

Even amid the beauty of Hawaii, a handful of places stand out as natural wonders. One such place on the island of Maui is Haleakalā, the "House of the Sun," the largest dormant volcano in the world. With a 10,023-foot peak and a crater streaked with shades of red, yellow, and black, the landscape here in the park's Crater District looks like no other wilderness on earth.

The island of Maui, like all the islands in the chain known as Hawaii, owes its very existence to volcanic eruptions. Maui actually began as two separate volcanoes on the ocean floor. As they repeatedly erupted, new layers of lava spread upon the old, building and building, until the volcano heads emerged from the sea. Lava, ash, and cinder eventually joined the two by an isthmus, forming Maui, "The Valley Isle."

Haleakalā, the larger volcano, finally reached its greatest height some 30,000 feet from the ocean floor; then, for a time, volcanic activity ceased. Falling rain caused streams to form on the volcano's slopes. Two of these streams carved out large depressions that eventually met, creating a long erosional "crater." When volcanic activity resumed, lava poured down into these stream valleys, nearly filling them. More recently, cinders, ash, and volcanic spatter were blown from the newer vents in the crater, forming multicolored symmetrical cones as high as 600 feet. Eventually, this water-carved basin was partially filled with lava and cinder cones, and it came to resemble a true volcanic crater.

Though Haleakalā is dormant now, in about the year 1790 (quite recent in geologic time) two minor flows along the volcano's southwest reached the sea and altered the coastline of Maui. Current records indicate that seismic adjustments are still taking place in the earth's crust under the weight of Haleakalā, but no volcanic activity of any kind is visible in the crater or at any other place on the island. There is a possibility that Haleakalā could erupt again; it just isn't known for sure.

Over millions of years of isolation, unusual native bird and plant life has evolved. A few species live nowhere outside of Haleakalā. The golden plover, commonly seen from September to May, is famous for its migratory flights to and from Alaska. The 'i'iwi is one of the most beautiful birds, with its vermilion body, its black wings and tail, and its inch-long curved bill. The 'apapane is a deep blood red, and the nēnē, or native Hawaiian goose, is the state bird.

One of the best-known native plants in Haleakalā is the silversword, called 'āhinahina ("gray-gray") by the Hawaiians. This spectacular plant, with its many daggerlike silvery leaves, will grow for some five to 20 years or more before blooming. After all that time, it develops a cluster of yellow and reddish-purple flower heads, each producing hundreds of seeds. Then, as the seeds develop, the remainder of the plant slowly dies.

In contrast to the brown, red, and black of the crater are the lush greenness and

NATIONAL PARK SERVICE

abundant waters of the Kīpahulu District. A chain of sparkling pools, some large and some small, is linked by a waterfall or short cascade. The water is usually placid here but 'Ohe'o, the stream joining the pools, becomes a torrent of white water at times, and the pools are buried as the water plunges toward the ocean. Surrounding the pools are rolling grassy fields and forested valleys of native kukui as well as alien plants like ginger, mango, guava, and bamboo. At the higher elevations is a vast native rain forest, thousands of years old. It receives up to 300 inches of rainfall a year.

Further Information

Write or call: Superintendent, Haleakalā National Park, Box 369, Makawao, Maui, HI 96768; (808) 572-9306

Visitor Information

Park Headquarters: Near park entrance; information.
House of the Sun Visitor Center: On the crater rim; exhibits on the geology, archaeology, and ecology of the park as well as on wilderness-protection programs.

Nuts and Bolts

Entrance Fee: $4/vehicle, $2/person arriving by other means.
Park Open: All year.
Permits: Required for camping in the crater.
In Emergency: Contact a park ranger or, after hours, call the emergency number posted at park telephones.
Acreage: 28,655.25

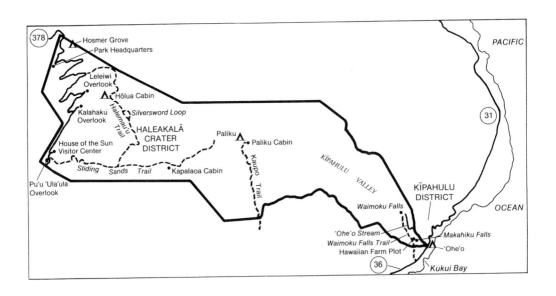

Practical Advisory

Seasons

Summit: Summers are generally dry and moderately warm, but occasional cold, windy, damp weather prevails. Winters are often clear, but cold, with occasional storms that can bring extended periods of heavy rain and wind. Crater: Can be very hot and sunny or very cold and rainy—often during the same day, although rain is more common from November through May. Nighttime temperatures range between 32° and 50°. Kīpahulu: Weather is subtropical; light showers can occur any day.

Special Advisory

• Bring a light raincoat, sun hat, and suntan lotion when hiking. Be prepared for weather changes.

Facilities for Disabled

All of the following, including rest rooms, are wheelchair-accessible: Summit Building at Pu'u 'Ula'ula, House of the Sun Visitor Center, park headquarters, Hosmer Grove picnic area, and Kīpahulu Ranger Station. There are three-dimensional models in the visitor center and headquarters for hands-on exploring by the sight-impaired.

Travel Advisory

Entrances

Crater District: Highway 37 to 377 to 378.

Kīpahulu District: Highway 36 or Highway 31.

Transportation

Airports: There are daily flights from Honolulu to Maui airport.

Bus and Train Service: There is no public transportation on Maui. There are bus tour companies in Kahului.

Rental Cars: Available in Kahului.

Attractions

The *Haleakalā volcano* is the major feature of the park. The one winding road leading to the summit of the volcano offers overlooks into the *crater*. It is possible to hike into the crater for short trips or even overnight. There are many unusual *plants* and *animals*, some of which are found nowhere else.

Other Points of Interest (Museums, Historic Sites, etc.)

A small traditional Hawaiian farm plot is a ¾-mile walk along a trail from the Kīpahulu parking area, over the bridge, past Oheo Stream.

Accommodations

There is no food or lodging available in the park.

Campgrounds and Picnic Areas

Stays are limited to two nights at any one location and three nights maximum per month. No wood fires; pack out all trash.

Hosmer Grove Campground: Tables, fireplaces, cooking shelter with grills, water, chemical toilets. Limited to 25 persons, 15 per group.

Backcountry Campgrounds: Two, Hōlua and Palikū, in the crater; pit toilets, water; 25 persons per campground, 15 per group. One campground in the Kīpahulu area, Oheo, near the ocean; tables, grills, chemical toilets, no water.

Backcountry Cabins: Three—Palikū, Hōlua, and Kapalaoa—in the crater. Each is allocated to one party, with a capacity of 12 people each per night. Bunks, limited water, firewood, cookstove, eating and cooking utensils. For reservations and fees, contact park superintendent (see "Further Information," above) at least 90 days in advance.

Picnic Areas: Three, near Hosmer Grove Campground, behind park headquarters, and in Kīpahulu area; tables.

Activities

Scenic Drives

There is one road leading to the summit. Overlooks with orientation panels and exhibits are located along the road at Leleiwi, the Summit Building at Pu'u 'Ula'ula, and at Kalahaku Overlook on the way down. Look for silverswords at the Kalahaku Overlook's Silversword Enclosure. No roads connect the two districts of the park. There is a separate road around East Maui (outside the park) to the Kīpahulu District.

Hiking

Thirty-six miles of trails offer many opportunities for walking and hiking; there are short self-guiding walks, and overnight hikes of several days. Keep in mind that the floor of the crater is some 3,000 feet below the summit. You can take part of the Halemau'u Trail for about one mile from the highway to the crater rim. With the aid of a brochure, the quarter-mile Hosmer Grove Nature Trail teaches about native and alien plants and animals.

Climb to the top of White Hill, a ⁴/₁₀-mile round-trip hike from the visitor center. A hike down Sliding Sands Trail returning via Halemau'u Trail is a 12-mile, 8-hour trip recommended for good hikers only. You can see groups of silverswords in various stages of growth on the Silversword Loop Trail. In the Kīpahulu District, the Makahiku Falls overlook is a half-mile hike from the parking area; Waimoku Falls is another 1½ miles up from the overlook.

Horseback Riding

Local companies provide trips through the crater on a one-day or overnight basis.

Bicycling

Bicycles are not allowed on the trails. Local tour companies sponsor bicycle trips down the park road.

Swimming

Swimming in the several pools along Oheo Stream is a popular pastime, though the water is usually quite cool. Never swim in high water; a stream can become a raging torrent in minutes. Be careful on wet rocks and check before diving or jumping: There are submerged ledges near the pools' edges. Strong ocean currents and hazardous surf make swimming in the ocean here dangerous.

Ranger-Led Activities

Park rangers give short nature talks at the Summit Building periodically during the day. They also lead hikes of varying length, including into the crater, during the summer months. Check at park headquarters for current schedules. Walks and hikes are provided during the summer in the Kīpahulu District as well.

To visit Hawaii Volcanoes National Park is to enter the nearly supernatural world of still-active volcanoes. Near the southeastern coast of the island of Hawaii, also known as "the Big Island," Mauna Loa and Kilauea stand tall; they are among the most active volcanoes on earth. Throughout the park are the remnants of their ancient and recent eruptions including craters, ash, and lava only a few years old.

All of the islands in the chain known as Hawaii are actually only the tops of volcanic mountains built up from the bottom of the Pacific Ocean over the last 25 million years. Deep inside the earth is a hot spot that continually heats up the rock around it, melting it into a fluid called magma. The magma forces its way up through the earth's crust in the form of lava. Layer upon layer of this lava builds up from the ocean's floor, until eventually the top of the mountain juts out of the water and an island is formed.

Since the Pacific Plate—the crust of the earth underneath the ocean here—is moving slowly to the northwest it actually pulls the island with it, away from the hot spot, and brings a new area of the plate into position for another island to eventually be formed. This is how all of the islands in the chain were created. At present, the hot spot is still under Kilauea and Mauna Loa, so they remain the most active. Since the year 1800, all of the eruptions in the Hawaiian chain have occurred on this island.

Kilauea rises 4,090 feet and Mauna Loa 13,680 feet above sea level. These and all the volcanoes in Hawaii are called shield volcanoes because they rise softly and are topped, not by peaks, but by calderas or basins. Recent eruptions in the park have been through vents in the volcanoes' sides, in areas known as rift zones. The activity here is actually fairly gentle, and not the violent eruptions you may think of as coming from volcanoes.

It is considered quite amazing that there is such a variety and number of plant and animal inhabitants on the Hawaiian Islands. Because of the nature of the islands' birth, all of the plants and animals had to find their way here. Winds, ocean currents, and distance-traveling birds carried seeds, spores, or even entire organisms across the ocean. Scientists believe that only one species has been introduced every 10,000 years on average. The only mammals to find their way here on their own were bats and seals. All others were introduced by humans. The special circumstances of the islands, especially the lack of any natural predators, has caused these species to evolve in unusual ways, and now most can be found only here.

The first human inhabitants of these islands most likely arrived about 1,200 years ago from Polynesia. They brought many plants and animals from their native land, including pigs, coconuts, bananas, and chickens. They had to live with the fiery volcanoes and their erratic anger. To them, the fire was the work of the goddess Pele, the daughter of Earth Mother and Sky Father. She came here to escape her cruel sister, goddess of the sea, and found her home in one volcano after another, where she rules as the goddess of fire.

NATIONAL PARK SERVICE, PHOTO BY KEPA MALY

Further Information

Write or call: Superintendent, Hawaii Volcanoes National Park, HI 96718; (808) 967-7184

Visitor Information

Park Headquarters/Kilauea Visitor Center: Near park entrance; eruption movie, information, exhibits, books for sale.

Nuts and Bolts

Entrance Fee: $5/vehicle.
Park Open: All year.
Permits: Required for backcountry camping.
In Emergency: Call 967-7311.
Acreage: 229,177.03

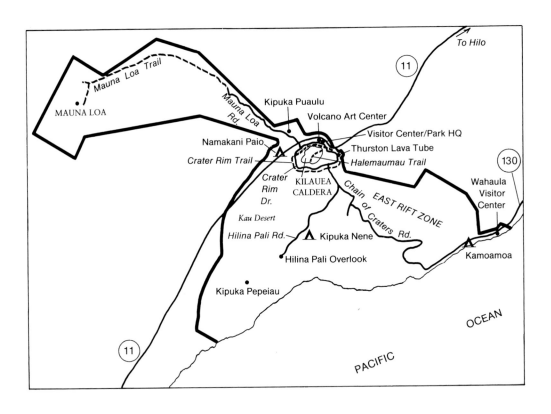

Practical Advisory

Seasons

The northern side of Kilauea's summit is 4,000 feet above sea level; the climate can be cool, and rain can fall any time of the year. Kilauea's leeward side is usually dry and warm. In winter the snow can extend down to 8,000 feet on Mauna Loa. At high elevations, snow and driving rain are possible any time of year, temperatures can drop below freezing at night, and sunlight is intense.

Special Advisories

- Stay on trails. There are many deep cracks hidden by vegetation on the surface of Kilauea, and recent lava flows are shelly and collapse easily.

- Fumes from volcanoes can compound respiratory problems; if in doubt, heed the warning signs.
- Be prepared for changes in weather.
- Altitude sickness is common when hiking at high altitudes under rigorous conditions; pace yourself.
- Volcanic eruptions can happen at any time; when hiking stay upslope from active lava flows and upwind of volcanic gases; remain on high ground.
- Fishing is prohibited.

Facilities for Disabled

All park buildings and some trails are moderately accessible; check with park authorities for more detailed information.

Travel Advisory

Entrance

Highway 11 for 29 miles southwest of Hilo.

Transportation

Airports: Hilo (30 miles away) and Kailua Kona (110 miles away).

Bus Service: Buses serve Hilo.

Train Service: There is no train service to the park.

Rental Cars: Available at Hilo and Kailua Kona airports.

Attractions

The two volcanoes, *Kilauea* and *Mauna Loa,* are the major features of the park. The *Crater Rim Drive* allows you to drive along the summit of Kilauea. Also of interest is the residue— *craters, ash,* and *lava*—from past volcanic activity.

Other Points of Interest
(Museums, Historic Sites, etc.)

The *Thomas A. Jaggar Museum,* on Crater Rim Drive three miles inside the park entrance, contains maps, models, and paintings concerning the story of the park, as well as excellent exhibits on volcanism, videos of recent eruptions, and a seismic-instrument display. The *Volcano Art Center*, housed in the historic 1877 Volcano House, includes a gallery; seminars and workshops on painting, printmaking, pottery, music, and dance are held there. The park also includes the remnants of one of ancient Hawaii's most sacred places: *Wahaula Heiau*, the Temple of the Red-mouthed God, dating from the 13th century.

Accommodations

Lodge

Volcano House: At 4,000 feet on the rim of Kilauea Crater; open all year. Reservations: Volcano House, Hawaii Volcanoes National Park, HI 96718.

Campgrounds and Picnic Areas

Seven-day limit; first-come, first-served. Bring wood. Fires are permitted only in designated camp and picnic sites. Pack out everything you pack in. Free.

Kipuka Nene Campground: Eating shelters, fireplaces.

Namakani Paio Campground: Eating shelters, fireplaces. Cabins with showers are also available. Contact Volcano House for information and reservations for cabins.

Kamoamoa Campground: Eating shelters, fireplaces.

Backcountry Campgrounds: Hiker shelters and cabins are available on a sharing basis; water available (should be treated); pit toilets.

Kilauea Military Camp: A rest-and-recreation camp for active and retired military personnel; one mile west of park headquarters.

Picnic Areas: Two, near Bird Park and off Crater Rim Road; tables.

Restaurant

Volcano House: On the rim of Kilauea Crater; open all year; dining room.

Activities

Scenic Drives

Crater Rim Drive offers the best orientation to the park in an 11-mile drive from the park headquarters. You will pass lush rain forest, raw craters, and great areas of devastation as you drive along the summit of Kilauea Volcano. Pumice is piled high from recent eruptions, and lava flows only a few years old cover much of the landscape. Allow one to three hours, depending upon how often and how long you stop. Chain of Craters Road explores the East Rift Zone and Coastal District, passing several huge pit craters formed in prehistoric time as well as several areas of recent volcanic activity, which temporarily buried the road. Allow two to three hours for this 65-mile round-trip drive, depending upon how often and how long you stop.

Hiking

There are many trails in the park, providing a range of hikes from self-guiding 1½-hour walks to day-long treks. Check on trail conditions and water supplies before you start. Many trails are easy, but to be properly prepared check with a ranger. In Bird Park (Kipuka Puaulu), a one-mile nature trail leads through open meadows and forest. Kipukas are islands of old soil surrounded by more recent lava flows. The Crater Rim Trail is 11 miles long and is fairly easy, going through cool rain forest and warm desert. Halemaumau Trail, 6½ miles round-trip, passes through a tree-fern forest and into the heart of the volcano. Trail guides are available at the visitor center.

Volcano Eruption Viewing

Volcano eruptions are the most exciting events at the park. You can get up-to-date information about ongoing eruptions or potential activity by calling (808) 967-7977 day or night. Temporary road signs will direct you to viewing points when conditions are safe.

Swimming

A few sheltered swimming sites exist in the coastal district of the park, but should be selected cautiously. Check with a park ranger first. Avoid entering the open ocean, as coastal waters generally present rough seas, high surf, and strong, unpredictable currents.

Horseback Riding

Horseback riding is permitted on the trails in the park's backcountry. Riders should tether their horses well away from campsites, in areas that present no hazard to other campers.

Ranger-Led Programs

Evening talks, nature walks, and other activities are offered at Kilauea and the Coastal Section during the summer. Schedules are at the visitor center.

Hot Springs is an unusual national park. The main attractions here are not natural wonders. Visitors come here to see attractions built by humans: the bathhouses. The bathhouses at Hot Springs have drawn people for over a century, offering therapeutic or just relaxing treatments. Of course, the most important component of the bathhouses is their water, and that *is* a natural wonder.

Hot springs bubble out of the earth here at an average 143°F. They flow out of the base of Hot Spring Mountain at the rate of about 850,000 gallons per day. Today only three of the springs are open for visitors to see. The others are covered in green concerete boxes that keep the water pure; it is piped to an underground reservoir for all the bathhouses' use. The hot water is unlike mineral water, which has substantial amounts of dissolved material. The water here is relatively soft, with a pleasant taste and no odor.

Earlier in the century, this was a booming vacation town; people traveled from all over to experience the curative effects of the natural hot springs. Beginning in the late 1800s private bathhouses, under the supervision of the federal government, began to be built. They ranged from the simple to the luxurious. By the 1920s, the popularity of the area had increased, and magnificent bathhouses were built along Bathhouse Row. The government even built two public facilities.

The bathhouses were beautiful structures with all the latest equipment to pamper guests in stylish surroundings. Vacationers would come to enjoy baths, sitzes, steam rooms, showers, and special treatments for specific ailments. In those days, many people believed, or wanted to believe, in the special healing powers of the water. Visitors enjoyed walks in the nearby woods, music and dancing, and racetrack betting as well as the baths.

Eventually, the popularity of the springs diminished; many of the bathhouses along Bathhouse Row closed and fell into disrepair. Today one is still operating as a bathhouse and another has been converted into the park's visitor center. The others are being restored to their original grandeur for other uses. Although some people still take the baths believing in their powers, most people come for the relaxation a total bath can offer.

Scientists now believe the water flowing out of the springs today once fell as rainwater and was absorbed by the very porous local rock known as Bigfork chert and Arkansas novaculite. It worked its way down through the rock for nearly 4,000 years, picking up minerals along the way, until it was between 2,000 and 8,000 feet below the surface. There it reached its highest temperature, came into contact with cracks and faults within the Hot Springs sandstone, and made a relatively rapid—one-year—ascent to the surface of the earth. It maintained most of its heat and thus flows out as hot water.

Visitors to the springs can enjoy the natural surroundings of the small but pleasant park as well. The Zig Zag Mountains are covered in dense forests of oak, hickory, and shortleaf pine. Flowering trees, including redbuds, dogwoods, and Southern mag-

nolias, are also common. Colorful birds and small animals are abundant in the forest. The park and the adjacent city are nearly intertwined; without a map, it can be difficult to know when you have left one and entered the other.

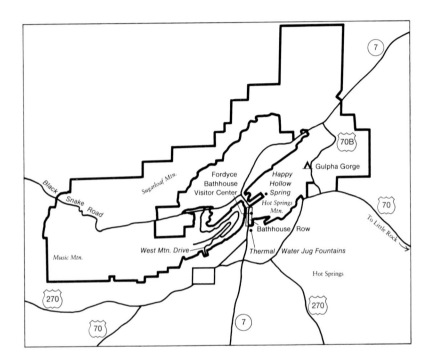

Further Information

Write or call: Superintendent, Hot Springs National Park, P.O. Box 1860, Hot Springs, AR 71902; (501) 623-1433

Visitor Information

Fordyce Bathhouse Vistor Center: In the 300 block of Central Avenue; restored bathhouse, information, and exhibits and films about thermal bathing.

Nuts and Bolts

Entrance Fee: None.
Park Open: All year. Visitor center closed December 25 and January 1.
Permits: None needed.
In Emergency: Call 624-3124.
Acreage: 5,839.24

Practical Advisory

Seasons

Favorable climate all year. Winters are mild and summers are usually hot and humid. Fall and spring are the best times to visit.

Special Advisories

- Be aware of mountain trails over uneven terrain.

- Be alert for stinging insects, ticks, snakes, and poison ivy.

Facilities for Disabled

Picnic and campground sites, comfort stations, parking areas, amphitheater, and visitor center all have facilities or services that are wheelchair-accessible.

Travel Advisory

Entrances

Southeast: U.S. 270 from Glenwood, Arkansas.

East: U.S. 70 from Benton, Arkansas.

North: Highway 7 from Hollis, Arkansas.

Transportation

Airports: Hot Springs, three miles from downtown.

Bus Service: Greyhound provides bus service to Hot Springs.

Train Service: Amtrak serves Little Rock (60 miles away) and Malvern (20 miles away).

Rental Cars: Available in Hot Springs.

Attractions

The *bathhouses* and the *hot-spring water* they use are the main attractions at the park. *Fordyce Bathhouse* on Bathhouse Row has recently reopened after having undergone extensive restoration to its original early-1900s look. It includes period furniture, steam cabinets, tubs, and more. Tours are available. A *thermal cascade* and three open *hot springs* have been set aside to be viewed. There are two thermal-water fountains and two cold-water springs where visitors can bring their own containers and collect the water to take home. *Hot Springs Mountain* is also of interest. The 216-foot *Hot Springs Mountain Tower* offers a spectacular view of Hot Springs. A fee is charged.

Accommodations

There is no food or lodging available within the park, but there are many choices in the adjacent city.

Campground and Picnic Areas

Build fires only in fireplaces.

Gulpha Gorge Campground: Two miles northeast of downtown; 45 tent and trailer sites; tables, fireplaces, water, toilets, dump station. First-come, first-served; 14-day limit; $6/night.

Picnic Areas: Tables, grills, rest rooms at Gulpha Gorge and at Hot Springs Mountain. Water is available at Hot Springs Mountain. Tables on the Grand Promenade, West Mountain.

Activities

Baths

The bathhouses are operated by private concessioners who provide services in accordance with regulations of and subject to inspection by the National Park Service. An attendant guides you through the process. No appointment is needed; just walk in and purchase a ticket. A full range of options is available: private baths, full steam cabinets or head-out cabinets, sitz (sitting) tubs, applications of hot packs, cool-down showers, and full-body Swedish massage. Available within the park, at Buckstaff Bathhouse, 623-2308, and Hot Springs Health Spa, 321-9664. Available in the adjacent city at Arlington Hotel Bathhouse, 623-7771; Downtowner Motor Inn Bathhouse, 623-5521; Majestic Hotel Bathhouse, 623-5511; and Park Hilton Bathhouse, 623-6600. Fees are charged.

Scenic Drives

Two tours from the visitor center through the park's scenic areas allow access to picnic areas, overlooks, and hiking trails. Hot Springs Mountain Drive is 2½ miles long and should take 45 minutes. Go north on Highway 7 to the first right on Fountain Street and follow the signs for Hot Springs Mountain. Several overlooks and the Mountain Tower at the summit offer views. West Mountain Drive is two miles long and takes about 40 minutes. Go north on Highway 7 to Whittington Avenue; turn left. Turn left again at the "West Mountain Drive" sign to begin the tour. After approximately one mile take the side trip to the summit of West Mountain.

Hiking

There are over 30 miles of trails, varying in length and difficulty. The Grand Promenade Trail, an easy half-mile, is designed to provide a transition between the developed bathhouse area and the mountains. The brick walkway begins behind the visitor center and travels behind Bathhouse Row and between several covered springs. The Peak Trail is a moderately strenuous half-mile walk from the visitor center to the summit of Hot Springs Mountain and the Mountain Tower. Dead Chief Trail is 1⁴/₁₀ miles starting from the visitor center and intersecting with the Short Cut Trail, which leads to the summit of Hot Springs Mountain and the Gulpha Gorge Trail.

Ranger-Led Activities

Walks, mountain hikes, and programs at the Gulpha Gorge campground amphitheater are offered. Schedules are reduced during spring and fall. In October a Volksmarsch ("People's Walk") is the highlight of Oktoberfest.

Rugged, unspoiled, and roadless, Isle Royale is the largest island in the largest freshwater lake on earth, Lake Superior. Tucked in the northwest corner of the lake, this 45-mile-long island lies completely within the boundary of the national park. Beautiful shorelines and lakes, wildlife, and dense forests all add to the secluded wilderness nature of the park.

Some 75 percent of the park consists of water—ponds, streams, rivers, and of course, Lake Superior. On the land, most of the northern shore of the island is made of rock; the rest of the shoreline is jagged, with peninsulas and islets. Inland are forests of spruce, fir, and hardwood trees. The island is also home to 17 wild orchid varieties including calypso and yellow lady's slippers.

Most of the landscape you see here today was formed by glaciers, from the last ice age, which left the area some 10,000 years ago. The heavy ice gouged out the lakes and mountains, and when it left, the land actually lifted and rose higher in the lake. Then began the development of soil, and plant and animal colonization. The types of plant and animal inhabitants have changed repeatedly since then as temperatures and other conditions have changed, and as different animals have found their way here in search of better feeding grounds.

The island is known as one of the few places in the Lower 48 states where wolves roam free. A small pack of Eastern timber wolves traveled over an ice bridge between Canada (only 15 or so miles away) and the island during the very cold winter of 1948–1949. The wolves travel in socially ordered packs. Every individual in the pack has a specific purpose and place in the hierarchy. Their numbers have varied over the years; today there are 12.

An important function of the wolves on the island is to maintain a crucial balance of life along with two other inhabitants, moose and beavers. For a time before the wolves arrived, the moose population rose so high that there wasn't enough food for all of them. This overgrowth was stemmed by the arrival of the wolves, who prey on the moose and keep their numbers down. Since only the oldest and most feeble fall victim to the wolves, the moose population remains healthy and strong. When the number of wolves decreases, the number of moose increases. As the moose population ages and grows weaker, the wolves flourish. The cycle continues and the populations are held in balance.

Beavers also contribute to this cycle: They provide a supplemental source of food for the wolves. They also build dams that foster the aquatic vegetation moose feed on. Biologists are continuing to study this interesting balance of nature.

Native Americans mined copper on the island for many years, probably most actively from A.D. 600 to 1450. More "modern" copper mining took place from the mid-1800s to late 1800s. Many forests were burned or logged and destroyed. The rem-

nants of mine shafts are still on the island. Commercial fishing became important in the 1830s, with the arrival of the American Fur Company. But by early in this century, the island was being used as a vacation and excursion spot.

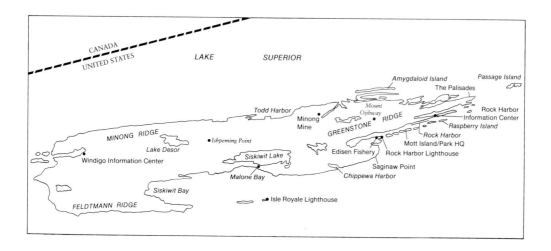

Further Information

Write or call: Superintendent, Isle Royale National Park, Houghton, MI 49931; (906) 482-0984

Visitor Information:

In the park: You can find information about the park, its wildlife, and activities at the following places:
Park Headquarters: Mott Island.
Windigo Information Center: On western side of the island.

Rock Harbor Information Center: On eastern side of the island.

Nuts and Bolts

Entrance Fee: None.
Park Open: April 16 through October 3.
Permits: Required for all campers and boaters. A Michigan fishing license is required in all Lake Superior waters.
In Emergency: Call park headquarters, (906) 337-4991/4992.
Acreage: 539,300

Practical Advisory

Seasons

Summer daytime temperatures rarely exceed 80°; evening temperatures can range from the high 30s to the low 40s. Dense fog is common in spring, and thunderstorms may occur throughout the season. Temperatures are quite cool on the ferries.

Special Advisories

- Insect repellent is helpful.
- Do not leave packs or food unattended because wildlife may damage or carry off items.
- Wheeled vehicles are not allowed in the park.

- To maintain the park's atmosphere, travel in small groups and be quiet.
- Don't damage trees when hiking.
- Beware of open mine pits at Island Mine, Todd Harbor, Siskowit Mine, Daisy Farm, Minong Mine, and other areas.
- Park waters are cold.
- U.S. citizens returning from Canada, and Canadian visitors to the island, must clear U.S. Customs at Rock Harbor, Amygdaloid, or Windigo ranger station.

Facilities for Disabled

Contact the park for information.

Travel Advisory

Transportation from the mainland to the park is by boat or floatplane only. Reservations are recommended.

From Houghton, Michigan: June to Labor Day: On the passenger vessel *Ranger III.* Contact the park at (906) 482-0984. May through September: By floatplane. Contact Isle Royale Seaplane Service: (906) 482-8850 in summer, or write Isle Royale Seaplane Service, P.O. Box 371, Houghton, MI 49931 off-season.

From Copper Harbor, Michigan: May through September: On a passenger vessel. Contact Isle Royale Queen: (906) 289-4437

summer, or (906) 482-4950 to make reservations off-season.

From Grand Portage, Minnesota: May through October: On a passenger vessel. Contact GPIR Transport Lines, (715) 392-2100.

On Your Own Boat: If you have your own boat, use Lake Survey Chart 14976, "Isle Royale," which may be purchased from the park. You should have an FM radio of sufficient power to reach shore. It is recommended that boats less than 20 feet in length not cross Lake Superior from the Keweenaw Peninsula, but they may be transported on the *Ranger III.*

Attractions

The island is wild and scenic throughout. The *shorelines, lakes, wildlife,* and *forests* are of interest. Access to all areas is by trail or boat only; private vehicles are not allowed. *Rock Harbor* is the most developed part of the island. Other popular destinations include *Windigo, Raspberry Island,* and *Passage Island.*

Other Points of Interest (Museums, Historic Sites, etc.)

Lookout towers are at Feldtmann Ridge, Ishpeming Point, and Mount Ojibway. The *Edisen Fishery* operates as a working commercial fishery. Two tours a week leave from the Rock Harbor Lodge.

Accommodations

Lodge

Rock Harbor Lodge: Along the shore of Rock Harbor; lodge and housekeeping rooms. For reservations: National Park Concessions, Inc., Box 405, Houghton, MI 49931; (906) 337-4993. Off-season: National Park Concessions, Inc., Mammoth Cave, KY 42259; (502) 773-2191.

Campgrounds

There are 36 campgrounds on the island, with three types of camping available: three-sided shelters for a maximum of six people; tent sites for a maximum of six people in one to three tents; and group sites for a group of seven to 10 people. First-come, first-served. Be prepared to travel to an alternate campground if the one you choose is full. From June 1 through Labor Day, stays at each campground are limited. Bring a self-contained stove; open wood fires are prohibited in most.

Restaurant

Rock Harbor Lodge: Dining room serving breakfast, lunch, and dinner.

Activities

Hiking

There are more than 166 miles of foot trails on the island. Cross-country, off-trail travel is not recommended because of dense vegetation, bogs, and swamps. You can arrange a combination trip, taking a boat or flying in one direction and hiking in the other (see "Boating," below). Starting at Windigo or Rock Harbor you can travel the length of the island (45 miles) along park trails. Five or more days are recommended for this hike. Side trips to Malone Bay, Chippewa Harbor, or Siskiwit Bay can add variety. Topographical maps are recommended.

Boating

The marina at Rock Harbor Lodge is open from the end of May through mid-September. Most park docks accommodate cruisers of moderate draft. Overnight docking is allowed only at the campgrounds and docks indicated in the park map brochure.

Canoe and motorboat rentals, sightseeing trips, and arrangements for boat pickups and drop-offs at various points are available from National Park Concessions, Inc., (906) 337-4993 in summer and (502) 773-2191 in winter.

Fishing

Michigan regulations apply in all Lake Superior waters as well as in inland lakes and streams. Sport fishers can catch lake, brook, and rainbow trout, northern pike, walleye, and yellow perch. Spring and fall produce the biggest catches, but fishing is considered good throughout the season. Do not dispose of fish remains near campgrounds or docks. Traps, seines, and nets (except landing nets) are prohibited. Artificial bait and lures are allowed in inland lakes and streams, but cut or live bait (including nonpreserved fish eggs) is prohibited. Digging for bait is not allowed. Guided fishing trips are available from Rock Harbor Lodge.

Mine Tour

A Minong Mine tour is conducted from the Rock Harbor Lodge once a week. This tour includes a 21-mile North Shore cruise and is led by a park ranger.

The vast and unspoiled natural beauty of the Alaskan wilderness is found in Katmai National Park. Rugged and remote, the park boasts dense forests, a vast system of lakes and streams, one of the world's most active volcanic centers, and the largest population of unhunted Alaskan brown bears in existence.

One of the greatest symbols of the wildness of Katmai is the population of brown bears. The Alaskan brown bear and the grizzly are considered the same species, although brown bears are slightly larger. Mature males in Katmai can weigh up to 900 pounds. The awesome bears emerge every April from dens that they entered in November, with cubs—born over the winter—in tow. They head down to the streams, where they know they can find superb meals of the park's other abundant inhabitants: salmon.

Sockeye salmon spawn in the gravel beds of the Naknek system of lakes and rivers. Beginning in late June, they return to the place of their birth from the North Pacific waters where they have spent two to three years. By the end of July close to 1,000,000 salmon have entered the waters here. They spawn in August and September. The bears know where to go to find good salmon-fishing opportunities. One of the more exciting aspects of a visit to the park is getting the chance to view this aspect of nature in action. Besides feeding the brown bears, bald eagles, and a few other creatures, the fish in the park have also provided important subsistence for local people and tremendous commercial fishing opportunities.

The land in the park is almost completely wilderness, with a variety of wildlife. Around the lakes and rivers, ducks, loons, grebes, and Arctic terns can be found. Sea lions and sea otters abound along the coast, and peregrine falcons nest among coastal cliffs. Grouse and ptarmigan inhabit uplands. Seacoasts and lakeshores provide nesting sites for bald eagles, hawks, and owls. Besides the bears, mammals include moose, red foxes, wolves, minks, and beavers.

Fifteen active volcanoes line the Shelikof Strait, the waters off the Katmai coast. Lying underneath this area is part of the Pacific Ring of Fire, an approximate circle of volcanic activity extending around the floor of the Pacific Ocean. There is still molten rock here, and thus real potential for these volcanoes to erupt. The most famous eruption in the park was that of Novarupta in 1912.

After the explosion, a lifeless valley remained filled with hissing and smoking vents in a landscape of ash hundreds of feet deep. The first explorer to visit the land named it Valley of the Ten Thousand Smokes in 1916. Although there are few smoking vents today, the name has remained. Streams have made their way through the ash, making for an even more surreal landscape.

The most recent devastation to the land was caused by human activity. Damage from the 1989 *Exxon Valdez* oil spill remains in the beach areas of the park. Rangers are monitoring the park's inhabitants, but long-term effects are still not known.

PHOTO BY JAMES GAVIN

Further Information

Write or call: Superintendent, Katmai National Park, P.O. Box 7, King Salmon, AK 99613; (907) 246-3305

Visitor Information

Park Headquarters: King Salmon; park information.
Summer Headquarters/Brooks Camp Visitor Center: Park information.

Nuts and Bolts

Entrance Fee: None.
Park Open: All year.
Permits: Required for backcountry camping. An Alaska fishing license is required.
In Emergency: Call 246-3305.
Acreage: 3,716,000

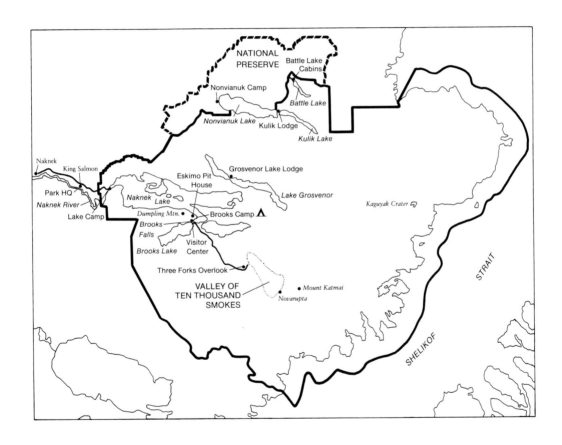

Practical Advisory

Seasons

Weather is stormy with some sunshine. Summer: Daytime temperatures range from about the mid-50s to the mid-60s; the average low is 44°. Strong winds and sudden gusts frequently sweep the area. Skies are clear about 20 percent of the summer. Light rain can last for days. Winds of 50–60 mph, with blowing rain, are not unusual.

Special Advisories

- Avoid encounters with bears, and know what to do if one occurs.
- You will need insect repellent.
- Cold winds and icy waters pose great hazards.
- Be prepared to wait out storms.
- Pets are not allowed in the park.

Facilities for Disabled

Contact the park.

Travel Advisory

Transportation

Daily commercial flights connect Anchorage with King Salmon, about six miles from the park's west boundary. Commercial floatplanes operate daily between King Salmon and Brooks Camp from June to September.

Year-round air charter services are available in King Salmon. A nine-mile dirt road connects King Salmon with Lake Camp, inside the park's west boundary. Make all charter arrangements before you arrive to ensure service that fits your schedule.

Attractions

Most of the park is wilderness. *Brooks Camp*, the most popular area of the park, is reachable via *Naknek Lake* and is near the scenic *Brooks Lake* and *Brooks Falls*. It is possible to hike from there to the unusual *Valley of Ten Thousand Smokes* as well as to *Dumpling Mountain*.

Other Points of Interest (Museums, Historic, Sites, etc.)

A *pithouse* at Brooks Camp is a replica of an actual early (about A.D. 1200) dwelling of native peoples. An excavation of this site was completed in 1967. The basic framework of split cottonwood logs and a partial covering of peat moss is completed.

Accommodations

Lodge

For reservations and information on lodging: Katmailand Inc., 4700 Aircraft Drive, Anchorage, AK 99502; (907) 243-5448; (800) 544-0551.

Brooks Lodge: At Brooks Camp on Naknek Lake; cabins with plumbing; four people per unit. Open from June to September.

Lodging is also available from June 1 into early September, at Grosvenor Lake, Kulik, Battle Lake, and Nonvianuk.

Campgrounds

Park authorities prefer that visitors use stoves, since firewood is limited. Only dead, downed wood may be used for fuel.

Brooks Camp Campground: On Naknek Lake; firepits, tables, water, pit toilets, and food-storage cache; seven nights out of 10 maximum; three shelters are available for cooking and are shared by all campers. The campground can accommodate up to 60 campers at a time. Reservations are required and can be made starting January 1. Contact Katmai National Park, P.O. Box 7, King Salmon, AK 99613; (907) 246-3305.

Backcountry Camping: Allowed anywhere in the park.

Restaurant

Brooks Lodge: At Brooks Camp on Naknek Lake; family-style meals.

Activities

Hiking

Katmai's rugged wilderness offers rewarding hiking experiences, but you should take reasonable precautions. There are several good short routes and unlimited opportunities for long trips. There are few trails, but passable routes can be found along lakeshores and gravel ridges. You can also arrange a van drop-off and pickup through Brooks Lodge (see "Accommodations"). A 23-mile dirt road between Brooks Camp and the Valley of Ten Thousand Smokes offers good views of the wilderness. A foot trail descends to the valley from road's end. Several commercial operators provide backpacking guide services.

Bear Viewing

A falls-viewing platform is located about ¾ mile from the lodge area at Brooks River Falls. The wooden platform is about 16 feet by 6 feet and holds 25 people comfortably. This area provides a rare opportunity to view bears gathered to feed at a salmon-spawning stream for a limited time in July. The bears stand at the falls and catch fish headed to their spawning areas.

Fishing

Catch-and-release fishing is encouraged throughout the park and required for rainbow trout fishing in the Brooks River. Brooks River is a fly-fishing-only river. The Naknek drainage offers grayling, Dolly Varden, northern pike, and the more abundant rainbow trout and sockeye (red) salmon. Coho (silver) and pink (humpback) salmon are sometimes taken in streams. Fishing at Brooks Camp can be peaceful and relaxing; at other times it can be hectic and crazy, as humans and bears compete. You must stay 50 yards away from single bears and 100 yards from groups of bears; this rule also applies when you are in the water. Operators provide fishing guides. Contact Brooks Lodge (see "Accommodations").

Boating

All state and federal boating regulations apply. Waters can become suddenly violent; know your boat and its operation before setting out. Beware of underwater rock outcrops. Watch the weather, and stay ashore when water is rough. Commercial operators can provide canoeing guides. Contact Brooks Lodge (see "Accommodations").

Sightseeing

Several commercial operators provide "flightseeing" trips. Vans also make daily round-trip excursions to the Valley of Ten Thousand Smokes; park rangers accompany these trips. Contact Brooks Lodge (see "Accommodations").

Ranger-Led Programs

The National Park Service conducts guided nature walks and evening programs at Brooks Camp from Memorial Day to Labor Day week. Evening programs on subjects such as brown bears, migration, and volcanoes take place in the visitor center. Nature walks—for example, to the pithouse, or to bird-watch or beachcomb—take place in the afternoons. Check at the visitor center for schedules.

The ice-capped coastal landscape of Kenai Fjords National Park offers a pristine stretch of mist-shrouded fjords, mountains, sea cliffs, and an ice-field wilderness. Seabirds and marine mammals add life to the beautiful seascapes of this very rugged and mostly remote Alaskan park.

Fjords are long, narrow ocean inlets between steep cliffs. Those for which the park is named are all along the coast here. These deep canyons full of ocean water, which look much like the fjords of Norway, were formed by glacial scouring. Glaciers are formed when snowfall exceeds snowmelt, and new snow piles on top of old. As the snow accumulates, the ever-increasing weight causes it to turn into ice. The weight of the snowmass eventually causes the glacier to begin to flow or stretch. As the ice moves along, it takes with it some of the land underneath, and thus carves and gouges out the landscape.

The Harding Icefield, the dominant feature of the park, is one of the four major ice caps in the United States. The source for most of the park's glaciers, it measures about 35 by 20 miles and its icy mass is interrupted only by a few mountains or nunataks. *Nunatak*, an Eskimo word, means "lonely peak." Because they reach down to the sea, eight of the park's glaciers are called "tidewater glaciers." At the water's edge they calve icebergs. The noise of the calving can be heard 20 miles away. Harbor seals can sometimes be seen riding on these floating icebergs in the sea. Exit Glacier, one of the glaciers flowing off the Harding Icefield, descends some 2,500 feet over its nearly three-mile-long flank. It is retreating, leaving in its wake bare land where vegetation is beginning to grow.

Also at work, changing the shape of the landscape here, are the movements of the plates below the surface of the earth. This movement is pushing the Kenai Mountains upward, but is slowy dragging the shoreline down along the coast of the park. Portions of the park's outer coast dropped six to eight feet in one dramatic event, the Good Friday, 1964, earthquake.

A rich rain forest, and the marine waters along the coast, support most of the surprisingly diverse wildlife in this rugged landscape. Mountain goats, moose, bears, wolverines, marmots, and other land mammals have reestablished themselves on the small area between the waters and the ice field's frozen edges. Bald eagles nest in the tops of spruce and hemlock trees. Sea lions and harbor seals gather on the rocky islands. Dall porpoises, sea otters, and gray, humpback, killer, and minke whales inhabit the fjord waters. Thousands of seabirds, including puffins, murres, kittiwakes, and gulls, breed on steep cliffs and rocky shores.

Another recent alteration to the land and marine system here was the 1989 *Exxon Valdez* oil spill in nearby Prince William Sound. Much of the coastline was affected by the spill. Although there is now little visible damage, only time will tell what long-term effects the spill has on the marine ecosystem.

NATIONAL PARK SERVICE

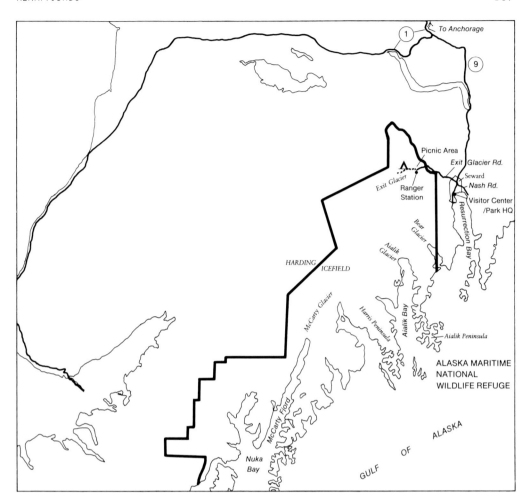

Further Information

Write or call: Superintendent, Kenai Fjords National Park, P.O. Box 1727, Seward, AK 99664; (907) 224-3175

Visitor Information

Park Headquarters/Visitor Center: At the Small Boat Harbor in the town of Seward; photo exhibit, slide programs, information. **Exit Glacier Ranger Station:** Exhibits on the glacier and Harding Icefield; information. (Closed fall to spring.)

Nuts and Bolts

Entrance Fee: None.
Park Open: All year.
Permits: Alaska fishing license is required.
In Emergency: At Exit Glacier, contact a ranger; in or around Seward, call 911.
Acreage: 669,541

Practical Advisory

Seasons

Spring/Summer/Fall: In this maritime climate of abundant rain, overcast, cool days may alternate with sunny, warm ones. Always be prepared for rain. May is the driest month; successive months see increasing precipitation. By mid-June daytime temperatures reach the mid-50s to mid-60s or higher. September initiates the wet and stormy fall. Winter: Weather is rainy, with temperatures in the 20s and 30s. The ice field receives 35–65 feet of snow annually.

Special Advisories

* Stay back from Exit Glacier; ice may fall unexpectedly at any time. This is an active glacier.

* Pay attention to all warning signs, and stay on designated trails.
* Hikers and boaters should beware of hypothermia.
* Black bears and brown/grizzly bears should always be considered dangerous. Beware of encounters and know what to do in case one occurs.

Facilities for Disabled

Exit Glacier Trail is wheelchair-accessible to within ¼ mile of the glacier.

Travel Advisory

Entrance

Exit Glacier Road from Seward is the only vehicle road into the park.

Transportation

Major airlines serve Anchorage; car rentals are in the airport. Bus service and commuter-flight services connect Anchorage with Seward. The Alaska Marine Highway (a ferry) connects Homer and Seldovia with Seward via Kodiak, providing further service to Valdez and Cordova. The Alaska Railroad serves Seward from Anchorage during the summer.

Attractions

Much of the park is ice-covered, the dominant feature being the *Harding Icefield*. Only one short road allows vehicle access into the park. The ice field and one of its glaciers, *Exit Gla-cier*, can be viewed by taking a strenuous trail accessible from this road. The *fjords* can best be seen by charter boat or kayak.

Accommodations

There is no food or lodging in the park. Seward provides full accommodations.

Campgrounds and Picnic Area

Exit Glacier Campground: Walk-in; 10 sites; ¾ mile from Exit Glacier; water, toilet; free.

Aialik Bay Cabin: Public-use cabin, available May through September; $20/night/group. Reservations should be made in advance by writing or calling the visitor center (see "Further Information," above).

Exit Glacier Cabin: For winter use, after Exit Glacier road is closed for season due to snow; $25/night/group. Reservations should be made in advance by writing or calling the visitor center (see "Further Information," above).

Picnic Area: Next to the parking lot at the Exit Glacier Ranger Station; tables.

Activities

Hiking

A half-mile trail with wayside exhibits begins at the Exit Glacier Ranger Station. A steep, rough-cut 3½-mile trail ascends the north side of Exit Glacier to a viewpoint overlooking the Harding Icefield. Allow all day for this strenuous hike. Backcountry hiking in this rugged wilderness requires good physical condition, proper equipment, and reasonable precautions. Get current specific local information before setting out. If hiking the Harding Icefield, be prepared to face sudden storms, high winds, blinding sunlight, and extreme temperature changes. Topographical maps are recommended and are available at the visitor center. Camping guides are available from commercial operators.

Scenic Drive

Exit Glacier is the only park area accessible by vehicle. A nine-mile gravel road at Mile 3.7 of the Seward Highway leads to the Exit Glacier Ranger Station.

Fishing

Saltwater fish taken in the waters off the park's coast include halibut, lingcod, and a variety of rockfish. Freshwater fish include Dolly Varden trout and silver, red, chum, and pink salmon. Fishing-guide services are available from commercial operations. Boat charters are available for fishing trips in Resurrection Bay.

Boating

The Gulf of Alaska is subject to strong winds and rough seas that can limit boat travel. Check at the visitor center for landing sites, mooring areas, weather conditions, and navigational hazards. A seaworthy craft and rough-water boating experience are important for safety. The more protected fjord waters are increasingly explored by sea kayakers, but the exposed outer coastline can be dangerous at times. Two areas frequently used by kayakers are Nuka Bay (McCarty Fjord) and Aialik Bay. Commercial kayaking-guide services are available.

Boat Trips

Charter boats from Seward offer scenic half-day or full-day tours. Scheduled daily charters operate from approximately mid-May to mid-September. You may observe calving glaciers, thousands of seabirds, and marine mammals including sea otters, the threatened northern sea lion, porpoises, and possibly humpback or killer whales. Boat charters are also available for overnight trips to the fjords.

Air and Bus Charters

Air charters from Seward or Homer are available. Scenic one-hour flights give views of the Harding Icefield. Landings can be arranged for day skiing or expeditions. Charters also overfly the coast for "flightseeing" and can take you to the fjords for extended kayak trips. In summer, bus excursions serve Exit Glacier from Seward.

Ranger-Led Activities

Activities include naturalist-led hikes to the glacier's base, Saturday evening campfire programs, and all-day hikes to the ice field from the ranger station at Exit Glacier. Interpretive programs are conducted daily in the visitor center auditorium during the summer as well.

Kobuk Valley is one of only two national parks north of the Arctic Circle. The valley for which the park is named is a gentle place bordered by the Baird Mountains to the north and the Waring Mountains to the south. Running through the valley is the slow-moving Kobuk River. Up to 1,500 feet wide in places, it falls only two to three inches per mile. Several rivers feed into the Kobuk, including the Salmon River, classified as a national wild and scenic river. Most visitors to the park come to float Kobuk's placid waters.

Within easy hiking distance from the river is one of the more interesting and unexpected sites in a park so far to the north: miles and miles of sand dunes. The 25 square miles of Great Kobuk Sand Dunes reach as high as 150 feet in places. This buff-colored sand, formed by the powerful forces of glaciers grinding down the earth, was blown here by winds and carried by water. Studies have shown that the dunes have been here for more than 30,000 years. In another part of the park are the Little Kobuk Sand Dunes, which cover another five square miles. Scientists believe the sand will continue to cover more ground as it slowly encroaches upon the surrounding boreal forest, at its northern limits here in the park.

The limited vegetation in the park provides important feeding grounds for native wildlife. The best-known inhabitants are the herd of western Arctic caribou that migrate annually across an extensive area of northwest Alaska. They spend a good part of late August through October in their fall range here in the Kobuk Valley. The herd, North America's largest, now numbers an incredible 340,000. The caribou must constantly search for plant food in the rugged tundra while watching out for their predators, most importantly wolves and bears. Other wildlife in the park includes moose, wolverines, foxes, eagles, weasels, and an abundance of migratory water birds.

The nomadic caribou have provided important subsistence for native people who live in this area. Their ancestors found their way here over the Bering Land Bridge, which at times has connected Alaska with Asia. Most likely, wildlife ventured over first, and the humans followed. Today's native people are living much as their ancestors did for thousands of years. During the long summer days, they fish in the water and dry the fish out in the sun. In the fall, they hunt for caribou and moose for their winter food supply.

Recent discoveries at Onion Portage in the park have proved that humans have hunted here for over 10,000 years. This area, below a bend in the river, is a crossing point for the migrating caribou. The artifacts found reveal that peoples of some seven different cultures have awaited the comings and goings of the caribou here. This is the most important archaeological site in the Far North. Archaeologists are hopeful that the park land will offer opportunities to uncover more clues to the earliest settlers in Alaska.

Further Information

Write or call: Superintendent, Kobuk Valley National Park, P.O. Box 1029, Kotzebue, AK 99752; (907) 442-3760, -3890

Visitor Information

Visitor Information Center: Outside the park in Kotzebue; information on river conditions, private land ownership, native subsistence activities.

Nuts and Bolts

Entrance Fee: None.
Park Open: All year.
Permits: Alaska fishing license is required.
In Emergency: Call park headquarters in Kotzebue at (907) 442-3890, or get assistance from local people, and/or report incident to a village search-and-rescue group.
Acreage: 1,750,421

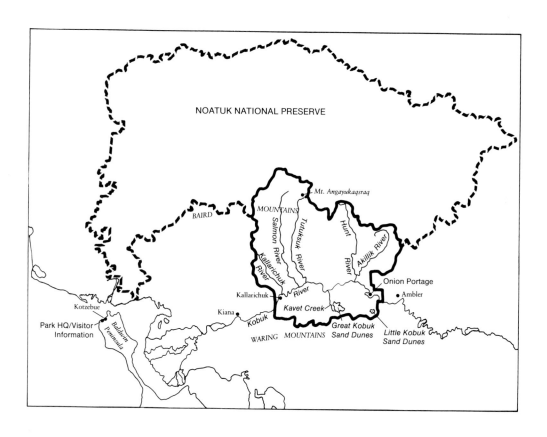

Practical Advisory

Seasons

Summer: Warm and brief. Temperatures in June, July, and August range from 40° to 90°, with daytime highs often in the upper 80s, but below-freezing temperatures may occur. June and July are usually clearest; rain increases in August and September. The midnight sun provides many hours of light through June and July. By September, nights are below freezing, but days can be clear and warm. The Kobuk River usually thaws by June 1 and freezes by the last week of September. Winter: Long and cold. Temperatures can drop to −60°, and −20° is common.

Special Advisories

- You must possess good backcountry skills for wilderness survival.

- Private lands are located within the park, generally along the rivers. Respect property and privacy; do not interfere with subsistence camps, fish nets, or other equipment.
- Sport hunting is prohibited, though it is legal to carry a firearm for bear protection only.
- Avoid encounters with bears and know what to do if one occurs.
- Head nets and insect repellent are recommended. Mosquitoes appear in late June, are at their worst in July, and disappear in August. Whitesocks and gnats hatch in August and continue into September.
- All visitors should be off the river by September 30; it will be freezing.

Facilities for Disabled

None.

Travel Advisory

Transportation

The park can be reached only by air. Scheduled flights from Fairbanks and Anchorage are available to Kotzebue airport and to Ambler and Kiana on the Kobuk River outside the park. Many Alaska package-tour companies, air taxis, and charter flights are also available. There are regularly scheduled flights from Kotzebue to the villages on the Kobuk. Flights may be chartered from Kotzebue, Kiana, Ambler, or Bettles to land on sandbars or beaches. There are no roads in the park.

Attractions

Most visitors to the park come to float the *Kobuk River* or, less often, the *Salmon River*. Also of interest are the unique *Great Kobuk Sand Dunes*, reachable via a fairly easy cross- country hike from the Kobuk River. There are no roads or trails in the park; you must be flown in, and then you are on your own.

Accommodations

There is no food, lodging, or campground facilities in the park. Tundra is often used for camping. Use caution when camping near rivers: Rapid changes in river levels can occur without warning. Campfires are permitted, and downed wood can usually be found. You may not cut live trees. A camp stove is recommended.

Activities

Floating the River

Motorboats, kayaks, canoes, and rafts are used on the Kobuk River for a variety of floating experiences. You should count on covering no more than 15 to 20 miles a day. Leave extra time in your itinerary for bad weather and side trips. The Kobuk is not a whitewater river; it is slow and winding. Tourists on the river fairly frequently encounter native people, since much of the land along the river is in private ownership. Native people will be engaged in subsistence activities; observe the courtesies due private citizens and their property. River-trip guides are available through operators outside of the park.

Hiking

There are no trails in the park. The northern tip of the Great Kobuk Sand Dunes can be reached—once you have floated the river into hiking range—by an easy cross-country hike from the Kobuk River, following the uplands near Kavet Creek. Hiking guides are available through operators outside of the park.

Fishing

Fishing can be good when rivers are clear and fish are running. Catches are best near or in the Kobuk's tributaries. Species include grayling, Arctic char, trout, sheefish, salmon, pike, and whitefish. Alaska fishing seasons and regulations apply. Sport-fishing guides are available through operators outside of the park.

Set in the heart of the Chigmit Mountains, Lake Clark National Park is where the mountains of the Aleutian Range and the Alaska Range join. The beautiful Chigmits, with gigantic glaciers flowing down their sides, are the centerpiece for the spectacularly lovely lakes, rivers, waterfalls, coastline, and tundra of the park.

On the eastern side of the jagged-peaked Chigmit Mountains, the land descends to Cook Inlet. Glacial rivers flow swiftly through Sitka spruce and white spruce forests down to the sea, where cormorants, puffins, and other seabirds nest on the rocky coast. The western side of the mountains offers a gentler slope down to the tundra-covered foothills, to the valleys with their boreal forests, and, eventually, to Lake Clark and the other lakes and wild rivers. In summer the park is ablaze with wildflowers. Two of the peaks, Redoubt and Iliamna, are semi-active volcanoes, part of the Pacific Ring of Fire which extends around the Pacific Ocean. These impressive peaks are each more than 10,000 feet tall.

The glacier-carved lakes in the park are numerous. The largest is Lake Clark, fed by hundreds of waterfalls cascading from the surrounding mountains. It is 50 feet long but is no more than 10 feet wide at any point. Native fish in the lakes include Arctic grayling; Dolly Varden, lake, and rainbow trout; and northern pike. The most awe-some display, however, is that of the red salmon that use the lake as a spawning ground.

Every year, beginning in late June, hordes of red salmon find their way here from any number of places in the Pacific Ocean. They will travel from Iliamna Lake up the Newhalen River to Lake Clark, arriving within three weeks of each other. They have numbered up to 9 million in any given year, sometimes creating a swath of red across the width of the lake as they head north. Those not caught by bears or humans will find their way to the exact place where they were born to begin their life cycle anew.

Other animals living in the park include brown and black bears, caribou, moose, Dall sheep, wolves, and lynx. Much of the wildlife in the park offers subsistence to the native people who live in the area. The park has been continuously occupied since prehistoric times. Archaeological studies are continuing to find clues to the earliest inhabitants. The Tanaina tribe lived in the area until the early part of this century, when they moved to adjacent areas. Around that time American and foreign settlers were attracted here for the commercial salmon-fishing possibilities. Now the sparsely populated park is becoming a popular fishing and river-running recreational destination; people can reach it from Anchorage in under two hours.

Further Information

Write or call: Superintendent, Lake Clark National Park, 4230 University Drive, Suite 311, Anchorage, AK 99508; (907) 271-3751

Visitor Information

Field headquarters: Located at Port Alsworth, outside the park.

Nuts and Bolts

Entrance Fee: None.
Park Open: All year.
Permits: Alaska fishing license is required.
Acreage: 2,636,839
In Emergency: Call (907) 781-2218

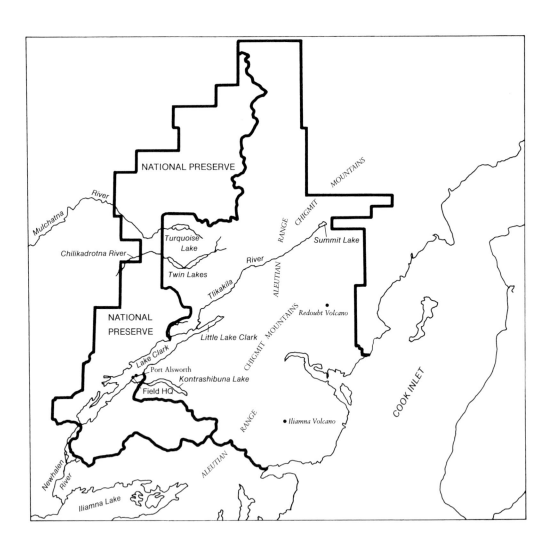

Practical Advisory

Seasons

Summer: From June through August, temperatures average between 50° and 65° and occasionally reach 80°, but even in midsummer there is evening frost. There is considerable precipitation, but the weather is warmer and drier west of the Chigmits. Fall, winter, and spring: Frost and snow can occur in September and October. Winter is long, lasting from October through April; temperatures in the interior can plummet to −40° and occasionally lower. Strong winds, severe in and near the mountain passes, can occur at any time. In some locations the sun does not rise for several months. Breakup in spring can immobilize the area, as ice melts and frozen ground turns to mud.

Special Advisories

• You are on your own and dependent on your own resources in the park. You must either be fully self-sufficient, with good skills for wilderness survival, or make arrangements with a guide. Winter travel can be recommended only to those experienced in cold-weather camping and survival techniques.
• The park is closed to sport hunting, but hunting is permitted in the adjacent preserve in accordance with State of Alaska regulations.
• Mosquitoes and biting flies may require a head net and/or repellent.
• Local residents carry on the subsistence way of life in the park with camps, fish nets, and other equipment. Practice courtesy and respect their property and their privacy.

Facilities for Disabled

None.

Travel Advisory

Transportation

Access to the region is almost exclusively by small aircraft. Floatplanes may land on the many lakes throughout the area. Wheeled planes land on open beaches, gravel bars, or private airstrips in or near the park. There is no highway access to the park. A one- to two-hour charter flight from Anchorage, Kenai, or Homer will provide access to most points within the park. Scheduled commercial flights between Anchorage and Iliamna, 30 miles outside the boundary, provide another means of access.

Attractions

The *mountains, lakes,* and *wild rivers* are the major features of this undeveloped park. Many visitors come to run the rivers, including *Tlikakila Wild River,* or to fish in the many lakes, including *Lake Clark.* The *Chigmit Mountains,* including *Redoubt Volcano* and *Iliamna Volcano,* provide a scenic backdrop.

Accommodations

There are no restaurants or campgrounds in the park.

Lodges

There are small lodges along the shore of Lake Clark; all but one are within the preserve.

Activities

Hiking

There is one established and maintained trail; it begins near the ranger station at Port Alsworth (outside the park, in the preserve) and leads to Tanalian Falls and Kontrashibuna Lake, ⅗ and five miles away from Port Alsworth, respectively. Other possible hiking areas include the western slopes of the park, higher and usually drier than the eastern portion of Lake Clark, which tends to have more precipitation and dense vegetation. The mountains themselves are steep, rugged, and subject to year-round inclement weather. Hiking guides can be hired through commercial operators.

Fishing

Fishing is generally good; the fish most commonly caught include grayling, Dolly Varden trout, red salmon, and lake trout. Commercial fishing trips may be arranged with outside operators.

Floating the Rivers

Float trips on the three designated wild rivers—Mulchatna, Tlikakila, and Chilikadrotna—as well as on other rivers in the area are popular. Commercial float trips may be arranged. Boats can be rented as well.

In the part of northeastern California where the Cascade Range meets the Sierra Nevada, lies Lassen Volcanic National Park. This scenic park is full of forests, lakes, streams, and meadows. It is most known, however, for its geothermal features including fumaroles, mud pots, hot springs, and one of the most recently active volcanoes in the United States, known as Lassen.

Lassen Peak, the volcano for which the park is named, actually began as a vent in the side of the mighty Tehama Volcano. The peak of Tehama eroded, however, and it is now extinct. Lassen's last active period began in the spring of 1914 and continued sporadically for seven years. The volcano's most awesome eruption took place in 1915, when an enormous cloud was blown seven miles straight up into the air. The fallout from the eruption profoundly affected all of the surrounding landscape. Although Lassen hasn't erupted since then, scientists believe it will again. Lassen is considered the world's largest plug-dome volcano, rising to 10,457 feet above sea level. It is one in a series of active, dormant, and extinct volcanoes that form the Pacific Ring of Fire, a ring of volcanoes nearly encircling the Pacific Ocean.

Other volcanic features can be seen in the park: lava pinnacles (huge mountains created by lava flows); smaller cinder cones; and, in the eastern part of the park, a vast lava plateau more than a mile above sea level. Cinder Cone is an 800-foot-high pile of volcanic cinders. During eruptions of this volcano, fragments of lava would often fall back around the vent. The accumulated lava is the huge cone of today. Most of the lava in the park was produced by eruptions of Mount Harkness. Chaos Jumbles, a 4½-square-mile area of shattered rocks and boulders, may be the result of a rockfall about 300 years ago from the collapse of an unstable volcanic dome in Chaos Crags. The tremendous avalanche sent boulders flying down the sides of the mountains at incredible speeds.

The park also contains the most extensive collection of active geothermal features in the Cascade Range. There are hot springs, mud pots, fumaroles, and steaming sulphur vents. Some of the waters are at temperatures above the boiling point, 212°F. Scientists say some of these thermal features are getting even hotter. Bumpass Hell is the largest area of geothermal activity in the park, containing acres of boiling pools, mud pots, and steam vents.

Lassen Park includes both barren-looking landscape destroyed by volcanic activity and areas of diverse and lush plant life. The park boasts over 700 species of plant life, mixing species of the Cascades with those of the Sierra Nevada. Lake Manzanita is surrounded by pines and firs, and beautiful meadows are covered with colorful wildflowers in spring. The Devastated Area of the park is a good representation of life coming back to a barren area as it slowly becomes reforested.

Four different Native American tribes frequented the land that is now the park:

NATIONAL PARK SERVICE

the Atsugewi, the Yana, the Yahi, and the Maidu. The California gold rush in the mid-1800s brought white settlers to the area. Two men, William Nobles and Peter Lassen, devised trails that traversed the area. Part of Nobles Emigrant Trail is still visible in the park. Lassen, for whom the park was named, tried unsuccessfully to found a city near the Sacramento River. He brought emigrants across the country on his trail to the town.

Further Information

Write or call: Superintendent, Lassen Volcanic National Park, P.O. Box 100, Mineral, CA 96063-0100; (916) 595-4444

Visitor Information

Manzanita Lake Visitor Center: Information; sales of books and maps.
Southwest Information Station: Sale of books and maps.

Nuts and Bolts

Entrance Fee: $5/vehicle or $2/person arriving by other means.
Park Open: All year. The park road is closed by snow from November to late May or early June, and most of the park trails are often snow-covered through early June.
Permits: Required for backcountry camping. California fishing license required.
In Emergency: Call (916) 595-4444, or 911
Acreage: 106,372.36

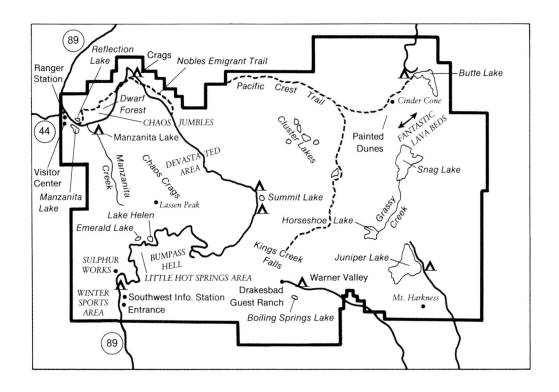

Practical Advisory

Seasons

Summer: Temperatures range from highs in the 80s to lows in the high 40s. Winter: Temperatures range from the 40s to the 20s. Most precipitation is in the winter. Annual snowfall is up to 700 inches.

Special Advisories

- Boiling water may be present at or near the surface in park thermal areas. The crusts over some geothermal feaures are brittle; breaking through them can plunge you into boiling water. Stay on trails and boardwalks where provided, and watch children.
- Bears are present, but not often encountered, in the backcountry. Give them the right of way.
- Volcanic rock is generally unstable and poorly suited to rock climbing.

Facilities for Disabled

The following are wheelchair-accessible. At the Manzanita Lake Visitor Center: Rest rooms, Indian Ways Program (with assistance), campsite rest rooms, amphitheater (with assistance). At the Summit Lake campsite: Rest rooms, picnic area (with assistance). At the southwest entrance: Information station, chalet rest rooms, campground rest rooms. At Butte Lake Campground: campsite rest rooms. At Lassen Park headquarters: Information desk, rest rooms. At Bumpass Hell: Portable rest room (with assistance). At Lassen Peak: portable rest room (with assistance).

Travel Advisory

Entrances

West: Highway 44 for 48 miles east from Redding to Manzanita Lake entrance.

South: Highway 36 (west) and Highway 89 (north) for 65 miles from Susanville or 52 miles east and north from Red Bluff to southwest entrance.

North: Highway 44 for 26 miles north and east of Manzanita Lake, then six miles south on a dirt road to Butte Lake entrance.

South: 13 miles on a paved and gravel road from Chester to Juniper Lake entrance.

South: 17 miles northwest of Chester on a paved and gravel road to Warner Valley entrance.

Transportation

Airports: Airlines serving Redding, Reno, and Chico. Private planes can land at Chester and Red Bluff.

Bus Service: Greyhound and Trailways bus lines serve Red Bluff (52 miles) and Redding (48 miles) daily from Sacramento (162 miles) and San Francisco (247 miles). Greyhound operates between Reno, Nevada (150 miles), and Susanville (65 miles) daily. Buses serve Mineral from Red Bluff (52 miles) and Susanville (65 miles).

Train Service: Amtrak serves Redding and Chico.

Rental Cars: Available at Redding, Red Bluff, Chico, Susanville, and Reno.

Attractions

Of special interest in the park are the *volcanic and geothermal features,* including *Lassen Volcano* which can be driven around on three sides or hiked up. *Cinder Cone* is a less accessible but interesting volcanic vent. Two of the most popular geothermal areas are *Sulphur Works* and *Bumpass Hell* (the largest). They contain boiling pools, mud pots, and steam vents, which can be viewed from boardwalks. Also of interest is the *Chaos Jumbles* area, the result of an avalanche from the *Chaos Crags* rocks, and the *Devastated Area,* which is slowly rejuvenating itself. The park has much natural scenery to enjoy as well, including the popular *Manzanita Lake.*

Accommodations

Lodge

Drakesbad Guest Ranch: Accessible by trail or unpaved road; full American plan; lodging; swimming pool, horses (for guests); open approximately June through September. Reservations: California Guest Services, Inc., Adobe Plaza, 2150 Main Street, Suite 7, Red Bluff, CA 96080; (916) 529-1512.

Campgrounds and Picnic Areas

First-come, first-served; 14-day limit per year (Lost Creek and Summit have seven-day limits); open (approximately) June to October. Fires are prohibited except in fire grates or grills. Use only dead and downed trees for firewood. Note: All campgrounds are above 5,600 feet in elevation.

Butte Lake Campground: Only accessible via unpaved road; 98 sites; fireplaces, tables, water, toilets, garbage collection; $8/night.

Crags Campground: 45 sites (overflow only), five miles from Manzanita Lake off the park road; fireplaces, tables, water, chemical toilets, garbage collection; accommodates trailers to 35 feet; $6/night.

Juniper Lake Campground: On east shore of Juniper Lake; 18 sites; accessible only via unpaved road; primitive; fireplaces, tables, pit toilets, garbage disposal; not recommended for trailers; free.

Manzanita Lake Campground: South of the lake off the park road; 179 sites; fireplaces, tables, flush toilets, water, garbage collection, dump station; accommodates trailers to 35 feet; $8/night.

Southwest Campground: Lassen Chalet parking area off park road; 21 walk-in sites; fireplace, tables, water, flush toilets, garbage collection; $6/night. (RVs may park overnight in Chalet parking for $3/night.)

North Summit Lake Campground: Off park road; 46 sites; fireplaces, tables, flush toilets, garbage collection; $8/night.

South Summit Lake Campground: Off park road; 48 sites; fireplaces, tables, pit toilets, garbage collection; $6/night.

Warner Valley Campground: Accessible only via unpaved road; 18 sites; fireplaces, tables, water, pit toilets, garbage collection; not recommended for trailers; $6/night.

Picnic Areas: At Manzanita Lake and Kings Creek, and near Bumpass Hell. All off main park road; tables.

Restaurants

Lassen Summer Chalet: Near southwest entrance; fast-food service, outside deck dining in summer.

Drakesbad Guest Ranch: 47 miles from southwest entrance; dining room.

Activities

Scenic Drives

The scenic 35-mile main park road loops around three sides of Lassen Peak. It offers access to trails, lakes, and volcanic and geothermal features. A *Road Guide to Lassen National Park* is a booklet available at information centers for a fee. Roadside markers keyed to the guide explain various natural and historic features.

Hiking

The park's 150 miles of trails include a 17-mile section of the Pacific Crest Trail. Trails vary in length and difficulty, winding through coniferous forests, alpine tundra and along waterways. The "Lassen Trails" booklet describes popular hikes. Self-guiding trails make good introductions both to hiking and to the park. If you are unused to them, the park's generally high elevations will likely leave you short of breath; take time to get acclimated.

Fishing

There are catch and possession limits. Lassen's waters are home to native rainbow trout as well as to introduced brook and brown trout. Emerald Lake, Manzanita Creek above Manzanita Lake, and the area of Manzanita Lake within 150 feet of the Manzanita Creek outlet are permanently closed to fishing. Grassy Creek connecting Horseshoe and Snag Lakes is closed from October 1 to June 15. Digging for bait in the park is prohibited. Do not clean fish in park waters.

Boating

Rowboats, canoes, and other unmotorized boats can be used on all park lakes except Reflection, Emerald, Helen, and Boiling Springs. Power boats, including boats with electric motors, are prohibited on park waters. There are no boat rentals in the park.

Bicycling

Bicycles are allowed only on paved roads and parking areas.

Winter Sports:

There is a winter sports area, including downhill and cross-country skiing, near the southwest entrance of the park.

Horseback Riding

Use of horses and other stock is permitted, subject to certain restrictions and regulations. Pack and saddle stock may stay overnight only in the corrals provided at Butte Lake, Summit Lake, and Juniper Lake. Reservations are required. There is a small corral near the northern park boundary for Pacific Crest Trail users.

Naturalist Programs

Check for schedules at visitor centers.

Below the ground at Mammoth Cave National Park is the world's most extensive system of underground passageways. The landscape of this multilevel cave is full of pits and domes, rivers, and a diverse collection of animals adapted to life in the cave. Ever since its discovery, new explorers have each attempted to go a little farther into the cave, trying to find its end. Over 335 miles of passageways have been found to date. But still the end has not been reached.

Parts of the massive Mammoth Cave were used by Native Americans as many as 4,000 years ago. Well-preserved artifacts, clothing, and even mummies from that time have been discovered. Modern exploration began in the late 1790s. The cave became commercially important during the War of 1812 between the United States and England. Cave sediments with large quantities of nitrate, an important ingredient in gunpowder, were mined by slaves for use in the war effort. Eventually, the cave came to be known as a popular tourist attraction, as it remains today.

The incredible wonders of Mammoth Cave are due to a very simple substance: water. Water has been eating away at the limestone for millions of years, carving out the passageways. The upper passages of the cave were hollowed out as long as 10 million years ago; they are dry today. The lower passages are still being enlarged by the flowing waters of Echo River and other underground streams.

Beautiful decorations in the caves are also the result of water. Water saturated with dissolved calcium carbonate trickles down into the cave, making its way to the floor or just to the ceiling. Although the water evaporates, the calcium carbonate remains, drop on top of drop eventually creating the surreal formations of the cave. Here in Mammoth are the more familiar stalactites, formed on the ceilings, and stalagmites, formed on the floor. But there are also examples of flowstone, draperies, and helictites. Other interesting formations are the gypsum flowers formed in the dry passages; some say they look alive.

Strangely enough, this dark, cool world actually does support life. Some unusual forms of animals have evolved to survive here. The rivers and streams are home to small, eyeless, albino fish. Eyes, of course, would be useless in the complete blackness of the cave. In place of sight the fish have developed extra-sensitive organs on their head and body that can detect when anything is near them. Other eyeless animals living in the cave include crayfish, beetles, and crickets.

A visit here affords the opportunity to explore not only the fascinating sights belowground at Mammoth Cave, but also the contrasting aboveground world. The park offers forests of oak and hickory, the Green and Nolin rivers, rugged hillsides, and other natural beauty.

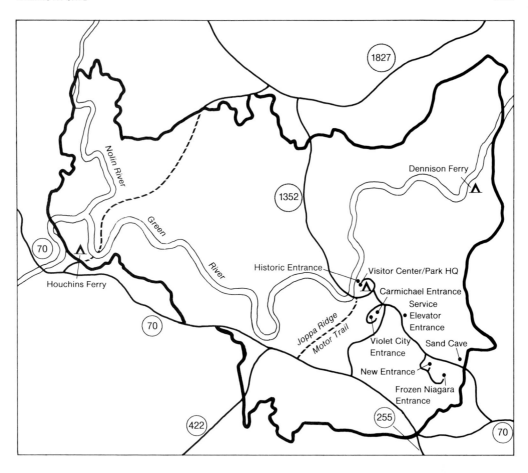

Further Information

Write or call: Superintendent, Mammoth Cave National Park, Mammoth Cave, KY 42259; (502) 758-2328

Visitor Information

Visitor Center: Cave-tour tickets sold here; orientation slide program, movie, exhibits, park activity schedules, park information.

Nuts and Bolts

Entrance Fee: None. A fee is charged for cave tours.
Park Open: All year. No services on December 25.
Permits: Required for backcountry camping.
In Emergency: Call 758-2251 or, after 7 P.M., 286-8917.
Acreage: 52,700

Practical Advisory

Seasons

Cave: The temperature remains nearly the same all year, in the mid-50s to low 60s.

Aboveground: Summer: Temperatures may range from 45° at night to 100° during the day. Average temperature is 90°; July and August are the hottest months. Winter: Temperatures range from below 0° to 70°. Average daily temperature is about 34°. Most snow occurs in January and February. Fog is possible.

Special Advisories

In the cave
• Sturdy low-heeled walking shoes are recommended for cave tours.
• Stay with tour and on cave trails.
• The cave is cool; you'll be most comfortable if you wear long pants and take a sweater or jacket.
• Persons with heart or respiratory problems or who have difficulty walking should talk with a ranger before taking a cave tour.
• Tripods and strollers are not permitted on cave tours.
• Smoking in the cave is prohibited.

Aboveground
• Be alert for ticks, chiggers, and poisonous snakes.

Facilities for Disabled

A special cave tour is offered for physically impaired persons. The visitor center is fully accessible; Loop D of the main campground, including rest-room facilities, is wheelchair-accessible; the picnic area is minimally accessible. The Heritage Trail is especially designed to accommodate people with disabilities.

Travel Advisory

Entrance

I-65 south to Highway 70 west for nine miles from Cave City; or I-65 north to Highway 255 west for eight miles from Park City.

Transportation

Airports: Airlines serve Louisville, Kentucky, which is 81 miles from the park, and Nashville, Tennessee, which is 85 miles from the park.

Bus Service: Southeastern Greyhound buses stop in Cave City. Taxi service is available from the bus station to the park.

Train Service: Not available.

Rental Cars: Available at airports.

Attractions

Mammoth Cave and its formations, including *stalactites, stalagmites, flowstone,* and *gypsum flowers,* are the major features of the park. Park rangers offer several diferent guided tours of the cave. There is also much natural beauty aboveground, including the *Green River.*

Accommodations

Lodges

For reservations at any of the lodges contact National Park Concessions, Mammoth Cave, KY 42259; (502) 758-2225.

Mammoth Cave Hotel: Hotel rooms; open all year.

Sunset Point Motor Lodge: Open all year.

Hotel and Woodland Cottages: Near the hotel; available from spring to fall.

Campgrounds and Picnic Area

Open all year on a first-come, first-served basis.

Headquarters Campground: 111 sites; ¼ mile from visitor center; rest rooms, grills, tables, water; $6/night.

Houchins Ferry Campground: 12 sites; on Green River near Brownsville; chemical toilets, grills, tables, water; free.

Dennison Ferry Campground: Four sites; at east boundary of park on Green River; chemical toilet, grills, tables; free.

Backcountry Camping: Allowed on the north side of the park, at designated sites along the trails.

Picnic Area: Near the visitor center; grills and rest rooms.

Restaurants

Snowball Dining Room: Lunch; underground, in the cave.

Mammoth Cave Hotel: Dining room; open all year.

Activities

Cave Tours

A variety of ranger-guided tours are offered, from ¼ mile and 1¼ hours long to five miles and 6½ hours long. Five tours are offered all year, four others only in the summer. Tours include the two-hour Historic Tour, which traces the long history of the cave; the Half Day Tour, which lasts 4½ hours; and the Frozen Niagara Tour, which lasts two hours and brings you to the fine example of flowstone in the Frozen Niagara room. The Lantern Tour, given only in summer, re-creates an old-time tour, when guides led the way with kerosene lanterns. Most tours are strenuous and require stooping, walking over irregular terrain, and climbing steps. Most follow dry, smooth, hard-surfaced trails, but portions can be wet and slippery. Cave tours sell out quickly. National Park officials strongly urge you to make reservations. Reservations can be made through MISTIX: Call (800) 365-2267 no earlier than 56 days and no later than one hour before the tour.

Hiking

Seventy miles of trails wind through the park. Approximately 60 miles is made up of backcountry trails located on the north side of the park. Roughly 10 miles of trails are on the south side of the park, concentrated near the visitor center. Maps are available at the visitor center. Guided hikes are offered in summer. The trails are appropriate for day hikes, overnight stays, or more extensive trips. The paved Heritage Trail begins near the Sunset Point Motor Lodge and is lighted for evening use.

River Trips

A scenic boat cruise along the Green River is available on the *Miss Green River II* from April through October. The cruise lasts one hour. For reservations, stop at the visitor center or call (502) 758-2243. Canoeists can float the Green and Nolin rivers. Canoe rentals are available from private operators outside the park.

Horseback Riding

Horseback riding is permitted in the park. Rentals are available from local concessioners.

Fishing

Fishing is permitted in the Green and Nolin rivers; state creel limits apply. Check at the visitor center for additional information and regulations.

Ranger-Led Activities

Evening ranger programs are given in the summer at an amphitheater and a campfire circle near Headquarters Campground.

About 1,450 years ago, on a high plateau in what is now known as the Four Corners region of the Southwest (near where Colorado, New Mexico, Arizona, and Utah meet), a tribe of nomadic Native Americans decided to try and settle.

These people and their descendants, whom we now call the Anasazi, "the ancient ones", stayed for more than 700 years. Over time, they grew in knowledge and experience in the ways of farming and living socially within a community. The last settlements they built were spectacular dwellings in the sheltered recesses of the canyon walls beneath the plateau. Many of their well-preserved homes remain today; these are the central feature of Mesa Verde National Park.

Originally, the Anasazi lived in pithouses and then in post and adobe houses. Among the many things archaeologists still do not know about these people is why they made the decision to move to homes on the sides of the cliffs. Since the Anasazi left no written records behind, only speculations can be made as to their reasons. But building these incredible cliff homes had to have been a difficult and time-consuming task.

Tree-ring dates indicate that Cliff Palace took more than 70 years to finish. The basic material was sandstone, which the builders shaped into rectangular blocks. The mortar between the blocks was a mix of mud and water. All of these materials had to be hand-carried down the sides of the cliffs to the recesses where the people were building.

It doesn't seem that there was any standard plan to these homes; the Anasazi fitted the structures into the available space.

The dwellings were built at around 7,000 feet above sea level, several hundred feet above the canyon floor and about 100 feet from the mesa tops. They usually had to be reached via ladders or handholds and toeholds that were built into the sides of the canyon walls. They ranged in size from one to over 200 rooms. Many were single-family homes, but the number of residents varied. It is believed that Anasazi society was made up of matrilineal clans—that is, property and family names were passed on from mother to daughter.

The front rooms of the dwellings, which averaged about six feet by eight feet, were living quarters, and the back rooms were mostly storage areas. The courtyards in front of the rooms were used by the women for making pottery, grinding corn, and preparing food, and by the men for making tools out of stones and bone. There was also a special room, the kiva, set aside for religious and ceremonial purposes. In the round kivas the Anasazi prayed for rain, good crops, or good luck on hunting expeditions.

In the fields on top of the mesa the men tended the crops of corn, squash, and beans and hunted for deer, rabbit, and squirrels. They also cut piñon and juniper for firewood. The Anasazi constantly struggled for survival. They had to depend on the goodwill of the weather for their crops. They

learned to build check dams along draws to conserve moisture. They knew they had to store enough food during the warm months for them to live on during the long winters. Remarkably, they did take the time and the energy to express themselves in the beautiful pottery they created. Their ancestors were known for their intricate basketmaking. But once they learned the uses of pottery they all but abandoned baskets. Black painted designs on white pottery are what the Ana-sazi are known for, and many relics remain today that show their fine artistic abilities.

No one knows for sure why in the late 1200s the Anasazi picked up and left these incredible homes after they took so long to build them. Many believe that there was a long drought and that the overused soil could not keep the Anasazi alive any longer. It is believed they headed south and became the ancestors of many of today's Pueblo tribes, including the Hopi.

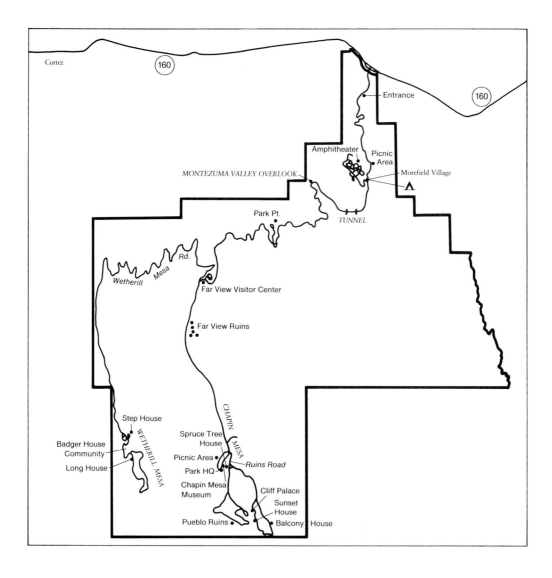

Further Information

Write or call: Superintendent, Mesa Verde National Park, Mesa Verde National Park, CO 81330; (303) 529-4461 or -4475

Visitor Information

Far View Visitor Center: Information; arts-and-crafts exhibits. Closed fall to spring.
Chapin Mesa Museum: Information; arts-and-crafts exhibits.

Nuts and Bolts

Entrance Fee: $5/vehicle or $3/person arriving by other means. Good for seven consecutive days.
Park Open: The main park road is open all year. Wetherill Mesa and the Cliff Palace–Balcony House loop of Ruins Road are closed in winter. There is limited access to the ruins in winter.
Permits: None needed.
In Emergency: Call 529-4469.
Acreage: 52,085.14

Practical Advisory

Seasons

Summer: High temperatures reach the mid-90s; evening temperatures are usually in the 60s. Thunder showers are possible. Fall and spring: Daytime temperatures are in the 50s and 60s; nighttime temperatures are in the 20s and 30s in fall and the 30s and 50s in spring. Winter: Daytime temperatures are in the 40s; nighttime temperatures are in the teens but can drop below 0°. There is an average of 80–100 inches of snowfall.

Special Advisories

* Entering a cliff dwelling without a park ranger present will result in a citation and fine. Only if a ranger is present in the dwellings may you tour them.
* Altitudes in the park vary from 6,000 to 8,500 feet. Trails may be uneven; steps and ladders must frequently be climbed. Not recommended for persons with heart or respiratory ailments.
* Trailers and towed vehicles are prohibited beyond Morefield Campground.

Facilities for Disabled

Six campsites with rest rooms at Morefield Campground are accessible to physically impaired persons.

Travel Advisory

Entrance

U.S. 160 for 10 miles east of Cortez or for eight miles west of Mancos.

Note: It is 21 miles from the park entrance to the Chapin Mesa ruins.

Transportation

Airports: There are daily scheduled flights to Cortez (10 miles from the park) and Durango (35 miles from the park).

Bus Service: Buses from Grand Junction, Colorado, and Gallup, New Mexico, serve Durango.

Train Service: Trains serve Grand Junction, Colorado, and Gallup, New Mexico.

Rental Cars: Rental cars are available in Durango and Cortez.

Attractions

The well-preserved *homes of the Anasazi* are the central features of the park. You can tour many of these, including *Spruce Tree House, Cliff Palace* (the largest cliff dwelling in the Southwest), and *Balcony House* on Chapin Mesa; *Long House, Step House,* and the *Badger House Community* of mesa-top villages on Wetherill Mesa; and the *Far View Ruins.* It is also possible to view many of the dwellings from overlooks on the park roads.

Other Points of Interest (Museums, Historic Sites, etc.)

Chapin Mesa Museum has dioramas that portray the life of the ancient Anasazi. *Far View Visitor Center,* open only in the summer, has exhibits on the arts and crafts of both the prehistoric and historic Anasazi and the Southwest.

Accommodations

Lodge

Far View Motor Lodge: Open May through October. For reservations: ARA Mesa Verde Company, Box 277, Mancos, CO 81328; (303) 529-4421 (summer) or (303) 533-7731 (winter).

Campgrounds and Picnic Areas

Camping is permitted only in designated campground; no backcountry camping. The gathering of firewood is prohibited. First-come, first-served; 14-day limit. Camps should not be left unattended for more than 24 hours.

Morefield Campground: 477 sites; four miles south of park entrance; modern toilets, tables, grills; some utility hookups are available; dump station; open mid-April through mid-October; $8/night without hookups, $15.50/night with hookups for one or two persons and $2/each additional person over 12.

Picnic Areas: Seven, off the park roads, at Wetherill Mesa, the museum area on Chapin Mesa, both loops of the Ruins Road, Morefield Campground, and two overlooks.

Restaurants

All open May through October, except Spruce Tree Terrace, which is open year-round.

Far View Motor Lodge: Restaurant.

Far View Terrace: Breakfast, lunch, and dinner.

Wetherill Mesa: Sandwiches and cold drinks.

Spruce Tree Terrace: Light breakfast, lunch, snacks; patio dining.

Knife Edge Cafe: At Morefield Village; snacks, meals, breakfast; patio dining.

Activities

Touring the Ruins

It is possible to visit many of the important cliff dwellings and mesa-top pueblos. Following are the major sites.

Spruce Tree House: Open on a self-guided basis in the summer. In the winter, ranger-led tours are conducted three times daily, conditions permitting.

Cliff Palace: Open on a self-guided basis in the summer and sometimes in late spring and early fall, conditions permitting.

Balcony House: This ranger-led tour requires climbing a 32-foot ladder and crawling through an ancient crawlspace. Tours offered in summer only.

Far View Ruins: Open on a self-guided basis mid-April to mid-November. A guide booklet to the mesa-top pueblos is available from the museum and visitor center.

Wetherill Mesa: Vehicles are allowed on the 12-mile stretch from the visitor center to the parking area on the mesa. From there, take the mini-tram to Long House for a ranger-led tour. The Badger House Community of mesa-

top villages and Step House are open on a self-guided basis. Offers excellent views of the surrounding area. There are size and weight restrictions on vehicles. Open only in summer.

Scenic Drives

Many cliff dwellings can be seen from canyon-rim viewpoints, where wayside exhibits explain the development of Anasazi culture from the Basket Makers through the classic period. Ruins Road offers two six-mile self-guiding loops on Chapin Mesa from which you can see two of the major cliff dwellings of the area—Cliff Palace and Balcony House—as well as others. Park Point offers a spectacular panoramic view of the Four Corners region.

Hiking

To protect fragile ruins, hiking is restricted to five trails within the park. Hikers must register at the rangers' office before attempting these trails. Two trails lead into Spruce Canyon. The Petroglyph Point Trail, 2⅖ miles, and Spruce Canyon Trail, 2¹⁄₁₀ miles, begin at points on the Spruce Tree House Trail. Prater Ridge Trail, 7⅘ miles; Knife Edge Trail, 1½ miles; and Point Lookout Trail, 2⅓ miles, originate at Morefield Campground. Soda

Canyon Overlook Trail on the Cliff Palace–Balcony House loop requires no registration and is about a 1½-mile round-trip walk. All trails are closed in the winter.

Bicycling

Permitted on all park roads except those on Wetherill Mesa. Lanes are not designated and roads are narrow and crowded, especially in summer. Use caution.

Bus Tours

Commercial tours of Chapin Mesa leave from Far View Motor Lodge from late May to mid-September. Tour pithouses, pueblo sites, and cliff dwellings with a stop at the museum and for lunch. The six-hour tours leave daily at 9 A.M. A fee is charged.

Ranger Talks

During summer, rangers give nightly talks in the amphitheater. Subjects vary but all concern the natural history and resources of Mesa Verde. Check bulletin boards at the visitor center and campgrounds for information.

Dense evergreen forests, wildflower-strewn meadows, cascading waterfalls of melting snow, and ice-white glaciers spilling down mountain slopes—all these define the beauty of Mount Rainier National Park. And towering above all this natural beauty is the mighty mountain itself, at 14,410 feet the highest point for miles around.

Mount Rainier is a volcanic mountain, part of a string of volcanoes in the Cascade Range, from Lassen Peak in California to Mount Garibaldi in British Columbia. Rainier is relatively young, as volcanoes go. Scientists believe it was only around a million years ago that its first eruption burst through the earth's surface. More violent eruptions followed, spewing out ash, lava, and pumice. The material from repeated eruptions slowly built up around the source, until layer upon layer created the mountain of today.

Rainier has been dormant for around 2,500 years, but that is not a long time in the world of volcanoes. And although scientists continue to study and watch it, they are still not able accurately to predict what it may do in the future. It could erupt again, as did nearby Mount St. Helens in 1980, or possibly it could just blow steam. Volcanologists do not know for sure, but they have not ruled out the possibility of future activity in Mount Rainier.

While it was the great force of volcanic fire that built up Rainier's impressive peak, another force of nature is now at work breaking it down. That other force is the much-slower-working power of ice. The icy glaciers on the mountain are still at work here, changing and reshaping the landscape. There are quite a number of them, covering nearly 34 square miles. All in all, there are 25 named glaciers and about 50 small, unnamed glaciers and ice patches. Emmons Glacier is the largest on the mountain.

Glaciers are formed when the level of snowfall exceeds the rate at which it can melt. The snow piles on itself, and eventually its weight forces the air out, compacting the snow and turning it to ice. Then gravity begins to work on the heavy ice, which is actually pulled down the side of the mountain, advancing at an incredibly slow pace. As the ice moves, it brings with it rocks, boulders, and debris, which often become a part of the ice. Near the tips of the glaciers, where the ice is melting, streams and rivers take more debris with them, depositing it along their way. This icy covering on Rainier creates special challenges for those attempting to scale its peak, making it very difficult to conquer.

The valleys and foothills of the mountain are free from ice and are made up of a wonderfully rich soil created from the nutrient-filled ash and pumice left by the volcano's eruptions. This soil has produced dense forests. The Carbon River section of the park, named for the coal deposits found there, gets the heaviest rainfall and has the most luxuriant forest. The lowland forest in the Ohanapecosh section is known for the Grove of the Patriarchs, full of Douglas fir,

NATIONAL PARK SERVICE, PHOTO BY L. LANE

western red cedar, and western hemlock.

Broad meadows in the park also benefit from the rich soil and are sprinkled in the late spring and summer with a profusion of brightly colored wildflowers. Paradise, the center of most of the park's activity, is a most beautiful flower-filled alpine meadow.

The native wildlife finds much in the park for its subsistence. Animal inhabitants include elk, black bears, cliff-dwelling mountain goats, and the more often seen deer, chipmunks, ground squirrels, marmots, and pika.

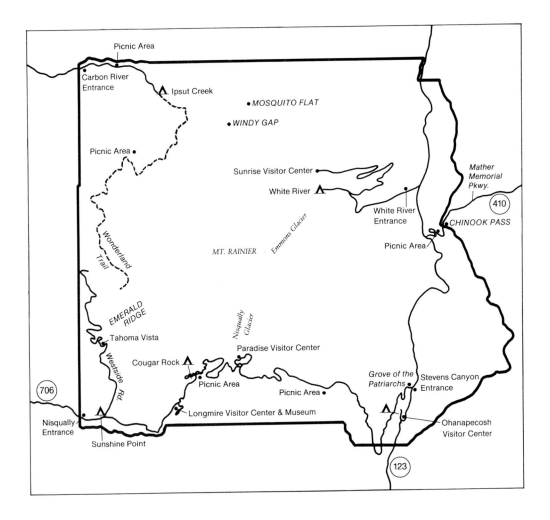

Further Information

Write or call: Superintendent, Mount Rainier National Park, Ashford, WA 98304; (206) 569-2211

Visitor Information

Longmire Visitor Center: Information and exhibits.
Paradise Visitor Center: Information, exhibits, and audio-visual programs.
Ohanapecosh Visitor Center: Information and exhibits on the Northwest forest.
Sunrise Visitor Center: Information and exhibits on the subalpine and alpine environments.

Nuts and Bolts

Entrance Fee: $5/vehicle or $3/person arriving by other means. Good for seven days.
Park Open: All year. Only the Nisqually entrance is open in winter.
Permits: Required for backcountry camping and mountain climbing.
In Emergency: Call 569-2211.
Acreage: 235,404

Practical Advisory

Seasons

Sudden and extreme weather changes. Mount Rainier is often said to create its own weather. The park has great amounts of rain and snowfall. The heaviest precipitation occurs between October and early May. Average summer temperatures range from the mid-70s to the upper 40s at Longmire, and from the mid-60s to the lower 40s at Paradise.

Special Advisory

• Always carry rain gear.

Facilities for Disabled

Limited facilities; visitor centers, some rest rooms, and some trails are wheelchair-accessible.

Travel Advisory

Entrances

Southwest: Highway 7 to Highway 706 for 47 miles southeast of Tacoma to Nisqually entrance.

Southeast: U.S. 12 to Highway 123 to Stevens Canyon entrance.

North: Highway 410 from Buckley to White River entrance.

Transportation

Airports: Scheduled flights serve Portland and Seattle/Tacoma airports.

Bus Service: Greyhound/Trailways provides bus service to major nearby towns and cities. Gray Line runs buses from Tacoma and Seattle to the park, from mid-spring to mid-fall.

Train Service: Amtrak provides rail service on both north–south and east–west routes stopping at Yakima, Ellensburg, East Auburn, and Seattle.

Rental Cars: Rental cars are available in Portland, Seattle, Tacoma, and Yakima.

Attractions

The central feature of the park is its namesake, *Mount Rainier*. It can be seen throughout the park, and you can hike a trail that completely encircles it. *Paradise Valley* is the center of most activity in the park. *Sunrise*, the highest point you can reach by road, offers good views of *Emmons Glacier*, the largest of the glaciers that cover much of the mountain. Also of interest is the lowland forest in the *Grove of the Patriarchs*.

Other Points of Interest (Museums, Historic Sites, etc.)

A *museum* tells of the early days of the park. It is at the site of the Mineral Spring Resort, which James Longmire opened in 1884 in Longmire, the oldest developed area of the park.

Accommodations

Lodges

For reservations: Mount Rainier Guest Services, 55106 Kernahan Road East, P.O. Box 108, Ashford, WA 98304; (206) 569-2275.

The National Park Inn: At Longmire; hotel rooms; open year-round.

Paradise Inn: Open only in summer.

Campgrounds and Picnic Areas

Make fires only in fire rings or grills at designated areas. First-come, first-served; 14-day limit.

Cougar Rock Campground: 200 sites; water, flush toilets, dump station; open late May to mid-October; $6/night.

Ipsut Creek Campground: 29 sites; water; open May through October; $5/night.

Ohanapecosh Campground: 205 sites; water, flush toilets, dump station; open late May to late October; $8/night.

Sunshine Point Campground: 18 sites; water; open all year; $5/night.

White River Campground: 117 sites; water, flush toilets; open late June to late September; $6/night.

Backcountry Camping: Allowed in remote areas; pack out everything. A portable camp stove is required; no wood fires.

Picnic Areas: Nine; at Carbon River, Sunshine Point, Longmire, Cougar Rock, Paradise, Stevens Canyon, White River, Sunrise, Tipsoo Lake.

Restaurants

The National Park Inn: At Longmire; dining room; open year-round.

Paradise Inn: Open only in summer.

Sunrise Lodge: Open only in summer.

Jackson Visitor Center: Open only in summer.

Activities

Scenic Drives

Major roads run from the southwest entrance through the southern and eastern parts of the park, with a spur to Sunrise on the northeast side of the mountain. The section between the entrance and Longmire is one of the world's most beautiful forest roads. There is also a separate road to Carbon River in the northwest. The roads were designed to make the least impact possible on the landscape and thus are very narrow, with trees growing very close to the road. Sunrise, at 6,400 feet, is the highest point in the park reachable by road. From here there are excellent views of Emmons Glacier; on clear days, this is also the spot for views of some of the other volcanoes in the Cascades. All but the 18 miles of road between the southwest entrance and Paradise are closed in winter.

Hiking

The more than 300 miles of trails that lead into the wilderness are usually snow-free from mid-July through September. Spending a few days in the backcountry is a great way to really see the park. The 93-mile Wonderland Trail completely encircles Mount Rainier, providing perspectives from every angle. A complete circuit takes about 10 to 14 days. There are also shorter trails for day hikes.

Mountaineering

Climbing the mountain is a hazardous adventure, which should be undertaken only by those sufficiently experienced, equipped, and fit. Those heading for the top are encouraged to use the long-established guide service in the park. You can get current information on rates, reservations, and equipment by contacting the guide service, Rainier Mountaineering, Inc., at Paradise, WA 98398 (from June through September), or 535 Dock Street, Suite 209, Tacoma, WA 98402 (from October through May).

Winter Sports

Snowshoeing, cross-country skiing, and "tubing" are the major wintertime activities. Paradise is the prime winter-use area in the park. Some winter sports equipment can be rented at Longmire.

Fishing

Fishing is allowed in the park's lakes and streams. There are some restrictions; check with a ranger for details. Since the waters are not stocked, catch-and-release fishing is encouraged. The daily limit is six pounds plus one fish, not to exceed a total of 12 fish.

Horseback Riding

The use of saddle and pack stock is permitted on more than 100 miles of trails. Most of these trails are in the lower forest.

Bicycling

Bicycles are not allowed on trails. Be cautious; there is little room to maneuver, since the roads are relatively narrow.

Naturalist Programs

Naturalists lead walks and give talks in the Paradise, Longmire, Ohanapecosh, and Sunrise areas, and lead snowshoe walks in winter at Paradise. Check information desk for schedules.

In the far northwestern reaches of the State of Washington is a scenic mountain territory called North Cascades National Park. The isolated and rugged park land is full of forested valleys; subalpine meadows; countless waterfalls, streams, and rivers; and hundreds of jagged snow-capped mountains. The mountains are part of the Cascade Range, which extends from Canada's Fraser River south beyond Oregon.

The park is actually part of a complex that also contains the Lake Chelan and Ross Lake national recreation areas. Only an invisible border separates the three; in fact, Ross Lake Recreation Area cuts through the middle of North Cascades, dividing the park's north unit from its south unit. Although some of the park, mostly near the Ross Lake Recreation Area, is fairly well traveled, many parts have remained virtually untouched and unexplored.

Adding to the park's pristine and remote beauty are the numerous glaciers and snowfields coating the tops of the mountains. Scientists count well over 300 glaciers in the park area; this is more than half of the glaciers in the contiguous United States. The glaciers in many ways set the scene in the park. Glacier meltwater flows down the mountains and eventually either joins with other streams to become a rolling river or, often, cascades over a high cliff, forming a picturesque waterfall. At times, loud rumblings can break the silence of the woods as glacier ice breaks off and crashes to the valley. All of the crevassed ice masses can present special challenges for those attempting to scale the mountains.

The glaciers are fed by moist air blowing from the Pacific Ocean. As it heads from the west over the top of the mountains it loses most of its moisture, in the form of snow and rain. The air that then reaches the eastern side of the slopes is warmer and drier. This unusual weather pattern makes for noticeable differences in the plant life. Because of the moisture, the western slopes have richer, lusher, and taller forests than the eastern slopes do.

More than 1,500 different species of plants have been identified in this area. In contrast to the evergreen forests of western red cedars and Douglas firs in the park's lowlands are the open meadows at higher elevations. Although the meadows are white with snow in winter, they come alive in spring and summer as colorful wildflowers bloom. Animals in the park enjoy the variety of plant life. Many animal species live here, including bears, wolves, mountain lions, bald eagles, blacktail deer, river otters, spotted owls, and hoary marmots. There are also hundreds of types of birds, reptiles and amphibians.

Prospectors came to this area in the late 1800s and attempted to mine for gold, lead, zinc, and platinum. Although they were fairly lucky, travel to this out-of-the-way and isolated land proved too difficult for theirs to be a profitable endeavor. The mines were abandoned by 1910. Unsuccessful efforts at logging were made early in the

century. The most successful commercial endeavor attempted in the park has been that
of the Seattle City Light Company. The utility recognized the potential electricity-gener-
ating power of the Skagit River and built
three dams here, which resulted in Ross,
Diablo, and Gorge lakes. The dams are still
in use today.

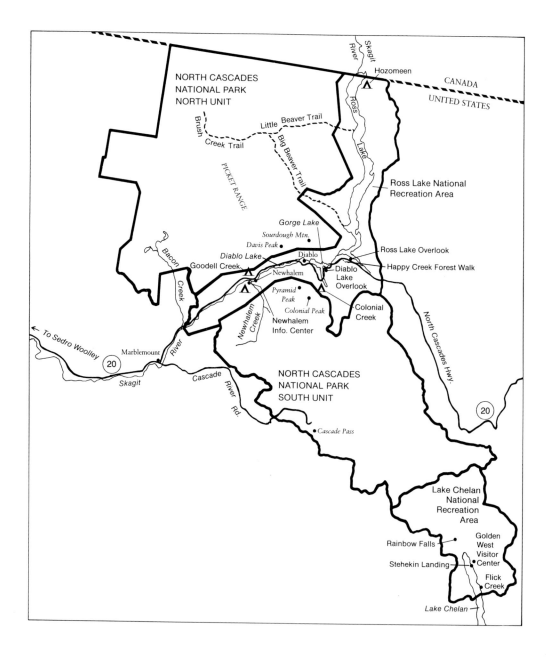

Further Information

Write or call: Superintendent, North Cascades National Park, 2105 Highway 20, Sedro Woolley, WA 98284; (206) 856-5700

Visitor Information

Park Headquarters: Sedro Woolley; information, books, maps, and pamphlets for sale.
Newhalem Information Center: Off North Cascades Highway near the Newhalem Creek; information, books, maps, and pamphlets for sale.
Golden West Visitor Center: At Stehekin on Lake Chelan; information, books, maps, and pamphlets for sale.

Nuts and Bolts

Entrance Fee: None.
Park Open: All year. Many areas are inaccessible during the winter because of snow.
Permits: Required for backcountry camping and mountain climbing. Washington State fishing license is required.
In Emergency: Marblemount Back Country Station, 873-4500 or Newhalem, 386-4495.
Acreage: 504,780.94

Practical Advisory

Seasons

The North Cascades get more rain on their western side than on their eastern side. Expect cooler weather and more cloudy days west of the range. East of the range you will find more sunshine and higher temperatures. Summer temperatures may reach almost to 100° and then return to nightly lows in the 40s and 50s. Average summer highs are in the high 70s, with lows in the 50s. Average highs in the winter are in the high 30s, with lows in the high 20s.

Special Advisories

- The park lakes are cold. Swimming is not recommended.
- Beware of the possibility of hypothermia caused by temperature drops during sudden summer storms. Be prepared.
- Be cautious crossing streams and traveling outside developed areas.
- Avoid encounters with bears and know what to do if one occurs.

Facilities for Disabled

Contact the park for information.

Travel Advisory

Entrances

There are no paved roads into the park. From Burlington on the west and Twisp on the east, Highway 20, the North Cascades Highway, will take you to the Ross Lake National Recreational Area and trailheads into the park. Vehicle access to Ross Lake is by unpaved road from Canada only. Stehekin is reachable only by boat, by floatplane from Chelan, or by trail.

Transportation

Airports: The nearest airport is in Seattle.

Bus Service: Greyhound/Trailways provides bus service to Seattle.

Train Service: Amtrak serves Seattle.

Rental Cars: In Seattle, at the airport.

Attractions

The many jagged peaks of the *Cascade Mountain Range* are the central feature of this undeveloped park. The mountains' numerous *glaciers* and the *lakes, rivers,* and *waterfalls* fed by their meltwater add to the natural beauty. No paved roads lead into the park. The highway through the recreational area provides many scenic views, however. Trails are also accessible from the highway. Many visitors remain in the more easily accessible Ross Lake Recreation Area, where the *Ross, Diablo,* and *Gorge lakes* are the major features and the sites of much activity.

Accommodations

Lodges

There is no lodging in the national park; the following lodgings are in the recreation areas.

Ross Lake Resort: Open in summer; accessible via the main road. Reservations: Ross Lake Resort, Rockport, WA 98283; (206) 386-4437.

North Cascades Lodge: Open in summer; on Lake Chelan; accessible only via boat, floatplane, or trail. Reservations: North Cascades Lodge, Box 275, Stehekin, WA 98852; (509) 682-4711.

Stehekin Valley Ranch: Open in summer; in Lake Chelan area; accessible only via boat, floatplane, or trail. Reservations: Stehekin Valley Ranch, Box 36, Stehekin, WA 98852; (509) 682-4677.

Silver Bay Inn: Bed and breakfast; open in summer; in Lake Chelan area; accessible only via boat, floatplane, or trail. Reservations: Silver Bay Inn, Box 43, Stehekin, WA 98852; (509) 682-2212.

Cabins for Rent: Open in summer; in Lake Chelan area; accessible only via boat, floatplane, or trail. For reservations: Flick Creek House, Box 25; Silver Bay Guest Cabin, Box

43; Stehekin Log Cabin, Box 288; all Stehekin, WA 98852.

Campgrounds and Picnic Areas

First-come, first-served. Fires are permitted only at designated locations; only dead and downed wood may be used.

Goodell Creek Campground: 22 sites; tables, water, vault toilets; accessible off main road.

Newhalem Creek Campground: 129 sites; tables, water, flush toilets; accessible off main road.

Colonial Creek Campground: 164 sites; tables, water, flush toilets; accessible off main road.

Hozomeen Campground: 122 sites; tables, water, vault toilets; on Ross Lake.

Backcountry Camping: Nearly 100 backcountry campgrounds and an additional 30 sites for horse campers. Campgrounds include the following, which are trail-accessible only: Cottonwood Campground, Flat Creek Campground, Park Creek Campground, Shady Campground, Dolly Varden Campground, Tumwater Campground, High Bridge Campground, Harlequin Campground, Purple Point.

Picnic Areas: At Goodell Creek, off main park road; Hozomeen, on Ross Lake; and nearly a dozen other places in southern unit of park and Lake Chelan area.

Restaurants

Diablo Lake Resort: Restaurant; open in summer.

North Cascades Lodge: Restaurant; open in summer.

Stehekin Valley Ranch: Restaurant; open in summer.

Activities

Scenic Drives

Few roads actually go into the park, but on clear days there are views of the park from the North Cascades Highway in the Ross Lake Recreation Area. Called the "most scenic mountain drive in Washington" by past visitors, the highway provides roadside vistas of Gorge, Diablo, and Ross lakes, but only Gorge and Diablo can be reached by vehicle from the highway. Diablo Lake Overlook offers superb views of Diablo Lake, Sourdough Mountain, Davis Peak, Colonial Peak, Pyramid Peak, and spectacular features of the Skagit River drainage. Wayside exhibits, mountain views (including a view of the Picket Range from Newhalem), and other points of interest are at roadside turnouts. Another road, the Cascade River Road—25 miles of improved dirt and gravel—gives summer and fall access into the park and to the Cascade Pass trail.

Hiking

More than 360 miles of maintained trails take you into the park and wilderness areas. Most hikers enter the park from trailheads along the North Cascades Highway. Others enter from trailheads along the Cascade River Road. Short, easy nature trails include the Trail of the Cedars and Ladder Creek Falls Trail near Newhalem, and the Thunder Woods Nature Trail from Colonial Creek Campground. Happy Creek Forest Walk is a short boardwalk through an old-growth forest. Longer, more strenuous hikes can take you to Cascade Pass, where flower-sprinkled hillsides and meadows enhance spectacular views of the Cascade and Stehekin valleys, or to Sourdough Mountain, with a view from the summit that overlooks nearly all of the park. Lower-elevation trails and lakes are usually free of snow from early April through mid-October. Some higher-elevation trails are not open until mid-July. Hiking guides are available from outside operators.

Mountaineering

Climbing trips can be arranged through concessioners. Write to the Superintendent for a list.

Boating

Much of the recreation in the North Cascades is water-oriented. Hundreds of lakes and streams drain into the major river valleys. Boat-launch ramps for Diablo Lake are at Colonial Creek Campground. Ross Lake has one launch ramp, at Hozomeen. Gorge Lake has a small ramp near the town of Diablo. There are boat-in campsites at Weaver Point, Manly Wham, and Flick Creek on Lake Chelan. Boats can be rented at Ross Lake Resort and North Cascades Lodge. Upper Skagit River raft trips (year-round) begin at Goodell Creek Campground and terminate near Bacon Creek. They can be arranged through concessioners. Write to the Superintendent for a list.

Boat Tours

Boat trips are available from Ross Lake Resort. Scenic ferryboat trips to Lake Chelan are available at Chelan; contact the Chelan Boat Company, (509) 682-2224.

Fishing

Sport fishing in the many streams and lakes is popular. The Skagit River and its impounded lakes, including Diablo and Ross, offer many species of trout, salmon, and whitefish. Salmon fishing is not allowed on the Skagit River inside the Ross Lake Recreation Area or in tributaries of streams on Ross Lake. Lake Chelan has freshwater cod and salmon. The Stehekin River offers a good chance at rainbow and cutthroat trout. You can rent fishing boats at Ross Lake Resort, and North Cascades Lodge at Stehekin. Washington regulations, seasons, and catch limits apply.

Bicycling

Many people tour the North Cascades Highway by bicycle. Travel single file, on the right edge of the road. Trails are closed to bicyclists. Bicycles can be rented at North Cascades Lodge.

Naturalist Activities

Nature-trail walks and evening programs are conducted by park naturalists in summer at Colonial Creek and Newhalem campgrounds, and at Hozomeen and Stehekin. Ask a park ranger for details.

Water sets the scene in Olympic National Park. From the 57 miles of Pacific Ocean coastline, to the snow-capped and glacier-peaked mountains of the Olympic Range, to the fine examples of Northwest rain forest, the Olympic Peninsula is steeped in moisture.

Moisture-laden winds from out over the Pacific Ocean are responsible for heavy levels of precipitation in the area. The winds blow eastward and drop their moisture in the form of rain, snow, and mist. This steady source of wetness sustains one of the more unusual features of the park: the rain forests. There are four on the peninsula—Bogachiel, Queets, Hoh, and Quinault—all nestled in ocean-facing valleys. Their cool, dark environments are pleasantly silent and lush with vegetation that seems to thrive everywhere. Plant life here ranges from mosses and mushrooms underfoot to enormous trees growing several hundred feet high. The most common trees in the Olympic rain forests are the Sitka spruce and Western hemlock.

Another very special environment in the park is the wild and scenic shoreline of the Pacific Ocean. This strip of land was added to the park but is not directly connected to the rest of the park land. Seals, sea lions, and whales can be seen swimming in the waves and around the rocky shores of this constantly changing coastline. Tide pools are home to an incredible variety of life, including snails, starfish, and sea urchins.

Beyond the coastline, forests seem to grow almost without interruption into the Olympic Peninsula and up the slopes of the Olympic Range. Moderate temperatures and heavy precipitation make for extremely healthy growing conditions. Although these forests do not receive as much precipitation as the rain forests, a good 100 inches of rain falls a year, encouraging dense stands of immense evergreens. Western red cedar, Western hemlock, and Douglas fir grow full and thick. The alpine meadows on the mountain slopes above the forests are rich in wildflowers. This area is home to about 4,000–5,000 Olympic elk, the largest herd of these oversize deer left anywhere in the country.

The Olympic Range, for which the park is named, covers about 40 miles. Mount Olympus, the tallest of the mountains, is actually at the center of the range. To the north and east, the mountains drop abruptly to the waters of the Strait of Juan de Fuca and the Hood Canal. To the south and west, the slopes descend more gradually. On many of the mountains' summits, snow falls on previous snow that has not had enough time and warmth to melt fully; the piled-up snow eventually turns to glaciers. There are some 60 glaciers, whose total area is about 30 square miles, scattered on the peaks throughout the park. Mount Olympus alone has six or so glaciers gracing its peak. The meltwater from these glaciers flows down the sides of the mountains, becoming streams and lakes. This moisture adds to the lushness and fertility that characterize the Olympic Peninsula.

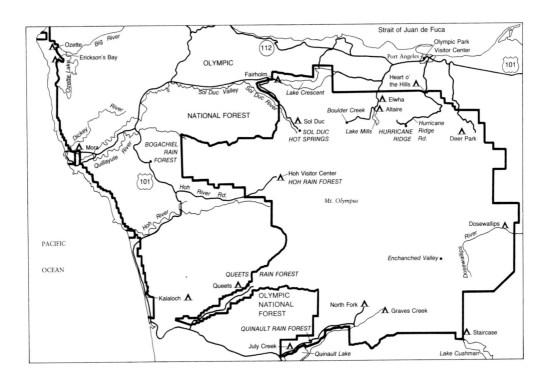

Further Information

Write or call: Superintendent, Olympic National Park, 600 East Park Avenue, Port Angeles, WA 98362; (206) 452-0330

Visitor Information

Olympic Park Visitor Center: At Port Angeles; houses the park's major exhibits, a small theater/auditorium, and a children's activity room.
Hoh Visitor Center: West side; exhibits.
Hoodsport Ranger Station: East side; information.

Nuts and Bolts

Entrance Fee: $3/vehicle or $1/person arriving by other means. Good for seven days. (Collected May through September.)
Park Open: All year.
Permits: Required for backcountry camping.
In Emergency: Call 911.
Acreage: 922,626

Practical Advisory

Seasons

Summer: Generally warm, but cooler at higher elevations. The western half of the park receives more precipitation than the eastern side, but rain is widespread throughout. High temperatures range from 65° to 80°; lows range from about 45° to about 55°. Winter: Colder; afternoon highs are about 32°–50°. Higher elevations are snow-covered from early November to late June. Rain is very frequent, and snow is common in the higher elevations. Spring and fall: Weather is variable, sometimes warm, sometimes wet. Temperatures range from 35° to 70°.

Special Advisories

• Quotas have been established for visitors to Dosewallips and Staircase areas of the park; reservations must be made.
• Avoid bears and know what to do if an encounter occurs.

Facilities for Disabled

There are wheelchair-accessible rest rooms in most of the campgrounds. Some trails are wheelchair-accessible; some are accessible with assistance. Contact the park for listings.

Travel Advisory

Entrances

North and West: U.S. 101 travels around the park.

Transportation

Airports: Regularly scheduled flights serve Port Angeles from Seattle or Portland, and serve Sequim from Seattle.

Bus Service: Port Angeles is served by Greyhound Bus Lines, operating several trips daily from Seattle.

Train Service: Not available to the park. Amtrak serves Seattle.

Rental Cars: Available in Port Angeles, Sequim, and Grays Harbor, and in all larger cities in the Puget Sound area.

Ferry Service: Regularly scheduled ferry service is available across Puget Sound with connections to the Hood Canal floating bridge and Bremerton. Schedules are available from Washington State Ferries: (800) 542-0810. Ferry service is also available most of the year between Victoria (in British Columbia, Canada) and Port Angeles (in Washington). Schedules available from Black Ball Transport: Call (206) 457-4491. Victoria Rapid Transit has seasonal service: Call (206) 452-8088.

Attractions

The central point in the park is *Mount Olympus*, which can be viewed from a distance. It is not possible to drive very near the mountain. None of the roads into the park meet each other and none crosses the park. To visit the different sections of the park, you must use separate roads. Trails offer access deeper into the park. The *rain forests* are a major feature; the *Hoh Rain Forest* is one of the more visited.

The *Pacific shoreline*, including the *Kalaloch, Mora,* and *Ozette* areas, is scenic. *Lake Crescent* is an area of much activity. Also of interest are the *Sol Duc River* and *Hurricane Ridge.*

Accommodations

Lodges

Kalaloch Lodge: U.S. 101 on the ocean beach; lodge and motel rooms, cabins; open all year. For reservations: Manager, HC 80, Box 1100, Forks, WA 98331; (206) 962-2271.

Lake Crescent Lodge: U.S. 101; lodge and motel rooms, cottages; open late April through late October. For reservations: Manager, National Park Concessions, HC 62, Box 11, Port Angeles, WA 98362; (206) 928-3211.

Log Cabin Resort: Northeast end of Lake Crescent; motel units and cabins; open late April through September. For reservations: Manager, 6540 East Beach Road, Port Angeles, WA 98362; (206) 928-3245.

Sol Duc Hot Springs Resort: In the Sol Duc River valley; cabins, hot mineral pools; open mid-May through September. For reservations: Manager, P.O. Box 2169, Port Angeles, WA 98362; (206) 327-3583.

Campgrounds and Picnic Areas

First-come, first-served; 14-day limit. Dead and downed firewood may be collected. All facilities have toilets, tables, and firepits or grills.

Altaire Campground: Elwha River Road; 30 sites; water; open June through September; $6/night.

Deer Park Campground: Blue Mount Road; 18 sites; tents only; dirt road; water; closed in snow; free.

Dosewallips Campground: Dosewallips River; 32 sites; water; open June through September; free.

Elwha Campground: 41 sites; water; open all year; $6/night.

Erickson's Bay Campground: Lake Ozette; 15 sites; tents only; open all year; walk-in; free.

Fairholm Campground: West end of Lake Crescent; 87 sites; dump station; water; open all year; $6/night.

Graves Creek Campground: 15 miles NE of Lake Quinault; 30 sites; dirt road; water; open all year; free.

Heart o' the Hills Campground: Hurricane Ridge Road; 105 sites; water; open all year; $6/night.

Hoh Campground: Hoh River Road; 89 sites; dump station; water; open all year; $6/night.

July Creek Campground: North Shore Road of Lake Quinault; 29 sites; tents only; water; open all year; walk-in; free.

Kalaloch Campground: Highway 101 on the ocean; 177 sites; dump station; water; open all year; $6/night.

Mora Campground: Rialto Beach Road; 94 sites; dump station; water; open all year; $6/night.

North Fork Campground: North Shore Road of Lake Quinault; 7 sites; tents only; dirt road; open all year; free.

Ozette Campground: 14 sites; gravel road; water; open all year; free.

Queets Campground: 20 sites; tents only; open all year; free.

Sol Duc Campground: Sol Duc Road; 80 sites; dump station; water; closed in snow; $6/night.

Staircase Campground: 59 sites; partly dirt road; water; open all year; $6/night.

Backcountry Camping: Pack out all trash; camp in an established site if one is available. Open, wood fires are prohibited in certain areas of the backcountry.

Picnic Areas: Seven, off park roads.

Restaurants

Kalaloch Lodge: Dining room, coffee shop, cocktail lounge; open all year.

Lake Crescent Lodge: Dining room, cocktail lounge; open late April through October.

Log Cabin Resort: Restaurant; open May through September.

Sol Duc Hot Springs Resort: Breakfast, dinner, snack bar; open mid-May through September.

Hurricane Ridge Lodge: Sandwiches and light meals; open May through September, and winter weekends and holidays when area is open to skiing.

Activities

Scenic Drives

There are several roads into the park, but none crosses it or even goes deep inside it. Heart o' the Hills Road, leading to Hurricane Ridge Road, offers scenic views, especially at Lookout Rock, a turnout area just before the tunnels. Other scenic paved routes include U.S. 101, west of Port Angeles, which travels part of the length of Lake Crescent. From there, another road leads to Sol Duc. Hoh River Road, from the west of the park, takes you into the Hoh Rain Forest. A road off U.S. 101 will take you past Quinault Lake, or you can continue north on it and travel up part of the coastal area of the park, passing Kalaloch.

Hiking

Since roads offer only limited access into the park, hiking the trails is an excellent way to see the beach, rain forest, and mountain wilderness. There are over 600 miles of trails, varying from those requiring a day or less to pathways taking up to a week or more. Self-guiding nature trails include those at Lake Crescent, Hurricane Ridge, Sol Duc Hot Springs, Hoh Rain Forest, and Ozette on the coast. Be sure to bring a tide table when hiking along the beach; you could be trapped by an incoming tide. Trails at higher elevations are normally accessible between July 15 and October 1.

Boating

There are paddleboat rentals and boat launching at the Log Cabin Resort on the eastern end of Lake Crescent and at Fairholm General Store on the western end. Motorized boats are prohibited on all park waters except Lake Crescent, Quillayute River, Dickey River, Lake Mills, Lake Cushman, Ozette Lake, and the Hoh River in the coastal strip. Waterskiing is prohibited except on Lake Crescent and Lake Ozette. Hand-propelled vessels and sailboats are permitted on park waters, except Dosewallips River.

Swimming

Swimming is available at Sol Duc and Lake Crescent.

Fishing

Check with the park for rules on seasons, limits, and regulations, which change frequently.

Winter Sports

The Hurricane Ridge Winter Use Area offers cross-country skiing and snowshoeing from November through April. Ski lifts and equipment rentals are available. Ski lessons are also available.

Naturalist Programs

Campfire programs, nature walks, and talks are offered during the summer. Check bulletin boards at campgrounds and visitor centers for locations, dates, and times.

Some 225 million years ago, during what is known as the Triassic Period, the land that is now in Arizona was not the dry tableland of today. It was a vast floodplain, covered by many streams and inhabited by early dinosaurs, reptiles, and amphibians, and by trees that grew as tall as 200 feet. These trees, now called Araucarioxylon, Woodworthia, and Schilderia by scientists, no longer exist. But the remains of many, turned to beautifully colored stone, can be found in Petrified Forest National Park.

Many of these trees died from old age, disease, or other natural causes; they fell down and were carried by heavy streams to the floodplain. As they traveled in the fast-moving water, they lost their roots and branches, ending up as solid logs in the plain. Silt and mud carried by the water eventually covered the logs, cutting off most oxygen from reaching them and thus dramatically slowing their decaying process. Volcanic activity in the area spewed ash containing silica into the air; some of the ash landed in the marsh. Gradually, silica-bearing water seeped through the logs, slowly surrounding the tissues of the wood with silica deposits. The silica crystallized into quartz—and the logs were preserved, full of semiprecious gems, including rose quartz, agate, jasper, and amethyst. Eventually, the land here sank and was flooded and the logs were deeply covered with sediments.

Over time, earth activity, including earthquakes and major uplifts of the land, cre-

ated stresses that cracked most of the logs into the smaller chunks found today. The uplifting also began the process of unearthing the logs from their long and deep burial. The effects of rain and wind helped to wash away the sediment, revealing the beautifully colorful chunks and logs of petrified wood. Of course, the process of erosion has not stopped. Sediments continue to be removed, breaking down logs and revealing others still below the surface. Up to 300 feet of fossil-bearing materials is still buried in some places.

The park land is a tremendous source of other Triassic fossils as well, including plants, fish, invertebrates, and early dinosaurs. Once exposed to the air and the elements, fossilized bones do not last as long as petrified wood, so most are not found intact. But scientists have been able to piece together much good information about the animals that lived in the forests of 225 million years ago, and fossil research continues.

The more visitors came to see the petrified forest, the more valuable petrified wood they took away. The establishment of the national park has lessened the taking of the wood, which is now protected by federal law. The signs throughout the park are a reminder to leave it alone. Petrified wood can be bought from commercial dealers who collect it from areas outside the park. It is from the same geological deposits and of the same quality as the wood in the park.

Although other areas of the world have petrified forests or deposits of petrified

NATIONAL PARK SERVICE, PHOTO BY CAT SYRBE

wood, this national park has the largest known concentration of the brightest-colored petrified wood. These fossilized trees are also much older than most. Other features of the park include part of the Painted Desert, as well as Native American ruins dating from A.D. 800 to A.D. 1400.

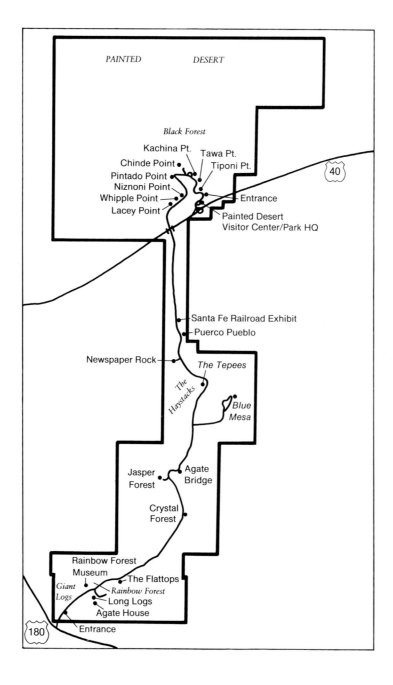

Further Information

Write or call: Superintendent, Petrified Forest National Park, P.O. Box 2217, Petrified Forest National Park, AZ 86028; (602) 524-6228

Visitor Information

Painted Desert Visitor Center/Park Headquarters: At north entrance; information; 17-minute orientation film on how wood is petrified.
Rainbow Forest Museum: At south entrance; information; exhibits of petrified wood, Triassic creatures, and the area's geological story and human history.

Nuts and Bolts

Entrance Fee: $5/vehicle or $2/person arriving by other means.
Park Open: All year except December 25 and January 1.
Permits: Required for backcountry camping.
In Emergency: Call 911.
Acreage: 93,532.57

Practical Advisory

Seasons

High winds may be expected in any season. Summer: Days may be quite warm and clear, with highs typically in the 90s; nights are in the 50s. Thunderstorms are frequent and sudden, accounting for 50 percent of the park's nine inches of precipitation per year. Winter: Highs are usually in the 40s, with lows in the 20s. Periodic storms may bring snow and ice, which can cause park road closures.

Special Advisories

- Federal law prohibits collection or removal of petrified wood or any other object.

- Do not climb on petrified logs. Stay behind barricades and on trails.
- Bubonic plague has been detected in this area. Check with park rangers for information.
- Because roads are narrow and traffic is heavy, bicycling is not recommended.

Facilities for Disabled

An "Accessibility Guidebook" is available from the park.

Travel Advisory

Entrances

North: I-40 for 26 miles east of Holbrook.
South: U.S. 180 for 19 miles east of Holbrook.

Transportation

Airports: Flagstaff, Phoenix, and Albuquerque.

Bus Service: Serves Holbrook, Arizona.

Train Service: Serves Winslow, Arizona.

Rental Cars: Available in Holbrook, Arizona.

Attractions

The petrified wood throughout the park is its main attraction. Some of the more notable areas for finding concentrations of the wood are *Rainbow Forest, Giant Logs, Long Logs, Jasper Forest, Agate Bridge,* and *Blue Mesa.* Also of interest is the *Painted Desert.* A road that travels the length of the park provides areas for viewing.

Other Points of Interest (Museums, Historic Sites, etc.)

There are several Native American ruins dating from before A.D. 1400. The *Puerco Pueblo* is the remains of a pueblo consisting of about 75 rooms surrounding a courtyard. *Newspaper Rock* is a sandstone block covered with petroglyphs; these signs and symbols have not been interpreted. *Agate House* is a partially restored pueblo made of petrified wood chunks. All are off the main park road.

Accommodations

There are no lodges or campgrounds available in the park.

Camping and Picnic Areas

Wilderness Camping: Allowed in the Painted Desert area and the Rainbow Forest area.

Picnic Areas: At Rainbow Forest and Chinde Point, which has water and toilets in warmer months.

Restaurants

Cafeteria: At north entrance; open all year.

Snack Bar: At south entrance; open all year.

Activities

Scenic Drives

The 28-mile park road will take you to all the park's main features as it winds along the rim of the Painted Desert, passes through archaeological areas, and leads to many petrified-wood sites. The road runs north–south through the length of the park, allowing you to enter at one end and exit at the other without doubling back. Several hours should be allowed to travel the road and stop at the frequent pullouts. The six-mile road along the desert rim has eight overlooks that offer sweeping views of portions of the Painted Desert. A three-mile spur road climbs Blue Mesa, where pedestal logs—hard logs acting as capstones to soft clays beneath—abound. The Jasper Forest Overlook shows the area's topography, with petrified logs strewn below.

Long Logs is near the south entrance; many trunks here are more than 100 feet long.

Hiking

The Long Logs and Agate House trails explore part of the Rainbow Forest. The trail through Giant Logs behind the Rainbow Forest Museum follows up and down the slopes. Other walking trails are at Crystal Forest, Blue Mesa, and Kachina Point to Tawa Point. Trails vary in length from ½ to ¾ mile. The two wilderness areas are also open for hiking.

Ranger-Led Programs

Available at Puerco Pueblo, Rainbow Forest, and Painted Desert Inn.

Visitors who walk through the redwood forests in Redwood National Park find themselves craning their necks as they look up in amazement. The trees here, named *Sequoia sempervirens,* or coast redwood, are not only the tallest trees, but the tallest living things on earth.

A walk among these giants is truly an amazing experience. One very special place in the park is the Tall Trees Grove, part of a long corridor known as the Emerald Mile. In the grove on the banks of Redwood Creek stands the earth's tallest known tree, 367.8 feet tall. In this grove are also the second-, third-, and sixth-tallest trees.

The redwood is often confused with its cousin, the giant sequoia. Redwoods are taller than giant sequoias, although they are not as large in total mass. Mature redwood trees are, on average, from 200 to 240 feet high, and when the trees are viewed from the ground this height seems to be increased by the lack of branches on the lower 100 or 200 feet of trunk. Another difference is that redwoods only live about half as long as giant sequoias. Although they can live to be as much as 2,000 years old, they usually average about 500 to 700 years.

For some reason redwoods, unlike other trees, do not have a distinct correlation between their age and their size. The oldest are not necessarily the tallest or the bulkiest. It is not known why this is true.

Redwoods' longevity is due largely to their natural resistance to disease and insects as well as to fire. Toppling is the cause of death in many redwoods. Their broad but very shallow root system, which lacks a deep taproot, sometimes provides inadequate support for their towering trunks, and wind can topple mature trees.

Once, coast redwoods could be found in North America, Europe, and Asia. However, the climate is no longer favorable anywhere else on earth. Today redwoods grow only in this small strip of land on the Pacific Northwest coast, stretching from Curry County in southern Oregon to south of Monterey, California. They grow within 30 miles of the coast and at elevations below 3,000 feet. The moist cool air blowing in off the Pacific Ocean is paramount to maintaining the correct conditions for these trees to survive. They need heavy levels of rain, fog, and a moderate temperature year-round, all of which can be found here.

The national park encompasses three California state parks, Jedediah Smith Redwoods, Del Norte Coast Redwoods, and Prairie Creek Redwoods, all known for their redwood groves. Besides the redwoods, however, there is much to see. The park also includes 40 miles of rugged Pacific coastline. Although the water here is cold (45°–55°), the beach with its pounding surf is full of life.

Gray whales can often be spotted offshore, traveling from their summer feeding ground in the Arctic to their winter calving area near Baja, California. These large mammals pass by here around December, and again in the spring, when the pods (as groups of whales

are known) travel back north with their new young. Also seen near the shore are harbor seals, playing in the water or on the rocks; porpoises; seals; and sea lions. Closer in, the tidal pools offer the perfect habitat for many animals including sea urchins, starfish, crabs, and barnacles clinging to the sides of the rocks. The intertidal zone boasts an incredible 168 invertebrate species.

Other animals seen in the park include the Roosevelt elk, the second-largest member of the deer family and found only in this part of the country; mountain lion; and blacktail deer. And beaver, mink, and otter thrive in the fresh water. The park is also home to some 300 species of birds, about half of which live near the water.

Further Information

Write or call: Superintendent, Redwood National Park, 1111 Second Street, Crescent City, CA 95531; (707) 464-6101.

Visitor Information

Park Headquarters: Corner of Second and K streets in Crescent City; park information, interpretive programs.
Hiouchi Information Center: On Highway 199; exhibits about the park, its trees and coastline, and related topics; interpretive programs. (Closed November to March.)
Redwood Information Center: In Orick; exhibits and information about the park, its trees and coastline, and related topics; interpretive programs.

Crescent Beach Information Center: South of Crescent City; exhibits, park information, interpretive programs.

Nuts and Bolts

Entrance Fee: None.
Park Open: All year.
Permits: Required for backcountry camping on the Redwood Creek Trail. A California fishing license is required.
In Emergency: Dial 911.
Acreage: 113,200

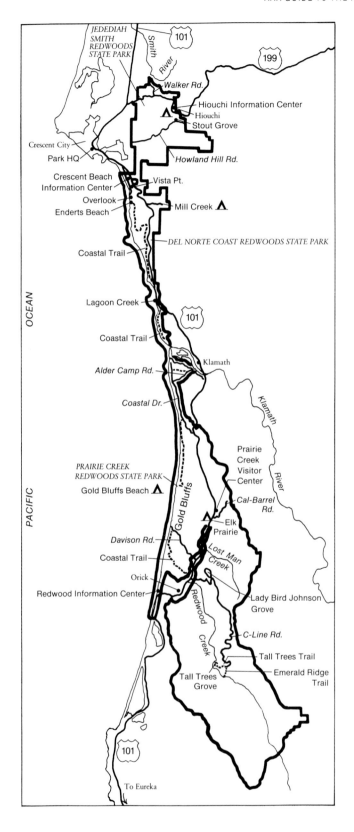

Practical Advisory

Seasons

The coastal climate is generally moist and mild, with wet winters, cool summers, and frequent fog or wind from the ocean. Seasonal temperatures are influenced by the ocean, becoming more extreme inland. In river and coastal valleys, it is warmer and less windy than on the coast. July temperatures inland are in the 70s to 90s, while on the coast they are in the 50s to 60s. Snow is uncommon, occurring at higher elevations within the park two or three times a year and usually melting rapidly.

Special Advisories

- You may gather fruits and berries for personal consumption.

Facilities for Disabled

Request a copy of "Access Redwood National Park" from the park.

Travel Advisory

Entrances

Crescent City: U.S. 101 south for 26 miles from Brookings, Oregon.

Orick: U.S. 101 north for 44 miles from Eureka.

Hiouchi: U.S. 199 southwest for 75 miles from Grants Pass, Oregon.

Transportation

Airports: Nearest major airport is in San Francisco (350 miles away); there is limited service to Eureka.

Bus Service: Greyhound serves Crescent City.

Train Service: None convenient.

Rental Cars: Available at airports and in Crescent City.

Attractions

The majestic *redwood trees* are the major feature of the park. *Tall Trees Grove, Lady Bird Johnson Grove,* and *Stout Grove* are some of the more notable sites. Along the Pacific Ocean is much scenic shoreline, including *Gold Bluffs Beach* and *Enderts Beach.* Also of interest are *Redwood Creek* and *Lost Man Creek.* Most of these areas are accessible by vehicle, except the Tall Trees Grove which requires some planning to see (see "Activities," below).

Accommodations

There are no lodges or restaurants in the park.

Campgrounds and Picnic Areas

All developed campgrounds are operated by the state parks. For reservations: MISTIX, P.O. Box 85705, San Diego, CA 92138-5705; (800) 444-7275. Cost is $14/night in summer and $12/night off-season; walk-in or bike-in campsites cost $3/person. Camp and build fires only where indicated.

DEL NORTE COAST REDWOODS STATE PARK

Mill Creek Campground: Highway 101; 145 sites; tables, grills, toilets, dump station; open May to October.

JEDEDIAH SMITH REDWOODS STATE PARK

Jedediah Smith State Park Campground: On Highway 199; 108 sites; toilets, tables, grills, dump station. Open all year.

PRAIRIE CREEK REDWOODS STATE PARK

Gold Bluffs Beach Campground: Tables, grills, toilets. Open all year.

Elk Prairie Campground: Tables, grills, toilets, dump station. Open all year.

There are also walk-in primitive campsites, with tables and toilets, at Nickel Creek, DeMartin, Flint Ridge, Little Bald Hills, and Butler Creek in Prairie Creek Redwoods State Park (permit required for the latter one).

Backcountry Camping: Available on the Redwood Creek Trail along the creek gravel bars, except within 1/4 mile of the Tall Trees Grove.

Picnic Areas: At Hiouchi Ranger Station, Jedediah Smith Redwoods State Park, Crescent Beach, Crescent Beach Overlook, Wilson Creek, Lagoon Creek, Klamath Overlook, Fern Canyon, High Bluff Quarry, Gold Bluffs Beach, Prairie Creek Redwoods State Park, Lost Man Creek, Lady Bird Johnson Grove, Redwood Creek Trailhead, Skunk Cabbage Trailhead, Redwood Information Center.

Activities

Scenic Drives

U.S. 101 runs north and south through the park, providing a scenic drive both along the coast and through the redwoods. Other roads offer more off-the-beaten-path scenery. The Crescent Beach Overlook, on the Enderts Beach Road, is a good place for whale watching. The partially unpaved Coastal Drive around the mouth of the Klamath River is scenic. Howland Hill Road, an alternative route to Crescent City, is an unpaved, narrow, scenic drive through redwood forest that gives you access to Stout Grove. Walker Road is an **unpaved scenic** road through redwood forest

that provides access to the Smith River. Davison Road, which is narrow and unpaved, goes to Gold Bluffs Beach, where resident herds of Roosevelt elk can often be seen. The Cal-Barrel road is an unpaved road through redwood forest.

C-Line Road

Thirty-five vehicles a day are allowed to enter the C-Line Road, which takes you to the 1 1/4-mile trail to the Tall Trees Grove. The daily permits are issued at the Redwood Information Center. Access time is 9 A.M.–2 P.M. only. The road closes at dusk.

Shuttle Bus Tour

A shuttle bus operates in summer between the Redwood Information Center and the Tall Trees Grove Trailhead. Allow four hours round-trip for the bus tour and hike (the hike is 2⁶⁄₁₀ miles round-trip). The trail is steep; you may wish just to take the bus tour. Purchase tickets and get information at the Redwood Information Center.

Hiking

It is possible to hike through many different environments in the park. Some established trails take minutes, some several hours, and some a few days. Self-guided nature trails include the Yurok Loop Trail, half a mile and about an hour's walk at Lagoon Creek, and the Lady Bird Johnson Grove Trail, a one-hour, one-mile trip. The Coastal Trail runs the length of the park. It is in six sections, which range in length from four to six miles and pass through ancient redwood forests, open prairies, high bluffs overlooking the ocean, and sandy beaches. The Redwood Creek Trail is an 8½-mile hike to Tall Trees Grove and the "Emerald Mile." It involves two creek crossings, over bridges that are provided in summer only.

Fishing

Both fresh water and salt water are fished here, for silver and king salmon and for rainbow, coast cutthroat, and steelhead trout. You can fish the Smith and Klamath rivers' famous salmon and trout waters.

Horseback Riding

Over 50 miles of trails are available for horseback riding in the Redwood Creek area, with several camps for overnight stays. Guided pack trips are possible through local outfitters in the Orick area.

Bicycling

The Ossagon Trail in Prairie Creek Redwoods State Park, and the Holter Ridge Trail in Redwood National Park, have been designated exclusively for biking. They take you through redwood forest and to the beach.

Swimming

Swimming in the Smith River and Redwood Creek is pleasant. Swimming in the ocean is not advised, because the water is quite cold and there is a strong undertow.

Ranger-Led Activities

In summer, the National Park Service and Redwood State Parks offer many interpretive activities, ranging from guided tidepool walks to kayak trips down a three-mile stretch of the Smith River. Reservations are needed, and a fee is charged for the kayak trips. Details are available from any park information center.

The Rocky Mountains have long been a symbol of the majestic beauty of the Western United States. The park presents the opportunity to explore the Front Range of the Rockies, the first wave of mountains rising out of the central Great Plains. The special mountain wilderness that is typical of the range is preserved here. This richly landscaped park straddles the Continental Divide.

The park includes some 60 mountains over 12,000 feet in elevation. The highest is Longs Peak, at 14,256 feet. There is snow nearly year-round on many of the peaks, including the Never Summer Mountains, with permanent snowfields. There are some small glaciers in the park; although active, these are not advancing very quickly. The natural environment changes here at each level of elevation with its range of soil, sun, and moisture. A variety of plants, hundreds of different species, is spread over the landscape.

At the lower elevations of the park the climate is relatively warm and dry. Ponderosa pine, western red cedar, and Douglas fir grow on these lowland slopes. Blue spruce and longpole pine can also be seen. Wildflowers cover the meadows during the summer. The term "parks" here refers to open, level sections of land surrounded by protective peaks and containing a body of water. Parks are generally the center of much life and activity for native animals.

On the mountain slopes are tall stands of spruce, fir, aspen, and pine trees in dense forests. Melting snow from the slopes feeds the streams that flow down the sides of the mountains into the clear lakes and valley rivers that dot the meadows below. Above 9,000 feet or so is the subalpine zoo. The Engelmann spruce, subalpine fir, and limber pine are the most common trees. Farther up these grow more twisted and bent: The fierce winds constantly blow and shape them as they grow.

Above the timberline, the last twisted trees give way to rocky alpine tundra, covering a full third of the park. Much like that in northern Alaska, this tundra is full of open areas of grass and mosses. Dwarf plants must be tough to survive here. Most living things grow very close to the ground to protect themselves from the biting, powerful winds. The blooming season is short—late June and part of July—so some plants need more than one year to complete a life cycle.

When blooming season does come, however, the land is covered with the brilliant colors of wildflowers. In fact, the entire park is home to a variety of wildflowers. Colorado's state flower, the blue columbine, grows at nearly every elevation but most abundantly in the subalpine zone. The tundra is home to alpine buttercups, dwarf clovers, and alpine forget-me-nots. Yellow violets are common on the mountain slopes, while wood lilies are found in the meadows of the lowland parks.

Bighorn sheep are the symbol of Rocky Mountain Park. They thrive in the upper mountain reaches. Other wildlife includes elk, beavers, mountain lions, moose, bobcats, golden eagles, pikas, yellow-bellied marmots, coyotes, mule deer, chipmunks, and ground squirrels.

NATIONAL PARK SERVICE PHOTO

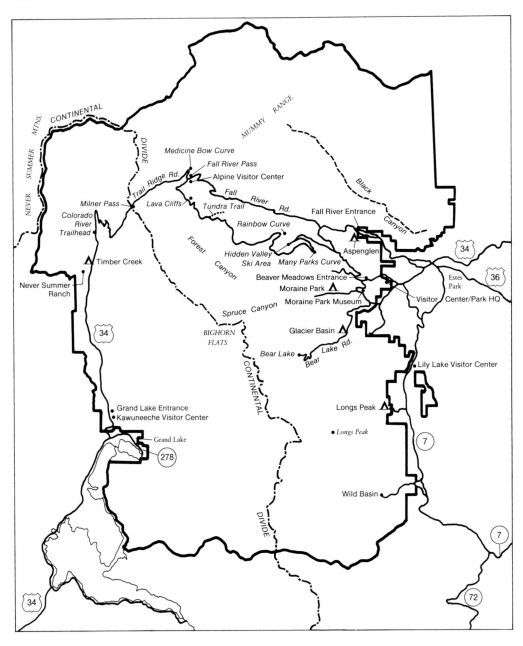

Further Information

Write or call: Superintendent, Rocky Mountain National Park, Estes Park, CO 80517-8397; (303) 586-2371

Visitor Information

Visitor Center/Headquarters: Near Estes Park; information.
Kawuneeche Visitor Center: Near Grand Lake; information.
Alpine Visitor Center: On Trail Ridge Road; information and exhibits. (Closed October to May.)
Lily Lake Visitor Center: South of Estes Park; information and exhibits. (Closed November to April.)

Nuts and Bolts

Entrance Fee: $5/vehicle. Good for seven days.
Park Open: All year. Trail Ridge Road is usually closed from mid-October until Memorial Day, and Fall River Road from mid-October until July 4.
Permits: Required for backcountry camping. A Colorado fishing license is required.
In Emergency: Call 586-2371.
Acreage: 265,668

Practical Advisory

Seasons

The park usually has pleasantly cool summers and bitterly cold winters. Below-freezing temperatures have been recorded in every month of the year, and snow has fallen in every month of the year. Temperatures vary widely at higher elevations, even in summer. The weather changes fast, and all types of weather are possible, including dangerous lightning.

Special Advisories

• No boats or flotation devices allowed on Bear Lake.
• There are extreme changes in elevation within the park; do not overexert yourself at high elevations.

Facilities for Disabled

Contact the park for a copy of their "Accessibility Guide."

Travel Advisory

Entrances

East: U.S. 36 for 65 miles northwest of Denver.

West: I-70 for 85 miles west of Denver to U.S. 40 to U.S. 34 north for 15 miles.

Transportation

Airports: Denver (65 miles) and Cheyenne (91 miles).

Bus Service: Buses serve Denver and Cheyenne. The Estes Park Bus Company makes connections with airlines, railroads, and buses at Denver. Call (303) 586-8108.

Train Service: Amtrak serves Denver and Cheyenne.

Rental Cars: Available in Denver and Cheyenne.

In-Park Transportation: Bear Lake Shuttle Buses are available along the Bear Lake Road. Take road from Estes Park entrance to parking area.

Attractions

The majestic *Rocky Mountain Front Range* is the central feature of the park, including *Longs Peak* (the highest in the park), the *Mummy Range,* and the *Never Summer Mountains.* The mountains are the highlight of the scenery throughout the park. Other areas of interest are *Bear Lake, Moraine Park,* and *Fall River.* A road travels across the park, offering many opportunities for scenic views. Trailheads can be found off the road.

Other Points of Interest (Museums, Historic Sites, etc.)

The *Moraine Park Museum* has colorful new exhibits including 3-D models, touchable specimens, and several "hands-on" exhibits that illustrate mountain building, glacier movement, and the creation of an ecosystem. Historic sites in the park are the *Never Summer Ranch* and the *William Alan White Cabin.*

Accommodations

There are no restaurants or lodgings in the park.

Campgrounds and Picnic Areas

Reservations for those noted below can be made through MISTIX at (800) 365-2267; all others are first-come, first-served. There is a seven-day limit. Gathering firewood is prohibited.

Moraine Park Campground: Reservations; 247 sites; open all year; water from mid-May, dump stations; $9/night.

Glacier Basin Campground: Reservations; 150 sites; open June 1; water, dump station; $9/night.

Aspenglen Campground: 54 sites; open mid-May; water; $7/night.

Timber Creek Campground: 100 sites; open all year; water as of June 1; dump stations; $7/night.

Longs Peak Campground: 26 sites; open all year; water as of late May; no RVs or motor homes; three-day limit; $7/night.

Picnic Areas: Nearly 20 in the park, most off the main park road.

Activities

Scenic Drives

Trail Ridge Road follows an ancient Native American trail and offers a beautifully scenic trip across the park. Beginning at Estes Park and ending at Grand Lake, the 48-mile road passes through the full range of environments and plant life in the park, from the lowlands up into the alpine tundra. The section of the road past Lava Cliffs is at an elevation of 12,183 feet, as high as you can go by vehicle anywhere in the national parks. The road crosses the Continental Divide at Milner Pass. Overlooks, including those at Many Parks Curve and Rainbow Curve, offer many scenery-viewing opportunities. Fall River Road is a one-way nine-mile road that loops north from the Estes Park entrance and joins the main road at Fall River Pass. It is very narrow and winding.

Hiking

There are 355 miles of hiking trails maintained within the park. Several self-guiding nature trails begin off the main park road, including the Tundra Trail and the Colorado River Trail. Other trails travel into the backcountry; topographic maps are needed. Get these and trail maps at the visitor centers.

Fishing

The mountain streams and lakes have four species of trout: German brown, rainbow, brook, and cutthroat. The waters are cold, so the fish are not very large. Fishing is not permitted in Bear Lake at any time. Other lakes and streams on the east side of the park are also closed to protect the fish. Check with the park for other regulations.

Horseback Riding

Many park trails can be traveled on horseback, but some cannot. Check with a park ranger on which trails are closed to horses. Two stables operate conducted rides at Moraine Park and Glacier Creek in the summer. For reservations: (303) 586-2327.

Winter Sports

Cross-country skiing is popular in the lower valleys and downhill skiing at Hidden Valley. Access roads from the east are kept open.

Mountaineering

There are a variety of challenging ascents possible throughout the year. A park concessioner operates a technical-climbing school and guide service. Write to the park superintendent for information and climbing regulations.

Ranger-Led Programs

Rangers lead walks, talks, and evening programs throughout the summer months. Check at visitor centers for schedules.

Descriptions of Sequoia and Kings Canyon national parks contain many superlatives. The two parks, which are administered as one, are home to the biggest tree on earth, the tallest peak in the Lower 48 states, part of the deepest canyon in the United States, and part of the longest single continuous mountain range in North America.

In total wood volume, giant sequoias stand alone as the world's largest living things. The only place on earth that these trees grow naturally is on the western slopes of the Sierra Nevada, most often at elevations between 5,000 and 7,000 feet. There are some 75 sequoia groves in all, and all but eight of them are south of Kings River in the park. Sequoias begin their lives as the tiniest of seeds, the size of oat flakes. With enough soil and sunlight, they begin their long and busy lives of growing.

Sequoias are as big as they are because they continue to grow throughout their entire long lives. They do not die of old age, and their chemical makeup makes them resistant to the effects of fire and disease. Because of their one major weakness—their shallow root systems—the main cause of death for sequoias is toppling. For all their enormous aboveground bulk, they lack the necessary taproots to keep them firmly anchored belowground. Soggy soil, root damage, and strong winds can lead to toppling.

One of the largest groves of sequoias is Giant Forest in Sequoia National Park. Given its name by John Muir, this forest is home to four of the world's five largest trees, including the 275-foot-tall General Sherman, the largest living thing on earth.

General Sherman's trunk weighs an estimated 1,385 tons, its circumference at the ground is nearly 103 feet, and its largest branch is almost seven feet in diameter. It is between 2,300 and 2,700 years old. Grant Grove, in Kings Canyon National Park, is home to the third-largest sequoia, the General Grant. The General Grant has officially been proclaimed the nation's Christmas Tree, and every year people gather here for a special holiday ceremony.

North of the sequoia groves is Kings Canyon, cut by the south fork of the Kings River. Outside the park, the canyon reaches a depth of some 8,200 feet from river level up to the peak of Spanish Mountain. There it is the deepest canyon in the United States, even deeper than the Grand Canyon in Arizona. In some places, it is V-shaped and in others it has the U shape characteristic of glacial gouging. Other canyons in the park include Kern Canyon in Southern Sequoia National Park at 6,000 feet deep, and several that are as deep as 4,000 feet.

To the east of the canyon and the sequoia groves, the jagged peaks of the Sierra Nevada stand tall, as North America's longest single continuous mountain range. The tallest of these peaks, the mighty Mount Whitney, is, at 14,494 feet, the tallest peak in the lower 48 states. The tall trees and dense forests found in other areas of the park cannot tolerate the harsh climate above 9,000 feet on the mountain; above 11,000 feet, very few trees grow at all. There, mostly boulders, rocks, and gravel can be found, interrupted by small alpine

lakes, meadows, and low-growing shrubs.

Dry, hot summers in the western foothills of the Sierra Nevada offer the perfect environment for low-growing chaparral vegetation. Chaparral is a drought-resistant shrub community adapted to rapid regrowth after periodic fire. Although winter rains bring wildflowers here in spring, the grass will all be brown by summer, and the chaparral retains its olive-drab color.

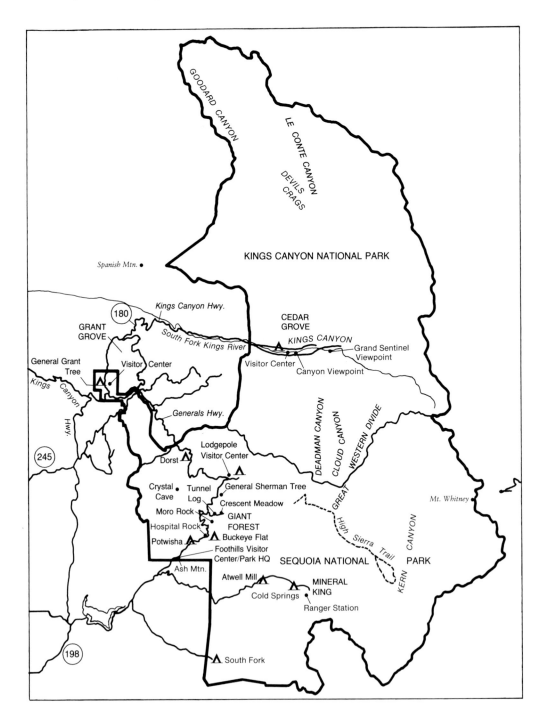

Further Information

Write or call: Superintendent, Sequoia and Kings Canyon National Parks, Three Rivers, CA 93271; (209) 565-3134

Visitor Information

Lodgepole Visitor Center: In Giant Forest; information; schedules; exhibits and audiovisual programs describe Sierra Nevada and sequoia natural history.
Grant Grove Visitor Center: In Grant Grove; information; schedules; exhibits explain the natural and human history of the area; 10-minute slide program.
Foothills Visitor Center: Park headquarters, at southwest park entrance off Highway 198; information; schedules.

Mineral King Ranger Station: South part of Sequoia National Park, accessible by road or trail. Open in summer only; information; schedules.
Cedar Grove Visitor Center. In Cedar Grove. Open May to October; information; schedules.

Nuts and Bolts

Entrance Fee: $5/vehicle or $2/person arriving by other means, motorcyclists, etc. Good for seven days in both parks.
Park Open: All year. Kings Canyon Highway and Mineral King Road are closed from about November to April.
Permits: Required for backcountry camping. California fishing license required.
In Emergency: Call 911.
Acreage: Sequoia, 402,482.38; Kings Canyon, 461,901.20

Practical Advisory

Seasons

Summer: Low elevations are hot and dry; rain is rare. In the middle elevations (where the sequoias grow), warm daytime and cool evening temperatures with occasional afternoon thundershowers. In the high elevations, pleasant with an occasional thundershower, and nighttime temperatures that often drop into the low 30s and occasionally the 20s. It can snow at any time. Winter: Low elevations have mild, wet winters with rain usually occurring from January to mid-May and averaging about 26 inches total. In the middle elevations, much of the 40–45 inches of precipitation comes during the winter, and a deep blanket of snow often covers the area from December to May.

Special Advisories

• Avoid encounters with bears and know what to do if one occurs.
• Be alert for high water levels and fast currents.
• Beware of snakes and ticks.
• Between Potwisha Campground and Giant Forest on the Generals Highway, trailers may not be longer than 35 feet, single vehicles may not be longer than 40 feet, and combination vehicles may not be longer than 50 feet. The width limit is eight feet.

Facilities for Disabled

Write to the superintendent for a copy of the "Access" handout.

Travel Advisory

Entrances

West Entrances: Highway 180 for 55 miles east of Fresno to Grant Grove; continue 30 miles to Cedar Grove in the Kings Canyon or south to Sequoia (via Generals Highway).

Sequoia: Highway 198, 35 miles northeast of Visalia.

Transportation

Airports: In Fresno and Visalia.

Bus Service: Available to Fresno and Visalia.

Train Service: Amtrak serves Fresno, and serves Visalia via bus connection from Hanford.

Rental Cars: Available in Fresno and Visalia.

Attractions

The parks' *groves of sequoia trees* are among their star attractions. Three of the most famous sequoias are the *General Sherman* (the largest living thing), the *General Grant,* and the *Tunnel Log,* a sequoia with a tunnel through it. Also of interest are *Crescent Meadow* and *Moro Rock.* Although much of the land is undeveloped, all of these areas can be easily reached by the one road that connects the two parks. The beautiful *Sierra Nevada Range,* including its tallest peak, *Mount Whitney,* can be viewed from many areas of the park. You can see a good part of the scenic *Kings Canyon* by driving along its rim.

Accommodations

Lodges

Reservations for all lodges: Reservations Department, P.O. Box 789, Three Rivers, CA 93271; (209) 561-3314.

Giant Forest: In Sequoia National Park; motel rooms, cabins, "semi-housekeeping" cabins without bath (closed in winter), and sleeping cabins without bath (closed in winter).

Grant Grove: In Kings Canyon National Park; cabins, "semi-housekeeping" cabins without bath, and sleeping cabins without bath (closed in winter).

Cedar Grove: In Kings Canyon National Park; lodge rooms; open late May through September.

Bearpaw High Sierra Camp: In Sequoia National Park; tent cabin with beds and showers; accessible only by 11 miles of trail; open late June to early September; reservations required.

Campgrounds and Picnic Areas

First-come, first-served, except Lodgepole. Lodgepole reservations can be made through MISTIX at (800) 365-2267 for the period from mid-May to Labor Day. There is a 14-

day limit for all campgrounds from June 14 through September 14. Bring wood or gather only dead and downed wood. All campgrounds have tables and fire grills; most have drinking water.

Atwell Mill Campground: In Mineral King area, near a sequoia grove; 23 sites; no trailers, RVs not recommended; open late spring to mid-November; no water and no fees after September; pit toilets; $5/night.

Azalea Campground: In Grant Grove area; 118 sites; open all year; flush toilets, dump station; $8/night.

Buckeye Flat Campground: In Foothills area; 28 sites; open mid-April to mid-October; flush toilets; no trailers or RVs; $8/night.

Cold Springs Campground: In Mineral King area; 37 sites; no trailers, RVs not recommended; open late spring to mid-November; no water and no fees after September; pit toilets; $5/night.

Crystal Springs Campground: In Grant Grove area; 67 sites; open Memorial Day to mid-September; flush toilets; $8/night.

Dorst Campground: In Lodgepole area; 218 sites; open Memorial Day–Labor Day; flush toilets; $8/night.

Lodgepole Campground: In Giant Forest area, near a sequoia grove; 260 sites; open all year but limited facilities after heavy snow; flush toilets, dump station from late May to mid-October; $10/night during reservations period; $8/night other times (no charge after significant snow cover).

Moraine Campground: In Cedar Grove area; 120 sites; open mid-May to mid-October; flush toilets; $8/night.

Potwisha Campground: In Foothills area; 44 sites; open year-round; flush toilets, dump station; $8/night.

Sentinel Campground: In Cedar Grove area; 83 sites; open mid-May to mid-October; flush toilets; $8/night.

Sheep Creek Campground: In Cedar Grove area; 111 sites; open mid-May to mid-October; flush toilets; $8/night.

South Fork Campground: In Foothills area; 13 sites; open all year but no fees from November through mid-May; pit toilets; $4/night.

Sunset Campground: In Grant Grove area; 184 sites; open Memorial Day to mid-September; flush toilets; $8/night.

Picnic Areas: One in Grant Grove area, three in Giant Forest area, one north of Ash Mountain entrance; all off the main park roads.

Restaurants

The Village Cafeteria: In Giant Forest; open all year; breakfast, lunch, and dinner.

The Lodge Dining Room: In Giant Forest; breakfast, lunch, dinner, and Sunday brunch; open late May through mid-October.

Grant Grove Coffee Shop: Open year-round; breakfast, lunch, and dinner.

Cedar Grove: Counter service for breakfast, lunch, and dinner; open late May to September.

Wolverton Ski Touring Area: In Giant Forest area; dining area with convenience foods during ski season.

Lodgepole Center: Deli sandwiches.

Activities

Scenic Drives

The Generals Highway and Kings Canyon Highway are the two main park roads. Both offer roadside pullouts with scenic viewpoints, including Canyon Viewpoint and Grand Sentinel Viewpoint along the Kings Canyon Highway. The Generals Highway connects the two parks, making loop trips possible. In Grant Grove, you can also take a separate park road to Panoramic Point, offering a spectacular view of the high Sierra. In Giant Forest, the Crescent Meadow Road is a three-mile dead-end road beginning at Giant Forest Village and traveling past the Tunnel Log (a tunnel through a fallen sequoia, 17 feet wide and eight feet high; there is no standing tunneled tree here), Moro Rock, and Crescent Meadow. In Cedar Grove, the Motor Nature Trail is a three-mile rough dirt road providing a leisurely drive along the river in Kings Canyon; a booklet is available to help guide you.

Hiking

There are over 700 miles of trails, including both relatively easy hikes and steep mountain trails. Short trails around Giant Forest include the two-mile-loop Congress Trail through the heart of the sequoia forest and the ½-mile paved Trail for All People, which circles around Round Meadow, surrounded by sequoia forest. Short trails around Grant Grove include the ⅓-mile trail to the General Grant Tree and the one-mile Big Stump Basin Trail. In the Cedar Grove area, the Roaring River Falls Trail is a five-minute walk to the waterfall. For serious hikers, the High Sierra Trail runs 71 miles to the summit of Mount Whitney. Trails below 10,000 feet are normally open by midsummer. Stream crossings may be hazardous any time, but especially before July. Trail maps should be used for extended day hikes and backcountry hikes.

Horseback Riding

Horses, burros, and llamas are allowed, but there are specific regulations for some trails and forage areas. Corrals with horses for hire are open from mid-May through September: Cedar Grove Pack Station, (209) 565-3464; Mineral King Pack Station, (209) 561-3404; Wolverton Pack Station, (209) 565-3445; and Grant Grove Stables (day rides only), (209) 335-2482.

Tours of Crystal Cave

Guided 45-minute tours of this marble cavern begin at the cave entrance (after a ½-mile downhill hike), and are available from mid-May through September. Light jackets are recommended. A fee is charged.

Motor Tours

All-day guided Kings Canyon Tours depart from Giant Forest and Grant Grove. Guided Giant Forest Tours are 1½ hours in the morning and evening and include Moro Rock, the General Sherman Tree, and Crescent Meadow. The tours stop frequently. Fees are charged. Telephone: (209) 565-3381.

Fishing

Rainbow, brown, eastern brook, and golden trout are caught. Ask for a copy of fishing regulations, including seasons, limits, and other rules, at any visitor center.

Winter Sports

Cross-country skiing and snowshoeing are available. Wolverton winter-use area has rentals and ski instruction; call (209) 565-3435. Grant Grove offers similar services; call (209) 335-2314. Marked cross-country ski trails connect Giant Forest, Wolverton, and Lodgepole. Grant Grove cross-country trails connect with ski trails in surrounding Sequoia National Forest. Maps are available at visitor centers and ski centers. Season opens with the first snow and lasts through mid-April.

Naturalist Programs

Naturalists offer walks, campfire talks, and other programs. Guided snowshoe walks may be offered on weekends and holidays in winter, as conditions permit. Check the free park newspaper and bulletin boards for schedules and locations.

A central feature of northwest Virginia's Shenandoah National Park is the beautiful Blue Ridge mountain range. The Blue Ridge Mountains, which really do look blue from a distance, are a part of the mighty Appalachian range, which stretches all the way up into the Northeast. The mountains here are surrounded by scenic landscape. To the west is the Shenandoah River, for which the park is named. To the east is the Piedmont Plateau. Lying between the north and south forks of the river is Massanutten Mountain.

This land of mountains and valleys, hardwood forests and open meadows, and streams and waterfalls had a history of human habitation long before the federal government turned it into a park. In the early 1700s, many years after Native American hunters left the area, settlers came through and decided it was a beautiful and fertile place to live. By the early 1800s the area was fully settled by farmers, who tilled the earth and logged the lush forests. But the land here could only take so much. Eventually the soil grew thin, the forests shrank, and the game animals grew scarce. Many people left. It was around this time that the government became interested in preserving the land. But it had to be bought and given to the government by the private owners.

Since the government took title in the early 20th century, the land has come back to its original beauty. The regeneration has been so successful, in fact, that 95 percent of the land is covered in forest today. These beautiful forests that blanket the Blue Ridge and the Shenandoah Valley are what the park is known for. The rolling hills and slopes, stretching for miles, are covered with about 100 species of trees. Growing side by side with pines and hemlocks are oaks, maples, hickories, black walnuts, and many others. The only large open area in the park is the Big Meadows, maintained as a meadow by the park administration and full of wildflowers, strawberries, and blueberries.

Shenandoah's wildlife includes deer and such smaller animals as chipmunks, raccoons, skunks, opossums, and the frequently seen gray squirrels. Bears are found mostly in the backcountry but are occasionally spotted elsewhere. About 200 species of birds have been recorded including grouse, ravens, various woodpeckers, and juncos. The park is also well known as the home of several species of salamanders.

The natural beauty of the park comes alive every year in the spring. Streams and waterfalls are full of meltwater and flow briskly. Wildflowers begin blooming in April and May, when trillium and bloodroot can be found. The greening of the trees moves up the slopes approximately 100 feet per day, with the peaks not green until May. Pink azaleas and mountain laurels bloom in the late spring, when the migratory birds are returning. With the onset of summer, the number and type of wildflowers increase. By late summer the open areas are covered with their bright colors. In fall,

NATIONAL PARK SERVICE

the leaves of the abundant trees change to their brightest shades of red, yellow, and orange.

The park's proximity to Washington, D.C., and other Eastern cities has made it a popular destination.

Further Information

Write or call: Superintendent, Shenandoah National Park, Luray, VA 22835; (703) 999-2266

Visitor Information

Park Headquarters: On U.S. 211; information.
Dickey Ridge Visitor Center: Mile 4.6; information, interpretive exhibits, illustrated programs. (Closed November to March.)
Byrd Visitor Center: At Big Meadows, Mile 51; information, interpretive exhibits, illustrated programs. (Closed intermittently in January and February.)

Nuts and Bolts

Entrance Fee: $5/vehicle or $3/person arriving by other means. Good for seven consecutive days.
Park Open: All year.
Permits: Required for backcountry camping. A Virginia fishing license is required.
In Emergency: Call 1-800-732-0911.
Acreage: 195,382.13

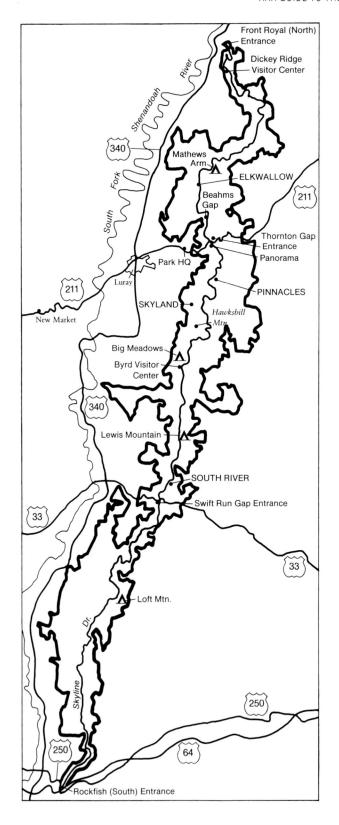

Practical Advisory

Seasons

Mountain weather is changeable. It can be cold and wet in any season. Summer days are warm; summer nights are cool. Fog may occur at any time. Overnight temperatures are lowest in the valleys. Winters are cold, with about 36 inches of snow per year.

Special Advisories

- Do not take shortcuts when hiking; terrain is steep and rocky.
- Do not play at the tops of waterfalls.
- Be careful when crossing streams in spring; water may be high.
- Respect the rights of private landowners.

Facilities for Disabled

Rest rooms, buildings, lodging at Skyland and Big Meadows lodges, some campsites, and toilets at picnic ground and campgrounds are wheelchair-accessible. Sign-language interpreting is available for some activities. Written information on exhibits, interpretive booklets or signs for self-guiding nature trails, and printed scripts of the orientation films are available. Tapes of much park information are available for loan. The history handout and nature-trail booklets are available in braille.

Travel Advisory

Entrances

North: U.S. 340 for 24 miles south of Winchester.

Thornton Gap: U.S. 211 east of New Market or 80 miles southwest of Washington, D.C.

Swift Run Gap: U.S. 33 for 24 miles east of Harrisonburg or northwest of Ruckersville.

South: I-64 for 91 miles west of Richmond or for 18 miles east of Staunton.

Transportation

Airports: Washington, D.C., and Richmond.

Bus Service: Various bus companies serve Washington, D.C., and Richmond.

Train Service: Amtrak serves Washington, D.C., and Richmond.

Rental Cars: Available at airports in Washington, D.C., and Richmond.

Attractions

The *Blue Ridge Mountains* are the central feature of the park. Offering a beautiful backdrop are the *Shenandoah Valley, Shenandoah River,* and *Massanutten Mountain* to the west of the park. The landscape consists largely of *thick forests* of many varieties of trees blanketing much of the land. *Big Meadows* is the only area kept free of forest cover. The main park road travels the length of the park, offering many scenic views as well as access to trails.

Accommodations

Lodges

Reservations for Skyland Lodge, Big Meadows Lodge, and Lewis Mountain Cottages: ARA Virginia Sky-Line Company, Box 727, Luray, VA 22835; (800) 999-4714.

Skyland Lodge: Miles 41–43; cabins and rooms; open April through mid-December.

Big Meadows Lodge: Mile 51.2; cabins and rooms; open mid-May through October.

Lewis Mountain Cottages: Mile 57.5; furnished cottages with outdoor cooking and living area; open mid-May through October.

Trail Cabins: Six trail cabins for hikers. Reservations: Potomac Appalachian Trail Club, 1718 N Street, N.W., Washington, D.C. 20036.

Campgrounds and Picnic Areas

Fourteen-day limit from June 1 to October 31. Reservation information: (703) 999-2282. Wood fires are permitted only in fireplaces in developed areas and are prohibited in the backcountry.

Mathews Arm Campground: Mile 22.2; tables, fireplaces, water, toilets, dump station; open late spring through October; $8/night.

Big Meadows Campground: Mile 51; tables, fireplaces, water, toilets, dump station; open March through December; $8/night.

Lewis Mountain Campground: Mile 57.5; tables, fireplaces, water, toilets; open May through October; $8/night.

Loft Mountain Campground: Mile 79.5; tables, fireplaces, water, toilets, dump station; open late spring through October; $8/night.

Backcountry Camping: Most of the park is open to backcountry camping; select sites out of sight of the trails. Seven huts along the Appalachian Trail are available for a fee of $1/night.

Picnic Areas: Located at Dickey Ridge (Mile 4.6), Elkwallow (Mile 24.1), Pinnacles (Mile 36.7), Big Meadows (Milepost 51), Lewis Mountain (Mile 57.5), South River (Mile 62.8), Loft Mountain (Mile 79.5). All have tables, fireplaces, water, and toilets.

Restaurants

Skyland Lodge: Dining room; breakfast, lunch, and dinner; open April through mid-Decemer.

Big Meadows Lodge: Dining room; breakfast, lunch, and dinner; open mid-May through October.

Big Meadows Wayside: Coffee shop; open May through October.

Panorama Restaurant: At Thornton Gap;

dining room; open April through November.

Loft Mountain Wayside: Coffee shop; open April through early November.

Activities

Scenic Drives

The Skyline Drive, a winding 105-mile road, runs along the Blue Ridge through the full length of the park, providing spectacular vistas of the landscape. There are concrete mile markers on the right-hand side of the drive as you head south. Numerous parking overlooks with interpretive signs offer panoramas of the Piedmont to the east and the Shenandoah Valley to the west. Skyland (Mile 41.7 and 42.5) is, at 3,680 feet, the highest point on the drive. Overlooks include the Shenandoah Valley Overlook (Mile 2.8) with a sweeping view across the valley; Range View Overlook (Mile 17.1) with an exceptional view of a large section of the Blue Ridge; and Calf Mountain Overlook (Mile 98.9) with a 300-degree view. Marys Rock tunnel at Mile 32.4 goes through 600 feet of rock with a 13-foot clearance.

Hiking

There are about 500 miles of trails in the park, varying in length from short walks to a 95-mile section of the famous Appalachian Trail. Many trailheads are located on Skyline Drive and in the developed areas. There are several self-guiding nature trails (these may be sign-posted, or the visitor may consult a leaflet), including the Stony Man Nature Trail from Skyland (Mile 41.7). Beahms Gap (Mile 28.5) provides access to the Appalachian Trail. A trail from Thornton Gap (Mile 31.5) leads to 360-degree views from Marys Rock. Near

Skyland, a five-mile round-trip hike leads to Whiteoak Canyon (Mile 42.6) and six waterfalls in an area of large hemlocks. Hawksbill Gap Trail (Mile 45.6) leads to Hawksbill Mountain, at 4,050 feet the highest point in the park. The Jones Run Trail (Mile 84.1) is a 3⁶⁄₁₀-mile round-trip hike to the 42-foot Jones Run Falls. Detailed maps are available at visitor centers.

Fishing

Those who are willing to hike to streams in the park may fish for native brook trout.

Bicycling

Bicycling is allowed on park roads.

Horseback Riding

Guided horseback trips are offered at Skyland Lodge from April through October. Pony rides are also available for children. Horse-drawn-wagon rides are available at Big Meadows Lodge.

Naturalist Programs

Evening programs, campfire talks, hikes, and demonstrations are offered at several locations during the summer and at a few sites during spring and fall. Activity schedules are posted on bulletin boards throughout the park and in the park newspaper, available at most visitor centers.

There is only one national park named after a president of the United States. Many people agree it is fitting that that president is Theodore Roosevelt. "T.R." spent a portion of the mid-1880s here in the colorful North Dakota badlands. The things he saw and learned had a lasting effect on his beliefs as a man and a conservationist.

The land in the park today looks much as it did when Theodore Roosevelt first traveled to this part of the country in 1883. Grasslands surround colorful, intricate canyons, cliffs, and buttes carved by the Little Missouri River. Roosevelt, in his twenties at the time, originally came for the prospect of big-game hunting. While he was here, though, his interest turned to cattle ranching. He invested in the Maltese Cross Ranch and later bought his own ranch, the Elkhorn.

Thus Roosevelt had the opportunity to witness firsthand the potential for destruction of the land from overgrazing. He saw some local cattle ranchers beginning to fail, and his beloved bison were disappearing from the area. He returned to his political life back East with a renewed sense of the importance of more careful management of the land. When he became president in 1901, he brought those feelings with him, and was later responsible for the establishment of several national parks, forests, monuments, and wildlife refuges to preserve our land's resources.

Today the park consists of three separate units—the North Unit, South Unit, and Elk-horn Ranch Site. A variety of animal and plant life flourishes in the park. Bison and elk, which had been driven from the area for a time, have returned, although the bison are confined to the park. Pronghorns, mule deer, and white-tailed deer also live here. Prairie dogs live in "towns" in the grasslands, and support such predators as badgers and coyotes. There are more than 170 species of birds, many of them songbirds. And golden eagles can be seen nesting in the badlands. The plains are covered with a mix of grasses, including needle-and-thread, an important component of the prairie that provides critical habitat and sustenance for native wildlife. Wildflowers add bright color to the scenery in the summer.

The interesting look and colors of the badlands are a result of erosional exposure of sediment that was laid down about 60 million years ago. Streams flowing east from the young Rocky Mountains brought a mix of sediment to the vast lowlands that are today's Great Plains. Erosion, much of it by the Little Missouri River in recent years, has sculpted the infinite variety of buttes, tableland, gorges, and valleys of the badlands and exposed the sediment in all of its bright and beautiful colors.

The lush semitropical vegetation that grew here at one time included ferns and palms. Deposits of these plants, buried by new layers of sediment, were eventually turned into thick, black beds of a soft coal called lignite. At times, lightning or grass

PHOTO BY G. T. ALTOFF, NATIONAL PARK SERVICE, THEODORE ROOSEVELT NATIONAL PARK

fires cause these beds to burn, sometimes for decades. Some vegetation has also been preserved as petrified wood, mostly found in the Petrified Forest.

Many of Theodore Roosevelt's attitudes about and interest in nature and conservation were sharpened and refined in this part of the country. It is in tribute to that fact that this national park has been named in his honor.

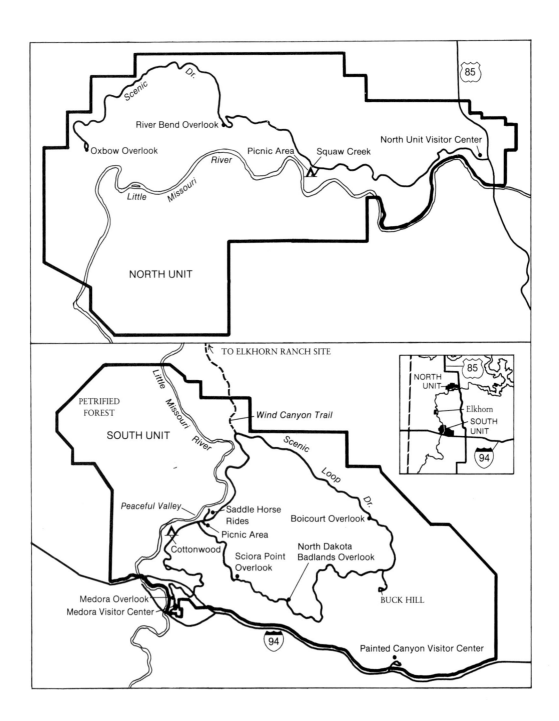

Further Information

Write or call: Superintendent, Theodore Roosevelt National Park, Medora, ND 58645; (701) 623-4466

Visitor Information

Medora Visitor Center: South Unit; personal items of Theodore Roosevelt, ranching artifacts, natural history displays, book sales, information.
Painted Canyon Visitor Center: South Unit; exhibits, audiovisual programs, book sales, information. (Closed fall to spring.)
North Unit Visitor Center: Information.

Nuts and Bolts

Entrance Fee: $4/vehicle or $2/person arriving by other means (charged May through September). Good for seven days.
Park Open: All year. Parts of the roads may be closed in the winter.
Permits: Required for backcountry camping.
In Emergency: Call 623-4466 (daytime) or 623-4379 (after hours).
Acreage: 70,416.39

Practical Advisory

Seasons

The badlands are subject to sudden, drastic weather changes. Summer highs are in the 80s; lows are in the 50s. Summer storms are frequently accompanied by lightning, hail, and high winds. Winter highs are in the low 30s, and lows are in the single digits to below 0°. About 30 inches of snow falls per year.

Special Advisories

- Rattlesnakes and black widow spiders often live in prairie-dog burrows.
- Watch out for poison ivy in wooded areas and for ticks in late spring and early summer.
- Climbing on the steep, barren slopes in the badlands can be dangerous: Slippery clays and soft sediments may yield underfoot.
- Remember, wild animals are dangerous.

Facilities for Disabled

The visitor centers are wheelchair-accessible. There are accessible campsites available.

Travel Advisory

Entrances

North Unit: Highway 85 for 15 miles south of Watford City or 55 miles north of Belfield.

South Unit: I-94 for 17 miles west of Belfield or 63 miles east of Glendive, Montana.

Elkhorn: Rough, poorly maintained dirt road for about 20 miles from the South Unit. You should inquire of park authorities before attempting this trip.

Transportation

Airports: Bismarck (135 miles from South Unit); Williston (75 miles from North Unit).

Bus Service: Greyhound serves Medora, near the entrance to the South Unit.

Train Service: Amtrak serves Williston.

Rental Cars: Available in Bismarck (135 miles from South Unit) and Williston (75 miles from North Unit).

Attractions

The *badlands* formations are the park's major attraction. The park roads offer many opportunities for scenery-viewing. Also of interest are the *Little Missouri River,* which runs through both sections of the park, and the *coal seams.* The *Petrified Forest* and *Wind Canyon,* in the South Unit, are best seen by taking the trails.

Other Points of Interest (Museums, Historic Sites, etc.)

The restored *Maltese Cross Cabin,* which Theodore Roosevelt used, is behind the Medora Visitor Center in the South Unit. Scheduled guided tours are available from mid-June through mid-September. Tours are self-guided the rest of the year.

Accommodations

There is no food or lodging available in the park.

Campgrounds and Picnic Areas

First-come, first-served; 14-day limit. Build fires only in fire grates at the campgrounds and picnic areas. Fires are prohibited in the backcountry. Gathering firewood is not permitted.

Cottonwood Campground: In the South Unit; water, toilets; open all year, but no services (and no fee) in winter; $7/night.

Squaw Creek Campground: In the North Unit; water, toilets; open all year, but no services (and no fee) in winter; $7/night.

Picnic Areas: At Painted Canyon and Peaceful Valley in the South Unit; at Squaw Creek in the North Unit.

Activities

Scenic Drives

In the North Unit, the 14-mile Scenic Drive goes from the entrance station to the Oxbow Overlook with turnouts and interpretive signs along the way. There are a number of trailheads off the road. In the South Unit, the 36-mile Scenic Loop Road has overlooks and interpretive signs along its course that explain some of the park's historical and natural phenomena. A Loop Road guide, for sale in the visitor center, gives detailed information about the landscape. Boicourt Overlook has one of the best views over the badlands in the park. There are a number of trailheads off the road.

Hiking

The 85 miles of backcountry trails in the park can be reached off the main park roads. In the North Unit there are short self-guiding nature trails. In the South Unit, a 16-mile trail takes you to the Petrified Forest, the greatest collection of petrified wood in the park. A one-mile trail takes you past impressive coal seams.

Horseback Riding

Riding groups with their own horses should write to the park superintendent to make special arrangements for camping. In the summer, saddle horses can be rented and guides hired at Peaceful Valley for trail rides of various lengths. Contact Peaceful Valley Ranch, P.O. Box 197, Medora, ND 56845. Horses are prohibited in campgrounds, in picnic areas, and on nature trails.

River Floating

You can float the Little Missouri River, which flows through both units of the park and past the Elkhorn Ranch. Canoes can be rented from Dixon Canoes, (701) 842-3448.

Ranger-Led Programs

From June to mid-September, varied programs are offered, including talks, campfire programs, demonstrations, films, and guided walks. Information is at the visitor centers and entrance stations, and is posted on bulletin boards.

Pristine white-sand beaches, clear blue-green water, green forested hills, the scent of lime and bay rum trees, and multicolored coral reefs fringing the shoreline—these are the hallmarks of Virgin Islands National Park. It is one of the tiniest national parks, comprising just over half of St. John, the smallest of the three major islands that make up the United States Virgin Islands. Since so much of St. John has been made a national park, it remains the least developed of all the islands, retaining much of its virgin natural state.

Christopher Columbus once landed in the Virgin Islands, giving them their name and claiming them for Spain. But they were rarely visited by Europeans for the next 200 years. In the late 1600s, they were settled by the Dutch. The Dutch, like the Danes who owned nearby St. Thomas, recognized that the climate here was perfect for sugarcane farming.

Coral Bay was the site of the first sugar plantation established on St. John, first settled in 1717. There the Dutch and Danes cleared much of the natural forest, imported slaves for labor, and began producing brown sugar, molasses, and rum for export. After slavery was abolished in the mid-1800s, the sugar plantations ceased operation. Remnants of those days remain on the island, however, most notably the partially restored Annaberg Plantation which can be toured. The United States bought the Virgin Islands from Denmark in 1917.

With the advent of air travel, the Virgin Islands have become a mecca for vacationers. The clear tropical seas are normally calm, warm, and placid, offering ideal swimming, sunbathing, and snorkeling conditions. The thickly wooded forests on St. John are excellent for hiking. The higher elevations and protected valleys contain subtropical moist forests, the type most common on the island. Although much forest was cleared for raising sugarcane, the trees are returning. The lower elevations, southern and eastern slopes, and less exposed coastal sites are primarily subtropical dry forests. Because of their exposure to the sun and the continuous easterly trade winds, the southern and eastern shores have a very dry landscape, almost desertlike; in fact, cactuses grow there.

The islands were created by volcanic activity that began nearly 100 million years ago. An uplift of the ocean floor around 70 million years ago helped raise the land above the water; seeds—brought by the wind and the water or carried by visiting animals—took root and began to flourish. Slowly but surely, the vegetation built up, until today the island's green lushness reaches nearly down to the water's edges.

At those edges are the famous white-sand beaches, and beyond them the coral reefs. The beaches could not exist without the growth of the living coral that makes up the reefs. Not only do the reefs protect the beaches from being washed away by distant storm-generated waves, they also provide the sand, which is composed of tiny pieces

NATIONAL PARK SERVICE

of broken-down coral. The reefs are a complex community of interacting marine plants and animals. These range from the hard corals (including brain, elkhorn, star, finger, and staghorn) to the soft corals (sea whips and sea fans), and are brilliantly colored in greens, yellows, oranges, and purples. There are over 450 species of fish in the community, including parrot fish, angelfish, grunts, and snappers.

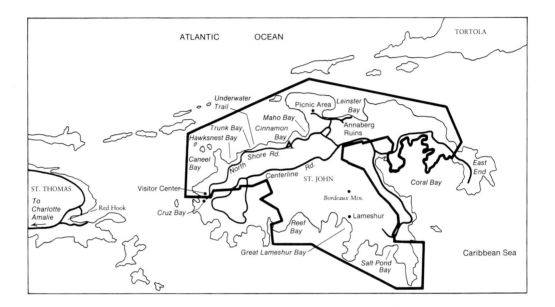

Further Information

Write or call: Superintendent, Virgin Islands National Park, Box 710, Cruz Bay, St. John, U.S. Virgin Islands 00830; (809) 775-6238 or (809) 776-6201

Visitor Information

Cruz Bay Visitor Center: Orientation talks, exhibits, information about park features.
Red Hook Contact Station: On St. Thomas; information.

Nuts and Bolts

Entrance Fee: None.
Park Open: All year.
Permits: Needed to use certain areas in the park. Check with park rangers for information.
In Emergency: Contact a park ranger, call visitor center at 776-6201, or go to Cruz Bay Clinic, across from public ferry dock.
Acreage: 14,688.87

Practical Advisory

Seasons

The yearly temperature averages 79° and varies little between winter and summer. Temperatures rarely exceed 98° or fall below 65°. Rainfall averages approximately 40 inches per year, coming mostly in brief afternoon or night showers. Cooling easterly trade winds temper the summer's heat and keep humidity down.

Special Advisories

• Possession of metal detectors is prohibited.
• Much of the land is still private property, and permission is necessary to enter or use these areas.
• Persons returning to the U.S. mainland from the Virgin Islands must go through customs and immigration at San Juan, Puerto Rico; St. Thomas; or other U.S. ports of entry. An import permit is required for fruits, vegetables, plant cuttings, and seeds.

Facilities for Disabled

There are ramps at Hawksnest Bay and Trunk Bay and wheelchair-accessible rest rooms at the visitor center.

Travel Advisory

You can fly from the mainland United States directly to Charlotte Amalie, St. Thomas, or to San Juan, Puerto Rico; or you can travel by ship. If you arrive in St. Thomas, taxis and buses can take you to Red Hook, where you can get a ferry that operates daily to Cruz Bay on St. John. Water-taxi service is available after hours. You can get scheduling information for ferries from Varlack Ventures, (809) 776-6412, or Transportation Services, (809) 776-6282, both on St. John. The campground is 20 minutes by taxi or car from Cruz Bay. Jeeps and other vehicles may be rented; reservations are necessary.

If you are only planning a day trip to the park, the package vehicle tours and scenic boat charters that leave from St. Thomas, with all transportation arranged, are most popular. Make arrangements in advance.

Attractions

The clear, warm *seas* and sandy *beaches* surrounding the island are the park's chief attraction. *Trunk Bay* and *Cinnamon Bay* are the center of much activity, mostly in the water. Other popular areas are *Leinster Bay, Coral Bay, Lameshur Bay, Reef Bay,* and *Salt Pond Bay*. The park road and trails offer access to places throughout the island.

Other Points of Interest
(Museums, Historic Sites, etc.)

The partially restored ruins of the *Annaberg sugar mill factory* complex are above Leinster Bay on St. John's north shore. Eighteenth-century and early-19th century Danes, Dutchmen, and slaves worked here to produce brown sugar, molasses, and rum for export.

Accommodations

Campground and Picnic Areas

Camping is allowed only at the campground.

Cinnamon Bay Campground: Five miles from Cruz Bay; tent sites, pre-erected tents, and cottage units with tables, grills, and water; can be rented with or without equipment including tent, cots, bedding, cooking utensils, eating utensils, and stove; 14-day limit. For information and reservations: Cin-namon Bay Campground, St. John, VI 00830, (809) 776-6330.

Picnic Areas: Scattered throughout the park.

Restaurants

Cinnamon Bay Camp Cafeteria: Breakfast, lunch, and dinner.

Tree Lizards Restaurant: At Cinnamon Bay; breakfast, lunch and dinner.

Activities

Swimming and Snorkeling

Swimming and snorkeling opportunities are excellent at St. John's many beaches when weather and sea conditions are good. Trunk Bay has one of the best beaches in the world and offers a self-guiding underwater nature trail (with underwater signs) for snorkelers. Lifeguards are on duty and snorkel equipment can be rented at Trunk Bay. Cinnamon Bay Water Sports Center, at the campground, has snorkeling-equipment rental, snorkeling tours, scuba-diving trips, windsurfing lessons, sea-kayak rentals, and Hobie monohull sailboats.

Scenic Drives

A 15-mile tour by auto or taxi over Centerline Road and back via the North Shore Road includes spectacular scenery; you can stop at the ruins of the Annaberg plantation and at some of the island's many beaches. Also popular are resident-guided taxi tours through the park. These are operated from Cruz Bay; a typical tour may take 2½ hours.

Hiking

The 22 hiking trails on St. John range from easy walks to difficult climbs; some are well maintained, others brushy. The longest is 2⁴/₁₀ miles. They travel to woodlands, beaches, bays, historic ruins, and beautiful views. Self-guided walking trails are at Annaberg and at Cinnamon Bay. Reef Bay Trail, from Center-line Road, is a 2²/₁₀-mile downhill trail that traverses an unusual subtropical moist forest—to—dry forest area.

Fishing

Saltwater fishing is good all year, and no license is required. Rod-and-reel fishing from the shore is permitted, but not in the vicinity of public swimming or snorkeling beaches. Boats for deep-sea fishing, drift fishing, or shoreline trolling may be chartered at St. John and St. Thomas. Spearfishing is prohibited. Fishing in Trunk Bay is prohibited.

Boating

Charter sail and power boats with operators are available on St. John, St. Thomas, and nearby British Tortola. All Coast Guard boating regulations are enforced. Waterskiing and jet skiing are prohibited. Cinnamon Bay Water Sports Center, at the campground, offers day sailing on a 42-foot yacht.

Ranger-Led Activities

Guided snorkel trips, hikes, cultural demonstrations, environmental talks, and evening programs are offered throughout the year. A schedule of interpretive activities is posted on the bulletin boards and in the visitor center. Some ranger-led hikes and activities require reservations. Spaces for popular activities can fill up a week in advance in peak season, December 15–April 15.

The most striking feature of Voyageurs National Park is the water: It is everywhere. In fact, past the main entry points, there are no roads in the park. The only way to get around is on the waters. Over 30 lakes of all sizes, as well as marshes, bogs, and streams, fill glacier-carved basins and depressions. The largest of the lakes, Rainy Lake, was a major link in the route traveled by the namesakes of the park, the Voyageurs.

During the late 17th and early 18th centuries, the North American fur trade was expanding westward. It had become the continent's most lucrative industry. French-Canadian men known as Voyageurs were responsible for transporting the prized animal pelts 3,000 miles along intricate waterways and trading them for other goods. Two sets of Voyageurs set out toward each other in May of every year. The group from Montreal carried firearms, ammunition, rum, tobacco, cloth, and other goods. The group setting out from northwestern Canada carried bales of animal pelts. The fur of beavers—called brown gold in the trade— was extremely popular for its warmth and stylishness.

The Voyageurs traveled in birch canoes across difficult terrain, paddling up to 16 hours per day. The enemies they faced along their way were rival fur traders, unfriendly Native Americans, and the sometimes treacherous forces of nature. Theirs was grueling and exhausting work. Their goal was to meet each other to exchange their goods near Minnesota sometime in mid-July. One of their major trading posts was on Rainy Lake.

The route traveled by the Voyageurs became so established that the 1783 treaty ending the American Revolution specified that the new international boundary should follow their "customary waterway" between Lake Superior and Lake of the Woods. Today, the park adjoins a 56-mile stretch of the water highway they traveled and named in honor of them.

The island-dotted waterscape that the Voyageurs traveled through was much the same as it is today and was mostly shaped by glaciation. At least four times in the past million years, continental glaciers two miles thick hammered through the area. The glaciers gouged the land, and now hundreds of ponds, lakes, and streams fill in the spaces they left behind. Here is some of the oldest exposed rock in the world, dating back 2.7 billion years. There is no young rock. Perhaps there never was any, but more likely it has been completely worn away by the glaciers.

The beavers, which were almost hunted to extinction by the early trappers, still live in the park. The ponds they build create separate environments that help not only themselves, but a host of other inhabitants as well. The pond environment encourages the growth of aquatic plants that fish feed on. The fish in turn make meals for birds. The beavers are food for coyotes and wolves.

The park is in the heart of the only area of the continental United States that is still

VOYAGEURS NATIONAL PARK, NATIONAL PARK SERVICE

home to Eastern timber wolves. Though it was once thought that these animals are dangerous to humans, that is not so. Wolves usually prey on smaller animals or, occa-sionally, on deer. Ospreys, eagles, and great blue herons nest throughout the park, and stands of fir, aspen, spruce, pine, and birch cover the land, reaching to the water's edge.

Further Information

Write or call: Superintendent, Voyageurs National Park, 3131 Highway 53, Interna-tional Falls, MN 56649; (218) 283-9821

Visitor Information

Rainy Lake Visitor Center: Information, navigational charts, films, exhibits, maps, and schedules of activities.
Kabetogama Lake Visitor Center: Informa-tion, navigational charts, films, exhibits, maps, and schedules of activities. (Closed seasonally.)
Ash River Visitor Center: Information, nav-igational charts, films, exhibits, maps, and schedules of activities. (Closed seasonally.)

Nuts and Bolts

Entrance Fee: None.
Park Open: All year. The lakes may be in-accessible during freeze-up in late autumn and ice-out in April.
Permits: A Minnesota fishing license is re-quired. (In adjacent Canadian waters, an Ontario license is required.)
In Emergency: Dial 911. Park rangers mon-itor marine band 16 for emergencies.
Acreage: 218,035.93

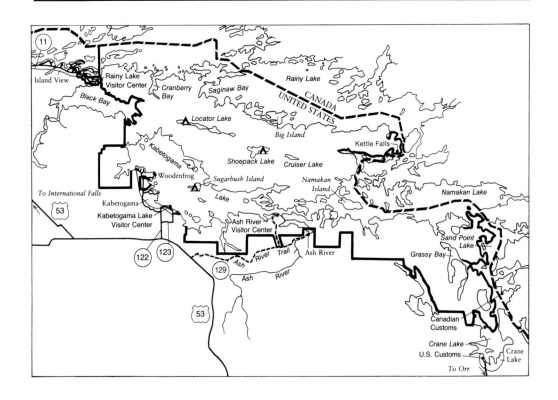

Practical Advisory

Seasons

Temperatures in summer range from highs in the upper 70s to lows in the low 50s. It is mostly cool and can be cloudy and rainy. From December through February, the temperature falls below 0° on most days and occasionally remains there for a week or more. Winter can bring some heavy snowfall, with blizzard conditions and severely drifting snow.

Special Advisories

* When the water is rough, stay ashore. Storms can arise quickly and high waves are hazardous. Heed weather forecasts; tune to local radio stations or monitor a weather radio for NOAA (National Oceanic and Atmopsheric Administration) weather broadcasts.
* Off-road vehicles are not permitted except on established roads leading to the entry points of the park and frozen lake surfaces.
* Do not trespass on private property in the park.
* Avoid contact with bears.
* Stay at least ¼ mile away from bald eagle, osprey, and great blue heron nests.
* Before going ashore in Canada and upon returning to the United States, you must report to customs offices. Canadian customs is at Portage Bay on Sand Point Lake and at Sand Bay on Rainy Lake. U.S. customs is at the Crane Lake Public Landing and at International Falls Bridge.

Facilities for Disabled

The Rainy Lake and the Kabetogama Lake visitor centers, including rest rooms, are accessible to the mobility-impaired. Braille park brochures and captioned park films are available upon request at all visitor centers.

Travel Advisory

Entrances

South: U.S. 53 to Highway 23 for 28 miles from Orr to Crane Lake.

Southwest: U.S. 53 to Highway 129 (the Ash River Trail) for 10 miles to Ash River.

West: U.S. 53 to Highway 122 for 4 miles to Kabetogama.

Northwest: U.S. 53 to Highway 11 east for 10 miles from International Falls to Island View.

Note: There are no roads beyond the edge of the park. Most of the park is accessible only by water. In winter, however, the seven-mile-long Rainy Lake Ice Road provides automobile access into the park.

Transportation

Transportation can be arranged from airports and bus depots to park entry points and to resorts outside the park.

Airports: Scheduled airlines serve Hibbing and International Falls, Minnesota, and Fort Frances in Ontario, Canada.

Bus Service: Buses serve U.S. 53 between Duluth and International Falls.

Train Service: None available.

Rental Cars: Available at International Falls airport.

Attractions

The *lakes* and other *waterways* are the major feature of the park; *Rainy Lake, Kabetogama Lake,* and *Namakan Lake* are the largest. Also of interest are the other *smaller lakes* dotting the major landmass, and the *small islands* in the larger lakes. Virtually all travel in and around the park is by water.

Accommodations

Lodges

Kettle Falls Hotel: At the junction of Namakan Lake and Rainy Lake; accessible only by boat. Boat service to the hotel is available. This historic hotel has been in business since the early 1900s. Reservations: (800) 322-0886. Open in summer.

Lodgings are also available year-round in the four resort communities adjacent to the park: Kabetogama Lake, Ash River, Rainy Lake, Crane Lake. For information: Kabetogama Lake Association, (218) 875-2621; Ash River Commercial Club, (218) 374-3141; for Rainy Lake, International Falls Chamber of Commerce, (218) 283-9400; Crane Lake Commercial Club, (218) 993-2346.

Campsites and Picnic Area

Campsites: 120 primitive boat-in campsites are scattered throughout the park, mostly on islands or near lakeshores. No fees; first-come, first-served; limit of 14 days at a site or 30 days total in a calendar year. Each site has a table, fire grate, pit toilet, and tent pad(s). Several sites have bear-proof food-storage lockers or poles. Use only dead and downed wood for campfires. Remove all trash from the park.

Picnic Area: At the Rainy Lake Visitor Center. Tables available for picnics.

Restaurant

Kettle Falls Hotel: At the junction of Namakan Lake and Rainy Lake; accessible only by boat. Boat service is available. Dining room. Open in summer.

Activities

Boating

In the summer, almost all travel within the park requires water transportation. Most visitors travel by motorboat, although many use canoes, sailboats, or houseboats. Boats, canoes, guides, and shuttle services are available at the four resort communities adjacent to the park. Boat rentals are also available at the Kettle Falls Hotel. You must comply with federal and state boating regulations. Nautical charts are essential, since there are few topographic landmarks. Along main travel routes, a U.S. Coast Guard–numbered buoy system guides you and marks navigational hazards. But off the beaten path, most rocks and reefs are unmarked.

Boat Tours

Concessioner-operated boat cruises are available from May through September; some have national park rangers as guides. Tour Rainy Lake aboard a 49-passenger tour boat, departing from the Rainy Lake Visitor Center, or a 12-passenger pontoon boat, departing from the Kabetogama Lake Visitor Center. For information and reservations: (218) 286-5470. Fees are charged.

Fishing

The fishing for walleye, northern pike, and smallmouth bass in this part of the North Country is world-renowned. Muskellunge, perch, sauger, lake trout, and crappie are also caught. In winter, ice fishing is popular. Guides can be hired through concessioners. Catch-and-release fishing is encouraged.

Hiking

Hiking the trails offers the opportunity to explore the park's interior and to fish and camp. Maintained trails for hiking are shown on the park map. Most trailheads are reached by boat.

Swimming

Be careful to choose a safe area for swimming, preferably a beach or protected cove with a gradual dropoff. Never swim in an area of boat traffic and never swim alone. Swimming from public docks and boat-launch areas is prohibited.

Winter Sports

Cross-country skiing, snowshoeing, and snowmobiling are popular from late December to late March when snow cover is sufficient. Equipment can be rented from local resorts. A map and guide to cross-country ski trails and snowmobile routes is available from the park.

Naturalist Activities

Park naturalists guide tour-boats and canoe trips, children's programs, and walks, and give campfire talks. Activities originate at the Kabetogama Lake and Rainy Lake visitor centers, as well as Woodenfrog State Forest Campground. Check at visitor centers for schedules.

Stretching for miles below the earth's surface is one of the world's oldest caves, full of underground passageways decorated with delicate formations. It is for this feature that Wind Cave National Park is named.

The wind for which the cave is named can be heard at the cave's only natural opening; it is caused by the differences in atmospheric pressure above and below the ground. The sound is what led two brothers, Jesse and Tom Bingham, to discover the cave in 1881. They followed the sound to the small hole in the ground that is the natural opening. Since then, many others have explored the fascinating network of passageways in the cave. At first, local people charged the curious who wanted to view the exciting underground wonder, and they sold some of the formations. Today the cave is protected for future visitors to discover. Much of the more than 66 miles of passageways still remain unexplored.

At least 60 million years ago, the limestone in this area cracked, allowing water to seep through and erode the stone. It took millions of years' worth of water trickling through the cracks to carve out the complex maze. Once the cave was formed, its decoration began. Groundwater seeping through the earth contained dissolved calcium carbonate that slowly crystallized into calcite. This calcite hardened, drop by drop, creating beautiful formations.

The type of formation most often seen in the cave is "boxwork," the honeycomblike structures that can be found on the walls and ceilings. Nowhere else in the world can so much of it be seen. Also here are "popcorn" and "frostwork" formations. The more commonly found stalactites and stalagmites are rare here. Since the water table has dropped below the level of the limestone, the decoration has slowed. But even though change is difficult to detect, the humidity, dripping water, and puddles in the cave signify that change is still taking place.

Because of its location in the plains of South Dakota, the park actually offers visitors two different but interconnecting worlds to explore. Besides the fascinating land below the ground, there is the world of the prairie above. The land here looks much as it did when white explorers first headed west in the early 19th century. This is a biological meeting place for plant and animal species from several geographical areas. Here the elm and burr oak of the Eastern forests and the yucca and cactus of the Southwest deserts coexist with the ponderosa pine and juniper of the Rocky Mountains.

Rolling grasslands fill much of the land with blue grama, wheat grass, and little bluestem. In the spring, wildflowers add color to the plains. Feeding in these pastures is a diverse mix of wildlife including the bison, elk, pronghorn, and prairie dogs that at one time covered much of the plains in the central United States.

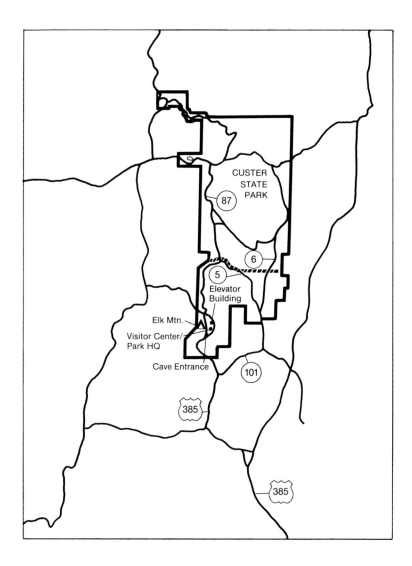

Further Information

Write or call: Superintendent, Wind Cave National Park, Hot Springs, SD 57747; (605) 745-4600

Visitor Information

Park Headquarters and Visitor Center: On a loop road off U.S. 385; cave-tour tickets; historical and nature exhibits; other exhibits and slide programs explaining park features; information about park facilities and activities.

Nuts and Bolts

Entrance Fee: None.
Park Open: All year. Cave and visitor facilities closed Thanksgiving, Christmas, and New Year's days.
Permits: Required for backcountry camping.
In Emergency: Call 911.
Acreage: 28,292.08

Practical Advisory

Seasons

Spring is short (mid-March to mid-May) and may be marked by cold weather and wet snows. Summer weather lasts through August, with daytime temperatures of 90°–100°. Evenings usually cool to the 50s. Afternoon thunderstorms are common, with spectacular lightning, rain, and hail at times. Fall (September–October) is usually warm and clear, with cold nights and infrequent snowstorms. Winters are often sunny and mild, with temperatures around 32°, or sometimes cold, with temperatures below 0°.

Special Advisories

- Wear low-heeled, nonslip shoes (not sandals or shoes with leather or hard composition soles) into the cave.
- The cave temperature is always about 53°, so a light jacket or sweater is suggested.
- Smoking is prohibited in the cave.
- Cave tours are not recommended for persons with heart, lung, or leg problems.

Facilities for Disabled

The visitor center and campground are accessible to wheelchairs. There is a complimentary cave tour for those with disabilities.

Travel Advisory

Entrances

South: U.S. 385 for 11 miles from north of Hot Springs.

West: U.S. 385 for 21 miles south of Custer.

North: Highway 87 from Custer State Park.

Transportation

Airports: Rapid City (45 miles from the park) or, for private planes, Hot Springs (5 miles from the park) and Custer, South Dakota (17 miles from the park).

Bus Service: Buses serve Rapid City.

Train Service: None convenient to the park.

Rental Cars: Available at Rapid City, Hot Springs.

Attractions

Wind Cave is the major feature of the park. Unusual formations include *boxwork*, *popcorn*, and *frostwork*. The cave may be visited only on tours led by rangers. The *prairieland* aboveground is also scenic. It may be viewed from the park road or by trails.

Accommodations

There is no lodging available in the park.

Campground and Picnic Area

Elk Mountain Campground: 100 sites; first-come, first-served; water, wood, tables, rest rooms, and fireplaces; limited services in winter; build fires only in fireplaces; $8/night.

Backcountry Camping: Permitted in northwest quarter of the park.

Picnic Area: North of the visitor center; tables.

Restaurant

Dining Room: In the visitor center building. Open mid-May to mid-September.

Activities

Cave Touring

Rangers lead tours through the cave. Enter through the entrance near the natural opening or by taking the elevator. Dim lighting and concrete stairs and walkways have been added along the routes. Tours follow the first passages explored in the cave 100 years ago; they vary in length. An elevator will return you to the surface at the end of the tour. There are several tours daily between Memorial Day and Labor Day and fewer during the rest of the year. A fee is charged. Special cave tours for handicapped visitors may be arranged through park headquarters.

Scenic Drives

Roadside exhibits along the main park road explain aboveground features of the park.

Hiking

Self-guided nature trails, a section of the South Dakota Centennial Trail, and other trails are available. Hikers are welcome to hike anywhere in the park; use of a topographic map is recommended.

Ranger Activities

Rangers give campfire talks nightly in the summer; they also lead hikes. A schedule is available at the visitor center.

Four major mountain ranges converge in southeastern Alaska in an area often referred to as the premier mountain wilderness of North America. The Wrangell, St. Elias, and Chugach mountains and the eastern end of the Alaska Range are all found within the park and preserve known as Wrangell–St. Elias. Scattered among these four mountain ranges are nine of the 16 highest peaks in the United States. Mount St. Elias, at 18,008 feet, is the second-highest peak in the country. Mount Wrangell is a still-active volcano, having last erupted in 1900.

The high country in the park is covered with snow year-round. This snow spawns massive glaciers and ice fields that overlie a good portion of the park's interior. In fact, the park has the largest collection of glaciers in North America. One of these glaciers, the Malaspina, flows out of the St. Elias Mountains in a mass larger than the entire state of Rhode Island. Also here is the largest subpolar ice field in North America, the Bagley Icefield.

The land here is crisscrossed with a multitude of streams and rivers flowing from the glaciers. Probably the most braided, the Chitina River, travels from the Chitina and Logan glaciers on the park's eastern boundary to the mighty Copper River. The Copper, the largest river in the park, forms its western border marker and empties into the Gulf of Alaska.

Few roads lead into this virtually unexplored park. All of the land has not always been considered uninhabitable, however. In fact, within the park are two formerly booming mine towns. The discovery of rich copper deposits in the Chitina River valley lured many people here, leading to the growth of the town of McCarthy, followed soon after by the town of Kennicott. From 1911 to 1938, ore was extracted from these highly productive mines, and a railroad was even built into the valley to transport the copper. Eventually, however, the ore deposits were emptied and most of the people left. The towns remain as living history. In fact, the ruins of the Kennicott mines have been placed on the National Register of Historic Places.

Native American populations have also come and gone in the surrounding areas. Copper Center, Chitina, Gulkana, and Chistochina were the homes of the native Athabaskans. Yakutat, on the coast, is a traditional Tlingit fishing village. The park still has residents, who hunt and fish for subsistence much as their ancestors did before them. Their property rights should be respected when visiting the park.

Although the ice fields and glaciers may make the land appear devoid of life, there is actually a substantial community of wildlife in the park. If any single species symbolizes the wildlife here, it is probably the Dall sheep. At least 12,000 Dall sheep—possibly the largest population in all Alaska—live in the interior highlands. The mountains are also home to mountain goats, who can make their way along the cliffs with amaz-

NATIONAL PARK SERVICE, PHOTO BY M.W. WILLIAMS

ing agility. Brown and grizzly bears as well as black bears inhabit the park. Moose can be seen foraging in the bogs in the coastal lowlands. Salmon use some of the waters as spawning ground. And sea lions and harbor seals live in the coastal areas.

Further Information

Write or call: Wrangell–St. Elias National Park, P.O. Box 29, Glennallen, AK 99588; (907) 822-5235

Visitor Information

Park Headquarters: At mile 105½ Old Richardson Highway near Copper Center. Ranger stations at Slana, Chitina, and Yakutat.

Nuts and Bolts

Entrance Fee: None.
Park Open: All year.
Permits: Alaska fishing license is required.
In Emergency: Contact Alaska state troopers, 822-3263, or park headquarters, 822-5234.
Acreage: National park, 8,331,604; national preserve, 4,856,720.99

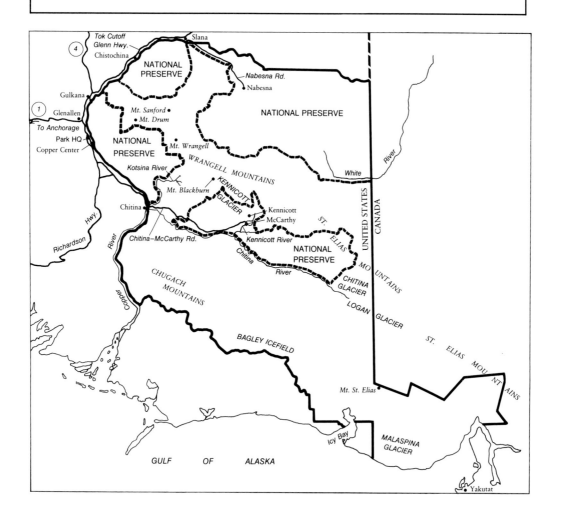

Practical Advisory

Seasons

Summer: Cloudy and cool. Clear, hot days are not uncommon in July, the warmest month. August and September tend to be cool and wet, but with fewer mosquitoes than July. Average summer temperatures range from the 50s to the 70s. Fall: Can be delightfully clear, but the season is short. Winter: Cold and dark, with temperatures dropping to − 50°. Average snow cover is two feet; days are often clear. Spring: Clear skies, and warming temperatures.

Special Advisories

- Visitors are mostly on their own and must be self-sufficient. Assistance may be days or miles away. Proper survival gear and skills to handle mountainous terrain are essential.
- Some areas within the park are private. Please respect the privacy of owners; check maps at headquarters or ranger stations for information.
- Within the national park, local rural residents may carry out traditional subsistence hunting, trapping, and fishing.
- Hunting is prohibited in the park but allowed in the preserve; a permit is required.

Facilities for Disabled

None.

Travel Advisory

Entrances

Two unpaved roads penetrate the park. High-clearance two-wheel-drive vehicles can usually make the trip in summer, but check for current conditions before starting. Both roads are reachable by the Glenn Highway from Anchorage, to the Richardson Highway at Glennallen. The Chitina–McCarthy Road, 61 miles long, follows the old Copper River and Northwestern Railroad route to the Kennicott River. The trip takes about four hours. At the Kennicott River you must hand-power two cable trams across the river to McCarthy and the privately owned Kennicott mining complex. 2. The Nabesna Road, from Slana on the Tok Cutoff, extends 45 miles to Nabesna, an inactive privately owned mining community.

Transportation

Airports: Aircraft may be used within the boundaries except to support subsistence hunting and fishing within the park. Charter aircraft are available in most communities, including Anchorage, Fairbanks, Northway, Glennallen, Cordova, Valdez, Tok, and Yakutat. Cordova and Yakutat are served daily by commercial jets.

Bus Service: In the summer, regularly scheduled buses run between Anchorage and Valdez with stops in Glennallen.

Train Service: Not available.

Rental Cars: Available in Anchorage and Fairbanks.

Attractions

The four mountain ranges—the *Wrangell Mountains, St. Elias Mountains, Chugach Mountains,* and *Alaska Range*—are the major features of this undeveloped park. *Glaciers, ice fields, roaring rivers,* and *streams* also add to the scenic wildness of the park.

Accommodations

Lodges

Most are open from Memorial Day through the end of September.

McCarthy Lodge: McCarthy/Kennicott area; hotel. Reservations: McCarthy Lodge, McCarthy, AK 99588.

McCarthy Wilderness B & B: McCarthy/Kennicott area; rustic rooms, cabin. Reservations: McCarthy Wilderness B & B, Box 111241, Anchorage, AK 99511; (907) 277-6867.

Kennicott Glacier Lodge: McCarthy/Kennicott area; hotel. Reservations: Kennicott Glacier Lodge, P.O. Box 103940, Anchorage, AK 99510; (907) 258-2350.

Silvertip Lodge: Nabesna Road; bunkhouse, cabins. Reservations: Silvertip Lodge, Mile 25.5 Nabesna Rd., SRA Box 1260, Slana, AK 99586; (907) 337-2065.

Sportsmen's Paradise Lodge: Nabesna Road; bunkhouse, cabins. Reservations: Sportsmen's Paradise Lodge, Mile 28.5 Nabesna Rd., Slana, AK 99586.

Devil's Mountain Lodge: Nabesna Road; bunkhouse, rooms. Reservations: Devil's Mountain Lodge, Mile 42 Nabesna Rd., SR Box 1455, Slana, AK 99586; (907) 822-3426.

Mount View Lodge: Nabesna Road. Reservations: Mount View Lodge, Mile 6 Nabesna Rd., SRA Box 1190, Slana, AK 99586.

Rustic accommodations are also provided at fishing camps and guide cabins in various parts of the park.

Camping

There are two private campgrounds on the McCarthy Road. Otherwise, you may tent-camp anywhere within the boundaries except on private property. Backcountry campers must be self-sufficient, carry enough food to cover unexpected delays, and be prepared for the wilderness. Only those with expertise in cold-weather camping and survival techniques should attempt winter camping.

Activities

Hiking

Most hikers start from points along the Slana–Nabesna or Chitina–McCarthy road. There are few trails, so most hiking is across what appears to be previously untraversed terrain. Hiking can take much more time than expected. From a distance the terrain may look like scrub land, but you can be knee-deep in water or flat on your back before you know it. Hikers must be familiar with safe techniques for crossing rivers and streams. Many are impassable even by experts. Others can change from trickling creeks to raging torrents quickly.

Boating

The Copper and Chitina rivers offer excellent opportunities for rafting and kayaking. The 77-mile trip down the Copper from Chitina to the Gulf of Alaska takes rafters through some of the park's most rugged terrain. Ocean kayakers increasingly are exploring the bays, inlets, and coast in the Yakutat and Icy Bay areas.

Moutaineering

The park's many glaciers, ice fields, rivers, and steep rock walls present challenges for mountaineers. Mounts Drum, Sanford, Blackburn, and St. Elias are favorites for climbing expeditions.

Fishing

Lake fishing for grayling, Dolly Varden, rainbow trout, and lake trout. Check with the park for specific locations and catch limits.

Skiing

The months of March, April, and May, after the severe cold weather but with the lowlands still snow-covered, are best for cross-country skiing.

Yellowstone National Park has the distinction of being the world's first national park. In 1872, the United States Congress decided that this rich and varied wilderness of forests, lakes, rivers, mountains, canyons, and unusual thermal features should be set aside for the enjoyment of all people, and so declared it a national park. Yellowstone remains the largest national park in the Lower 48.

The park is best known for its thermal features: It contains the world's greatest concentration of geysers, hot springs, steam vents, and mud pots. The most famous of these, in fact, many would say the symbol of Yellowstone Park, is the geyser called Old Faithful. Of the 300 geysers in the park, some are bigger and some erupt on a more regular schedule. But none is quite as spectacular in all ways as Old Faithful. It keeps its own timetable on its own terms. Since park rangers have continuously monitored it for so long, however, they can usually predict the time of the next eruption within five minutes. The average interval between eruptions is 76 minutes. Eruptions begin with a few mere sputters and splashes and grow into an intense fountain of water, blowing out of the earth more than 100 feet into the air. For up to five minutes, these spectacular eruptions amaze awestruck visitors.

The cause of Old Faithful's behavior and the source of all the thermal features in the park lies one to three miles below the surface of the earth. Historically, the park's landscape has been shaped and reshaped by great volcanoes that date back as much as 55 million years. Although the volcanic activity has stopped on the surface, the hot molten rock in the interior of the earth remains, closer to the surface here than anyplace else on earth.

As water from rain or snow seeps through cracks or faults in the earth's crust, it finds its way down to this extreme heat, where the pressure is also greater. Since water under pressure has a higher boiling point, this water gets intensely hot—it can reach temperatures of 400°F. As the hottest water rises it begins to bubble and move up the passageways to the surface. At first it merely spurts a bit. Some geysers never do more than spurt. But others, like Old Faithful, eventually explode with a roaring pressure.

Geysers are not the only form this hot water takes as it reaches the earth's surface. Interestingly colored hot springs contain water that never erupts out of the earth at all, but rather just flows steadily. Fumaroles are vents or holes from which no water, only steam escapes. Many of the most famous geysers and hot springs here are located on the west side of the park.

Not to be overlooked amid the unusual thermal features are the other scenic natural wonders of the park. The Grand Canyon of the Yellowstone is known for its rich yellow stone, for which the park is named. This steep rock-walled gorge, as deep as 1,500 feet, with its carving rush of water from the

Yellowstone River, offers breathtaking views of waterfalls. It is approached through thick lodgepole pine forests. Cold, clear Yellowstone Lake, with 110 miles of shoreline, is North America's largest mountain lake. The area is favored habitat of a variety of birds and animals, including the native trout. The park as a whole shelters an abundance of wildlife including moose, grizzly bears, bighorn, bison, coyotes, and great gray owls.

You will still see evidence today of the fires of 1988; about a third of the park was affected. But you will also see that life here has gone on and is as beautiful as ever.

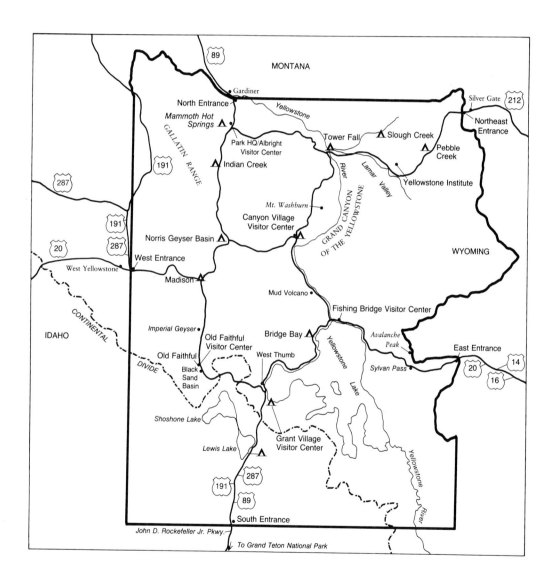

Further Information

Write or call:
Superintendent, Yellowstone National Park, P.O. Box 168, Yellowstone National Park, WY 82190; (307) 344-7381

Visitor Information

Park Headquarters/Albright Visitor Center: Mammoth Hot Springs; information, exhibits about the park's natural and human history, movie and slide program shown throughout the day. This is the site of Fort Yellowstone, built during the army era of park administration.
Old Faithful Visitor Center: Information, geyser eruption predictions, nine-minute movie shown throughout the day. (Closed November through early April.)
Canyon Visitor Center: Canyon Village; information, geology exhibit designed and produced by students, movies. (Closed October through mid-May.)
Fishing Bridge Visitor Center: Information; exhibits concerning birds, wildlife, and lake geology. (Closed early September through late May.)
Grant Village Visitor Center: Information, "Yellowstone and Fire" exhibit. (Closed mid-September through mid-May.)

Nuts and Bolts

Entrance Fee: $10/vehicle or $4/person arriving by other means. Free to those under 17. Good for seven days and includes entrance to Grand Teton National Park. Those 62 and older may purchase a $10 Golden Age Passport allowing free entry forever.
Park Open: All year. In winter, all roads are closed except the road from Gardiner, Montana, through the north entrance to the northeast entrance and on to Cooke City, Montana.
Permits: Required for backcountry camping, fishing, boating, and some day hikes.
In Emergency: Call 911 or a ranger at 344-7381.
Acreage: 2,219,823

Practical Advisory

Seasons

Weather changes suddenly and unpredictably. Summer: Average maximum temperature is usually in the 70s, and occasionally the 80s in the lower elevations. Nights are cool and temperatures may drop into the 30s and 40s. June can be cool and rainy; July and August tend to be somewhat drier although afternoon thundershowers are common. Fall: Pleasant, although temperatures average 10°–20° lower than summer. Nighttime lows can fall into the teens and single digits. Winter: Temperatures near zero, occasionally reaching highs in the 20s. Subzero nighttime lows are common. Spring: Cold and snow linger into April and May. Average daytime temperatures are in the 40s or 50s, reaching the 60s and 70s by late May and June. Nighttime lows fall below freezing.

Special Advisories

- Swimming is prohibited in thermal pools or streams whose waters flow from a thermal spring or pool, and is discouraged in other waters.
- Stay on boardwalks and designated trails; scalding water can burn you seriously.
- Be prepared for sudden changes in weather; exposure can cause hypothermia.

Facilities for Disabled

Request a copy of "Guide to Accessibility for the Handicapped Visitor" from the park.

Travel Advisory

Entrances

North: Highway 89 for 58 miles south of I-90 at Livingston, Montana.

West: U.S. 20 for 110 miles northeast of Idaho Falls, Idaho.

South: John D. Rockefeller, Jr. Memorial Parkway, north of Grand Teton National Park.

East: U.S. 16 for 53 miles west of Cody, Wyoming.

Northeast: U.S. 212 for 69 miles southwest of Laurel, Montana.

Transportation

Airports: Commercial airlines offer service to Cody and Jackson, Wyoming; Idaho Falls, Idaho; and Bozeman and Billings, Montana. The West Yellowstone, Montana, airport is serviced from June to early September.

Bus Service: Available to West Yellowstone, Montana, all year, with service from Idaho limited to the summer months; available to Gardiner, Montana, daily during the summer and winter but limited to one day per week from October to mid-December and from mid-March to the summer; available from Cody and Jackson, Wyoming, during the summer.

Train Service: There is no train service convenient to the park.

Rental Cars: Available at airports.

Attractions

The park's most famous attractions are its *thermal features. Old Faithful Geyser* is the most popular of these. Some of the other well-known geysers and hot springs are at *Mammoth Hot Spring Terraces, Norris Geyser Basin,* and *Black Sand Basin. Mud Volcano* and *West Thumb Geyser Basin* are other remarkable thermal areas. The *Grand Canyon of the Yellowstone* is of interest, and *Yellowstone Lake* is scenic. All of these major areas of the park can be reached via the park road, although some require short walks.

Other Points of Interest (Museums, Historic Sites, etc.)

The *Norris Museum* has exhibits on thermal features and geyser-basin life. Part of the *Madison Museum–Caldera Arts Center* will be used as studio space for a resident artist and the rest will be used to exhibit the resident artist's works. The *Museum of the National Park Ranger,* located at Norris in the historic soldier station, has exhibits that trace the development of the park ranger's profession, with a video shown on request. All museums are open only in summer.

Accommodations

Lodges

For reservations or information on any of the lodges, contact TW Recreational Services, Yellowstone National Park, WY 82190; (307) 344-7311.

Mammoth Hot Springs Hotel & Cabins: Open late May through mid-September.

Roosevelt Lodge Cabins: Open June through August.

Canyon Lodge Cabins: Open mid-June through August.

Lake Yellowstone Hotel & Cabins: Open mid-May through late September.

Lake Lodge Cabins: Open early June through mid-September.

Grant Village AAA Rated: Hotel rooms; open June through September.

Old Faithful Inn: Hotel rooms; open May through mid-October.

Old Faithful Lodge Cabins: Open late May through mid-September.

Old Faithful Snow Lodge & Cabins: Open mid-May through mid-October.

Campgrounds and Picnic Areas

All campsites are first-come, first-served except Bridge Bay, part of which is run on a first-come, first-served basis, and part run on a reservation system through MISTIX, (800) 365-2267. Stays are limited to 14 days between July 1 and Labor Day, and to 30 days the rest of the year. Campfires are permitted in designated campgrounds and in picnic areas where fire grates are provided; dead and downed material may be used as firewood.

Mammoth Campground: 85 sites; flush toilets; open all year; $8/night.

Madison Campground: 292 sites; flush toilets, dump station; open May through October; $8/night.

Bridge Bay Campground: 420 sites; flush toilets, dump station; open late May through mid-September; reservations available; $10/night.

Norris Campground: 116 sites; flush toilets; open mid-May through September; $8/night.

Slough Creek: 29 sites; pit toilets; open late May through October; $6/night.

Tower Fall Campground: 32 sites; pit toilets; open late May through mid-September; $6/night.

Canyon Village: 280 sites; flush toilets, dump station; open June through early September; $8/night.

Indian Creek Campground: 75 sites; pit toilets; open June through mid-September; $6/night.

Grant Village Campground: 403 sites; flush toilets, dump station; open late June through mid-October; $8/night.

Pebble Creek Campground: 36 sites; pit toilets; open mid-June through early September; $6/night.

Lewis Lake Campground: 85 sites; pit toilets; open mid-June through October; $6/night.

Fishing Bridge Trailer Village: No tents or tent trailers allowed; open early June to early September. For reservations contact TW Recreational Services (see "Lodges," above). Full hookups are available for $18/day.

Backcountry Campsites: Park has a designated-campsite system. Check with visitor center for information.

Picnic Areas: Off the park's roads; tables; most have pit toilets. Fires may be built only in fire grates, where available, or in fuel stoves where no grates are available.

Restaurants

Old Faithful Inn Dining Room: Dinner reservations required; open early May through mid-October.

Old Faithful Inn, Pony Express Snack Shop: Open early May through mid-September.

Old Faithful Snow Lodge Family Restaurant: Open mid-May through mid-October; no lunch after early September.

Old Faithful Lodge Snack Shop and Cafeteria: Both open late May through mid-September.

Old Faithful Four Seasons Snack Shop: Open late May through early September.

Grant Village Restaurant: Dinner reservations required; open early June through late September.

Grant Village Steak House: Open early June through late September.

Lake Yellowstone Hotel Dining Room: Reservations required for dinner; open mid-May through late September.

Lake Lodge Cafeteria: Open early June through mid-September.

Canyon Lodge Snack Bar, Cafeteria, and Dining Room: All three open mid-June through August.

Roosevelt Lodge Dining Room: Open early June through August.

Roosevelt Lodge Dinner Cookout: Old West dinner cookout; early June through August.

Mammoth Hot Springs Hotel Dining Room: Dinner reservations required; open late May through mid-September.

Mammoth Fast Foods: Open mid-May through mid-September.

Activities

Scenic Drives

There are over 350 miles of paved roads in the park; most are narrow, rough, and busy. The park's major scenic attractions can be seen on a drive along the Grand Loop Road, the figure-8-shaped road in the center of the park. The distance around the entire Loop is 142 miles, but driving time is difficult to estimate because the roads are narrow and winding, road surfaces may be poor, and traffic may be slow-moving. Major attractions like Old Faithful Geyser and the Grand Canyon of the Yellowstone can only be seen by driving to a parking area and walking to the spot. While it is possible to drive the Grand Loop in a day, if you want to see these things, you will need more time. The most famous and spectacular section of the Grand Canyon of the Yellowstone is seen from overlooks along the North and South Rim roads in the Canyon Village area.

Hiking

Over 1,200 miles of trails are available for hiking. Some offer easy part-day trips off the main park roads; others take you deep into the backcountry and require strength and endurance because of their elevation, length, and ruggedness. Good topographical maps, which can be purchased at any visitor center, are highly recommended. Check at ranger stations for current trail and stream conditions. Certain parts of the park are designated as Bear Management Areas because they have a higher-than-average concentration of bears. Human access is restricted in these areas; check at ranger stations and visitor centers for information.

Fishing

Yellowstone is known for its fishing for native species of wild trout. There are certain restrictions on fishing in the park to maintain a program of species management. The fishing season begins on Memorial Day weekend and continues through the first Sunday of November. Exceptions are Yellowstone Lake, where the season opens on June 15, and Yellowstone Lake's tributary streams, which open July 15. The Bridge Bay Marina offers guided fishing trips. Contact TW Recreational Services (see "Lodges," above) for information.

Boating

All kinds of vessels are allowed in the lakes, but all are barred from park rivers and streams except the channel between Lewis and Shoshone lakes, where hand-propelled vessels only are permitted. Bridge Bay Marina has dock rental as well as boat rental and scenic-cruiser excursions. Contact TW Recreational Services (see "Lodges," above) for information. A Coast Guard–approved flotation device is required for each person boating.

Bicycling

Bicycling is permitted on established public roads, parking areas, and designated routes. There are no bicycle paths along roadways. Bikes are prohibited on backcountry trails and boardwalks. Be aware that park roads are narrow and winding, with relatively long distances between services and facilities; note also that road elevations range from 5,300 to 8,860 feet. A list of routes is available at visitor centers.

Horseback Riding

Trail rides are available at Mammoth Hot Springs, Canyon Lodge, and Roosevelt Lodge. Roosevelt Lodge also has "Stagecoach Outings." Outfitters (located outside the park) will plan short or long trips.

Tours

TW Recreational Services (see "Lodges," above) provides bus tours within the park through the summer season and snowcoach tours during the winter season.

Winter Sports

Snowmobiling, skiing, and snowshoeing are becoming increasingly popular. Groomed roads and trails can be used for cross-country skiing and snowshoeing; snowmobiles are restricted to groomed roads.

Ranger-Led Activities

A full schedule of hikes, walks, campfire programs, and other activities is offered from mid-June through late August. Check at visitor centers for current schedules.

Yellowstone Institute

Outdoor courses for all age groups on topics such as wildlife photography, grizzly bears, wildflowers, geysers, birds of prey, ecology, and Yellowstone history are offered. Write P.O. Box 117, Yellowstone National Park, WY 82190, or call (307) 344-7381.

Yosemite National Park, in the heart of the Sierra Nevada, offers spectacular natural scenery including broad wildflower-strewn meadows, groves of giant sequoias, and some of the nation's largest waterfalls cascading from the mountains' cliffs.

The Sierra Nevada, unlike other major mountain ranges in the country, is not a chain of separate mountains. Rather, it is one solid block of granite uplifted from the earth's crust, standing stern and barren. Although Mount Lyell is the park's highest mountain at 13,110 feet, the two most famous peaks flank the Yosemite Valley. El Capitan at over 7,500 feet and Half Dome at over 8,800 feet are huge hulking shapes with sheer walls of granite. Yosemite Valley, the pleasantly grassy meadow corridor between them, is seven miles long and up to a mile wide.

Flowing over the high cliffs of the mountains are some of the country's largest and most beautiful waterfalls. Springtime finds them at their fullest, as meltwater from the winter's snow adds to slow-moving streams to create incredible displays of rushing water. The park is home to more than half of the highest waterfalls in the country. Ribbon Fall is the largest single waterfall in the park, at 1,612 feet. Bridalveil Fall is 620 feet high. Probably the most famous, Yosemite Falls, is the highest falls in the country and the fifth-highest in the world. Although it looks from below like one continuous waterfall, it actually falls in two levels; the Upper Fall drops 1,430 feet and the Lower Fall 320. The falls eventually feed into what Spanish explorers called *El Rio de Nuestra Señora de la Merced*, "The River of Our Lady of Mercy." It is now called simply the Merced.

Adding to the grandeur of the park are three stands of giant sequoias. The Mariposa (the largest), Tuolumne, and Merced groves all have trees hundreds of feet tall. They dwarf other plants and the animals and humans that walk beneath their shady silence. These huge trees are known for their longevity. The Grizzly Giant, 2,700 years old, is one of the oldest known living sequoia trees in the world. At a weight of 2 million pounds and a height of more than 206 feet, it is also the world's 23rd-largest tree.

Other evergreen trees that grow in the park's magnificent forests are ponderosa pines, white fir, and incense cedars. Beautiful wildflowers bloom in the meadows in spring and add brilliant color to the scene. The mule deer is the commonest large mammal found in the park, which is also home to bobcats, coyotes, and black bears.

Natural forces sculpted the landscape over millions of years. Glaciers from the Sierra Nevada dramatically carved the land, widening valleys and creating canyons. Yosemite National Park turned 100 years old in October 1990. Time has changed the face of the park. In August 1990, lightning-caused fires closed parts of the park and destroyed many of the park's trees; but life

YOSEMITE COLLECTIONS, NATIONAL PARK SERVICE

has a way of rejuvenating itself, and new growth can be seen there now. The seasons still come and go as the multicolored wild- flowers of summer turn to the blazing oranges and yellows of autumn and the snow-white cover of winter.

Further Information

Write or call: Superintendent, Yosemite National Park, P.O. Box 577, Yosemite National Park, CA 95389; (209) 372-0200

Visitor Information

Yosemite Valley Visitor Center: In Yosemite Village; general information, backcountry information, orientation slide show, "One Day In Yosemite" program, natural-history displays, changing art exhibit, maps and books for sale.
Big Oak Flat Information Station: At Highway 120, west entrance; information, maps, publications.
Tuolumne Meadows Visitor Center: Exhibits, maps, information. (Closed October to late spring.)
Wawona Information Station: On Chilnualna Falls Road; information about the Wawona area and the Mariposa Grove; publications.

Nuts and Bolts

Entrance Fee: $5/vehicle or $3/person arriving by other means. Good for seven days.
Park Open: All year, but the Tioga Pass, Glacier Point, and Tuolumne Grove roads generally close in early November and open in late May.
Permits: Required for camping in the backcountry; advance reservations for summer must be postmarked between March 1 and May 31 and mailed to: Wilderness Permit Reservations, P.O. Box 577, Yosemite, CA 95389; include your name, address, phone number, the number of people in your party, trip dates, starting location, trail head, first overnight point, ultimate destination and a second choice of date and route. California fishing license is required.
In Emergency: Call 911.
Acreage: 748,542

Practical Advisory

Seasons

Weather can change rapidly in all seasons. Elevation plays a major role in temperature and precipitation. Summer: Warm and dry. Daytime temperatures in Yosemite Valley sometimes reach 100°; nights are cool. Temperatures in Tuolumne Meadows are usually in the 70s during the day and in the 30s at night. Winter: Relatively mild, though between November and March 70%–90% of the total precipitation falls. Yosemite Valley receives an average of 29 inches of snow during this season. Spring: Waterfalls and cascades are at their fullest; May and June are the best months for viewing the waterfalls of Yosemite Valley.

Special Advisories

- Never swim or wade in streams above waterfalls or in cascade areas.
- Store food properly to protect it from bears and other wildlife.

Facilities for Disabled

A "Changing Yosemite" trail and the trail through the Village of the Ahwahnee are wheelchair-accessible and have materials available for the visually impaired. Disabled visitors are allowed to drive to Mirror Lake if they display a disability placard available from the visitor center.

Travel Advisory

Entrances

South: Highway 41 for 63 miles north of Fresno.

Southwest: Highway 140 for 70 miles northeast of Merced.

West: Highway 120 for 71 miles east of Oakdale.

East: Highway 120 for 12 miles west of Lee Vining.

Transportation

Airports: San Francisco (183 miles from the park) and Fresno (63 miles from the park).

Bus Service: Greyhound serves Merced and Fresno. Transportation to the park is available from Yosemite Gray Line or VIA Bus Lines.

Train Service: Amtrak serves Merced (70 miles from the park) and Fresno (63 miles).

Rental Cars: Available at airports and in Fresno (63 miles) and Merced (70 miles).

In-Park Transportation: The Valley Shuttle Bus offers transportation to the visitor center and many other stops in the eastern portion of Yosemite Valley. If you are just visiting for the day, you can park in the Day Use Parking Area at Curry Village and use the shuttle. The Wawona Shuttle Bus stops at the Wawona Campground, the store, the south entrance, and the Mariposa Grove.

Attractions

The most visited area of the park is *Yosemite Valley*, flanked by the peaks *El Capitan* and *Half Dome*. The park is well known for its spectacular and numerous *waterfalls*, most notably *Yosemite Falls* and *Bridalveil Falls*. The park is also known as the home of many *sequoia trees*, including the magnificent *Mariposa Grove of Giant Sequoias*. Other areas of special beauty are the *Merced River, Tuolumne Meadows*, and *Hetch Hetchy Reservoir*. You can tour most of the park by road.

Other Points of Interest (Museums, Historic Sites, etc.)

The *Indian Cultural Exhibit*, located next to the Yosemite Valley Visitor Center, displays the cultural history of the native Miwok and Paiute people from 1850 to the present. The *Museum Gallery* is located next door and offers changing displays including "Yosemite Renaissance" exhibits. A short self-guiding trail leads through the reconstructed *Village of the Ahwahnee* starting behind the visitor center. Also nearby is the *Ansel Adams Gallery*. The *Pioneer History Center*, in Wawona, is a collection of historic buildings with volunteers dressed in pioneer clothing who answer questions about the pioneer period. Closed in winter, but a self-guiding tour is available. The *Mariposa Grove Museum* and the *Happy Isles Nature Center*, offering exhibits of plants and animals, are also available.

Accommodations

Lodges

Reservations for all lodging: Central Reservations, Yosemite Park and Curry Company, 5410 East Home, Fresno, CA 93727; (209) 252-4848. Advance reservations are recommended and may be made up to one year in advance.

Curry Village: In Yosemite Valley; rooms, cabins, and canvas tent cabins.

Curry Housekeeping Camp: In Yosemite Valley.

Yosemite Lodge: In Yosemite Valley; rooms and cabins.

The Ahwahnee Hotel: In Yosemite Valley; rooms and cottages.

Wawona Hotel: Rooms.

White Wolf Lodge: Cabins and canvas tent cabins.

Tuolumne Meadows Lodge: Canvas tent cabins; open in summer.

Campgrounds and Picnic Areas

Reservations for campgrounds in the Yosemite Valley, Hodgdon Meadows, Crane Flat, and part of Tuolumne Meadows Campgrounds may be made through MISTIX, no earlier than eight weeks in advance; call (800) 365-2267. Other campgrounds are first-come, first-served. No gathering of wood in Yosemite Valley, in Sequoia Groves, or above 9,600 feet. All sites have tables and fire pits or grills. All have space for RVs and tents except where noted.

North Pines Campground: In Yosemite Valley; 85 sites; water, flush toilets; open May through October; $12/night.

Lower Pines Campground: In Yosemite Valley; 172 sites; water, flush toilets; open all year; $12/night.

Sunnyside Walk-in Campground: In Yosemite Valley; 35 sites; tents only; water, flush toilets; open April through November; no reservations; $2/person/night.

Backpackers Walk-in Campground: In Yosemite Valley; 25 sites; tents only; water, flush toilets; open May through October; no reservations; $2/person/night.

Upper Pines Campground: In Yosemite Valley; 238 sites; water, flush toilets, dump station; pets allowed; open April through November; $12/night.

Upper River Campground: In Yosemite Valley; 124 sites; tents only; water, flush toilets; open April through October; $12/night.

Lower River Campground: In Yosemite Valley; 138 sites; water, flush toilets, dump station; open May through November; $12/night.

Wawona Campground: On Highway 41; 100 sites; water, flush toilets; pets allowed; open all year; $7/night.

Bridalveil Creek Campground: Glacier Point Road; 110 sites; water, flush toilets; pets allowed; open June through September; $7/night.

Hodgdon Meadow Campground: Highway 120; 105 sites; water, flush toilets; pets allowed; open all year; $10/night.

Crane Flat Campground: Highway 120; 166 sites; water, flush toilets; pets allowed; open May through October; $10/night.

Tamarack Flat Campground: Highway 120 east; 52 sites; not suited for large RVs or trailers; pit toilets; open June through mid-October; $4/night.

White Wolf Campground: Highway 120 east; 87 sites; water, flush toilets; pets allowed; open June through mid-September; $7/night.

Yosemite Creek Campground: Highway 120 east; 75 sites; not suited for large RVs or trailers; pit toilets; pets allowed; open June through September; $4/night.

Porcupine Flat Campground: Highway 120 east; 52 sites; pit toilets; open June through mid-October; $4/night.

Tuolumne Meadows Campground: Highway 120 east; 314 sites; water, flush toilets, dump station; pets allowed; open June through mid-October; $10/night.

Backcountry Campsites: No camping is allowed in the Tuolumne Grove or the lower grove of the Mariposa Grove of Big Trees. Limited number of campers allowed.

Restaurants

Degnan's Delicatessen and **Degnan's Fast Food:** In Yosemite Village; breakfast, lunch, and dinner.

Loft Restaurant: In Yosemite Village; lunch and dinner.

The Village Grill: In Yosemite Village; breakfast, lunch, and dinner.

Yosemite Lodge. Cafeteria, Four Seasons, and **Mountain Room Broiler:** Breakfast, lunch, and dinner.

The Ahwahnee Main Dining Room: Breakfast, lunch, dinner. Reservations suggested for dinner; (209) 372-1489.

Curry Village. Cafeteria and **Hamburger Stand:** Breakfast, lunch, and dinner.

Tuolumne Meadows. Grill and **Lodge Dining Room:** Breakfast and dinner. Dinner reservations advised; (209) 372-1313.

White Wolf: Breakfast and dinner. Dinner reservations advised; (209) 372-1316.

Wawona Hotel: Breakfast, lunch, dinner, Sunday brunch. Dinner reservations advised; (209) 375-6556.

Glacier Point Snack Stand.

Activities

Scenic Drives

"The Yosemite Road Guide" is a self-guiding auto tour sold at visitor centers. "Yosemite Valley Tour" is a tour on cassette, available at the Yosemite Valley Visitor Center. Tioga Road, generally open from late May through October, offers a 39-mile scenic drive through forests and past meadows, lakes, and mountains between Crane Flat and Tuolumne Meadows. There are many pullouts with broad views, some with signs explaining the local natural history. Vehicles are prohibited beyond the parking area of the Mariposa Grove, but several giant sequoias can be seen in the immediate vicinity of the parking area.

Hiking

There are 800 miles of trails, of all difficulty levels, in the park. Many day hikes originate in Yosemite Valley. "A Changing Yosemite" is a one-mile trail, beginning near the visitor center, that explores the changes that have taken place in Yosemite. A self-guiding nature trail goes through the Mariposa Grove of giant sequoias. The John Muir Trail starts at Happy Isles and travels through Tuolumne Meadows and along the Sierra Crest. Check at park information stations for current trail conditions. Detailed maps and hiking guides are sold at visitor centers.

Sightseeing Tours

A range of scenic open-air tram and bus tours is available. Narrated by guides, they operate daily to most points of interest in the park, including Yosemite Valley (year-round), Tuolumne Meadow (July and August), and Glacier Point, Wawona, and the Mariposa Grove of giant sequoias (through October). Two-hour moonlight tours are available during summer months. In winter, tours are conducted on heated and enclosed motor coaches, with stops in Yosemite Valley. Also in winter, one-hour snowmobile tours from Badger Pass offer views of the Sierra Nevada. For reservations and information, check at Tour/ Transportation Desks or call (209) 372-1240. Fees are charged.

Bicycling

There are more than eight miles of bikeway through the eastern end of the Yosemite Valley. Most of the way is flat, though some moderate grades exist. Bicycles may be ridden only on these bikeways or on paved roads. Bicycles can be rented at Curry Village in the summer—(209) 372-1200—or at Yosemite Lodge year-round—(209) 372-1208.

Fishing

Check with the park on current fishing regulations, including catch-and-release requirements for rainbow trout.

Saddle Trips

There are two-hour, half-day, and all-day rides available from four locations in the park: Yosemite Valley, Wawona, White Wolf, Tuolumne Meadows. Reservations are recommended; call (209) 372-1248. All trips are led by guides. The Valley stables are open from

Easter to mid-October; others are open in summer.

Mountaineering

The climbing season runs approximately from mid-April to mid-October. Contact Yosemite Mountaineering School, Yosemite National Park, CA 95389.

Winter Sports

Snow conditions are often favorable for skiing and snowshoeing in the Upper Grove of the Mariposa Grove of giant sequoias, in the Tuolumne Grove of giant sequoias in Crane Flat, and at the Badger Pass Ski Area. Ski maps are sold at the visitor center. Ski lessons and equipment rental are available at Badger Pass; call (209) 372-1244.

Yosemite Theater

Theatrical programs including live performances and films are offered. All shows are given at the Valley Visitor Center Auditoriums. Fees are charged; tickets may be purchased at the Yosemite Valley Visitor Center.

Ranger-Led Programs

A variety of ranger-led walks, talks, and evening programs are available in Yosemite Valley, Badger Pass, Wawona, and the Mariposa Grove. Ranger-led snowshoe walks are offered during the winter at Badger Pass.

Yosemite Association

Outdoor seminars are offered, some for college credit. Call (209) 379-2646.

The name of this beautiful national park in southwestern Utah, "Zion," evokes a sense of spirituality and peace, just as this multi-colored, cliff- and canyon-filled landscape has done for centuries of visitors. Zion inspires a feeling of wonder and awe that is not easy to describe.

The heart of the park is Zion Canyon. Carved out of solid rock millions of years old, the towering sandstone cliffs of the canyon reach heights of 2,000 to 3,000 feet and are barely 18 feet apart in some sections of the Zion Narrows. They dwarf humans. The vivid colors of the sandstone are among the brightest of any rock on earth.

The north fork of the Virgin River is responsible for this sculpting. It still flows along the bottom of Zion Canyon, generally looking more like a creek than a canyon builder. In reality, it is quite a powerful force. For more than 13 million years, it has cut its way down and through the layers of rock, carrying debris away with it. Most times, the river flows along at a peaceful pace. But when a sudden storm strikes, flash floods carry large trees and even boulders along, further eroding the cliffs. Bit by bit, Zion is still being sculpted today. Eventually, it will be destroyed by the same forces that formed it.

Outside of the Zion Canyon area, spectacular formations abound. Arches include the Great Arch of Zion, an arch carved high in a cliff wall, and Kolob Arch, the largest free-standing arch in the world, with a span of 310 feet. Checkerboard Mesa, a mountain of sandstone etched with odd patterns of cracks and grooves, is a prominent example of naturally sculpted art. In the northwest corner of the park, at the edge of the Kolob Terrace, streams have carved the spectacular Kolob Finger Canyons. Some of the most unusual formations are "hoodoos," iron-capped rocks that look like enormous mushrooms.

Despite these rocky landscapes, some areas of the park are so beautifully lush it is hard to believe they are actually in the middle of semidesert country. The riverbanks support an abundance of cottonwoods, box elders, and ashes offering cool shade. Springs and seeps make for small waterfalls and clear pools as well as mini-oases along the cliffs of rock, where plants and animals thrive. One of the most famous oases in the park is Weeping Rock: The water dripping out of the overhanging rock makes it appear to be crying. Over 900 species of wildflowers bloom throughout the park in the spring and to a lesser extent in fall. The spring blooming season lasts from March through June, peaking in May. Wildlife in the park includes mule deer, desert bighorn, mountain lions, bobcats, gray foxes, squirrels, and rabbits.

The earliest visitors to the park were very aware of its spiritual feeling. Paiute Native Americans; Mormon pioneers; and other early explorers—all seemed to feel inspired by the landscape. This is apparent in the names they chose for the park's features. Frederick Vining Fisher, a Methodist minis-

ter, named the Great White Throne and Angels Landing. John Wesley Powell, of Colorado River exploration fame, named the East and West Temples. It was Mormon settlers who named the park itself as well as the Kolob area. They built several small set-

tlements along the river in the mid-1800s. These settlements included orchards and fields in Zion Canyon and the lower parts of Parunuweap Canyon, at the east fork of the Virgin River.

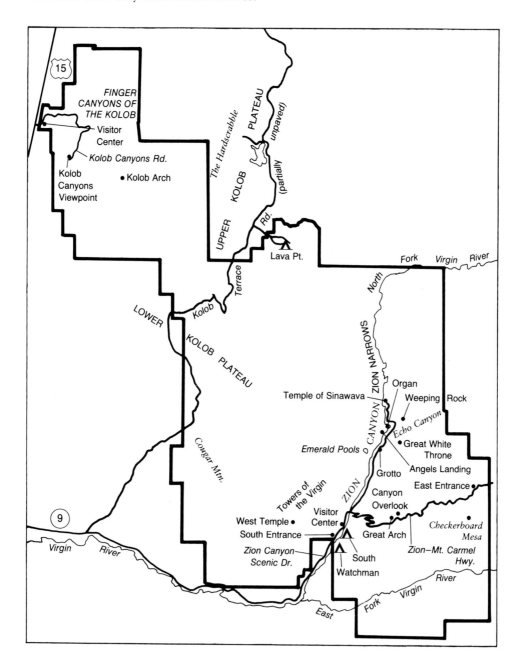

Further Information

Write or call: Superintendent, Zion National Park, Springdale, UT 84767; (801) 772-3256

Visitor Information

Zion Canyon Visitor Center: Information, exhibits, introductory slide program, books and maps for sale.
Kolob Canyons Visitor Center: Information, books and maps for sale.

Nuts and Bolts

Entrance Fee: $5/vehicle or $3/person arriving by other means.
Park Open: All year.
Permits: Required for backcountry camping, and for all trips through the length of the Narrows and its tributaries. The number of permits is limited and they are not issued in advance.
In Emergency: Call 772-3322.
Acreage: 146,597.64

Practical Advisory

Seasons

From May to October, temperatures range from 70° to 105° in the day and from 45° to 75° at night. Thunderstorms are common in July, August, and early September. Winters are mild in Zion Canyon, with high temperatures often reaching above 40°. Little snow falls in Zion Canyon, but it does accumulate on the plateaus, making the trails there impassable during winter and early spring. March is often rainy. Spring and fall temperatures range from freezing at night to 80° during the day. Humidity is very low most of the year in this semidesert area.

Special Advisories

• Steep slopes and cliff edges are dangerous.
• Do not roll or throw things from high places: People may be below.
• Avoid drainages during and after thunderstorms or severe weather: Flash floods are possible.

Facilities for Disabled

Contact the park for a copy of "Access to Zion for People with Disabilities."

Travel Advisory

Entrances

South: I-15 to Highway 9 east for 35 miles.

East: U.S. 89 to Highway 9 west for 13 miles.

West: I-15 to Exit 42, Kolob Canyons Road.

Note: Road in from east entrance goes through narrow tunnels; escorts are required for RVs, trailers, and buses. A $10 fee is charged.

Transportation

Airports: The nearest commercial airports are St. George (45 miles) and Cedar City (60 miles). International airports are in Las Vegas (150 miles) and Salt Lake City (322 miles).

Bus Service: Commercial bus lines serve St. George (45 miles) and Cedar City (60 miles).

Train Service: None available to the park.

Rental Cars: Available in St. George (45 miles) and Cedar City (60 miles).

Attractions

Zion Canyon is the centerpiece of the park. Some highlights of its beautifully carved rock landscape include the *West Temple, Towers of the Virgin*, the *Great White Throne*, the *Great Organ, Angels Landing*, the *Temple of Sinawava, Weeping Rock*, and the *Emerald Pools*. Many areas of the canyon can be viewed from the park road. Other significant park features are *Checkerboard Mesa* and the *Great Arch*; areas for viewing these are accessible via a spur road. In the northwest section of the park, which must be reached via a separate road, the *Finger Canyons of the Kolob* and *Kolob Arch* are of interest.

Accommodations

Lodge

Zion Lodge: Motel units, cabins; open all year. For reservations: Zion Lodge Reservations, TW Recreational Services, P.O. Box 400, Cedar City, UT 84720; (801) 586-7686.

Campgrounds and Picnic Areas

First-come, first-served, 14-day limit, $7/night. Gathering of wood not permitted.

Watchman Campground: Fire grates, tables, water, rest rooms, dump station.

South Campground: Fire grates, tables, water, rest rooms, dump station.

Lava Point Primitive Campground: Accessible only by trail or unpaved road; open from May to October; fire grates, tables, toilets; free.

Backcountry Camping: Number of permits issued is limited; permits are not available in advance. Fires are prohibited.

Picnic Areas: Grotto Picnic Area in Zion Canyon has fire grates, tables, water, and rest rooms. Area at end of Kolob Canyons Road has tables and pit toilets.

Restaurant

Zion Lodge: Restaurant and snack bar; open all year.

Activities

Scenic Drives

It is possible to see a great deal of Zion's spectacular landscape by driving the roads. Keep in mind that they are narrow, winding, and sometimes steep. The Zion Canyon Scenic Drive follows the river along the floor of Zion Canyon. The Zion–Mount Carmel Highway connects lower Zion Canyon with the high plateaus to the east. There are two narrow tunnels on this road, including one 1$\frac{1}{10}$ miles long. All buses and almost all RVs are too large to pass through the long tunnel without an escort; a \$10 fee is charged for this service. The Kolob Canyons Road, which leads from I-15 into the northwestern corner of the park, is not connected to any other road in the park. The partly unpaved Kolob Terrace Road goes across the Kolob Plateau and is usually closed by snow from late November until mid-May, or later in some parts.

Hiking

Trails range from easy 10-minute walks to multiday backpacking trips. Easy and short trails include Weeping Rock off Zion Canyon Scenic Drive, and Canyon Overlook off the Zion–Mount Carmel Highway. Gateway to the Narrows and Emerald Pools are also very popular trails, both in Zion Canyon. Carry a topographical map when hiking longer trails or off-trail. The Zion Narrows is one of the most popular, and most strenuous, off-trail hikes. It is a 16-mile trip requiring at least one very full day. Much of the trip involves wading through the Virgin River over slippery water-rounded rocks. The Narrows may be closed much of the time because of cold water, high water, bad weather, or flash-flood danger. A concession-operated service shuttles hikers to and from backcountry trailheads. Contact Zion Lodge (see "Accommodations:Lodge" above) for information.

Bicycling

Bicycles are allowed on the park roads but must be transported through the long tunnel in a vehicle. Ranger escorts are provided at nine A.M. and three P.M. on request.

Horseback Riding

Private horseback parties should check with the park before arriving. Most trails are closed to horses. Guided concession-operated rides in Zion Canyon are available from late March to early November. Reservations and information are available from Bryce-Zion Trail Rides, (801) 772-3967.

Climbing

Technical climbing is permitted in the park. The rock is soft sandstone and does not hold pitons. A climbing guide is available for study at the visitor-center information desk. Climbing alone is not recommended. Certain areas may be closed for reasons of public safety or resource-management.

Guided Tram Tours

Concession-operated tours of Zion Canyon aboard open-air trams run several times daily in the summer. Reservations and information are available at Zion Lodge (see "Lodge" above).

Naturalist Programs

From late March to November, naturalists guide trips along many of the trails as well as off-trail hikes through canyons, up the Virgin River, and over slickrock country. There are also evening programs and talks. Activity schedules are posted in the visitor centers and on bulletin boards throughout the park.

	Exhibits/Museums	Historic Sites/Ruins	Lodging	Campgrounds	Picnic Areas	Restaurant	Scenic Drives	Hiking	Boating/River Floating	Mountain/Rock Climbing	Swimming/Snorkeling	Horseback/Saddle Trips	Winter Sports	Fishing	Bicycling	Interpretive Programs	Tours (Bus, Boat, etc.)	Cave Tours	Scuba Diving
ACADIA	*			*	*	*	*	*	*		*	*	*	*	*	*	*		
AMERICAN SAMOA								*											
ARCHES	*	*		*	*		*	*		*		*			*	*	*		
BADLANDS	*		*	*	*	*	*	*								*			
BIG BEND		*	*	*	*	*	*	*	*	*		*		*		*			
BISCAYNE	*			*	*			*	*		*			*			*		*
BRYCE CANYON	*		*	*			*	*	*			*	*		*	*			
CANYONLANDS	*	*		*	*		*	*	*	*		*			*	*	*		
CAPITOL REEF	*	*		*	*		*	*				*			*	*			
CARLSBAD CAVERNS	*				*	*	*	*								*		*	
CHANNEL ISLANDS	*	*		*	*			*	*		*			*		*	*		*
CRATER LAKE	*		*	*	*	*	*	*					*	*		*	*		
DENALI			*	*	*	*		*		*				*	*	*	*		
EVERGLADES	*		*	*		*	*	*	*						*		*		
GATES OF THE ARCTIC								*						*					
GLACIER			*	*	*	*	*	*	*	*	*	*	*	*		*	*		

305

	Exhibits/Museums	Historic Sites/Ruins	Lodging	Campgrounds	Picnic Areas	Restaurant	Scenic Drives	Hiking	Boating/River Floating	Mountain/Rock Climbing	Swimming/Snorkeling	Horseback/Saddle Trips	Winter Sports	Fishing	Bicycling	Interpretive Programs	Tours (Bus, Boat, etc.)	Cave Tours	Scuba Diving
GLACIER BAY	*		*	*		*		*	*					*		*	*		
GRAND CANYON	*	*	*	*	*	*	*	*	*			*		*	*	*	*		
GRAND TETON	*	*	*	*	*	*	*	*	*	*	*	*	*	*	*	*	*		
GREAT BASIN	*	*		*	*	*	*	*						*		*		*	
GREAT SMOKY MOUNTAINS	*	*	*	*	*	*	*	*				*		*	*	*			
GUADALUPE MOUNTAINS	*	*		*	*			*				*				*			
HALEAKALĀ	*			*	*		*	*			*	*			*	*			
HAWAII VOLCANOES	*	*	*	*	*	*	*	*			*	*				*			
HOT SPRINGS	*	*		*	*		*	*								*			
ISLE ROYALE	*		*	*		*		*	*					*			*		
KATMAI		*	*	*		*		*	*					*		*	*		
KENAI FJORDS	*			*	*		*	*	*					*		*	*		
KOBUK VALLEY								*	*					*					
LAKE CLARK			*					*	*					*					
LASSEN VOLCANIC			*	*	*	*	*	*	*			*	*	*	*	*			
MAMMOTH CAVE	*		*	*	*	*		*				*		*		*	*	*	
MESA VERDE	*	*	*	*	*	*	*	*							*	*	*		
MOUNT RAINIER	*		*	*	*	*	*	*		*		*	*	*	*	*			

	Exhibits/Museums	Historic Sites/Ruins	Lodging	Campgrounds	Picnic Areas	Restaurant	Scenic Drives	Hiking	Boating/River Floating	Mountain/Rock Climbing	Swimming/Snorkeling	Horseback/Saddle Trips	Winter Sports	Fishing	Bicycling	Interpretive Programs	Tours (Bus, Boat, etc.)	Cave Tours	Scuba Diving
NORTH CASCADES			*	*	*	*	*	*	*	*				*	*	*	*		
OLYMPIC	*		*	*	*	*	*	*	*		*		*	*		*			
PETRIFIED FOREST	*	*			*	*	*	*								*			
REDWOOD	*			*	*		*	*			*	*		*	*	*	*		
ROCKY MOUNTAIN	*	*		*	*		*	*		*		*	*	*		*			
SEQUOIA and KINGS CANYON	*		*	*	*	*	*	*				*	*	*		*	*	*	
SHENANDOAH	*		*	*	*	*	*	*				*		*	*	*			
THEODORE ROOSEVELT	*	*		*	*		*	*	*			*				*			
VIRGIN ISLANDS	*	*		*	*	*	*	*	*		*			*		*	*		*
VOYAGEURS	*		*	*	*	*		*	*		*		*	*		*	*		
WIND CAVE	*			*	*	*	*	*								*		*	
WRANGELL–ST. ELIAS		*	*				*	*	*				*	*					
YELLOWSTONE	*		*	*	*	*	*	*	*			*	*	*	*	*	*		
YOSEMITE	*	*	*	*	*	*	*	*		*		*	*	*	*	*	*		
ZION	*		*	*	*	*	*	*		*		*			*	*	*		

NATIONAL PARKS BY GEOGRAPHIC LOCATION

Alaska
Denali
Gates of the Arctic
Glacier Bay
Katmai
Kenai Fjords
Kobuk Valley
Lake Clark
Wrangell–St. Elias

American Samoa
American Samoa

Arizona
Grand Canyon
Petrified Forest

Arkansas
Hot Springs

California
Channel Islands
Kings Canyon
Lassen Volcanic
Redwood
Sequoia
Yosemite

Colorado
Mesa Verde
Rocky Mountain

Florida
Biscayne
Everglades

Hawaii
Haleakalā
Hawaii Volcanoes

Idaho
Yellowstone

Kentucky
Mammoth Cave

Maine
Acadia

Michigan
Isle Royale

Minnesota
Voyageurs

Montana
Glacier
Yellowstone

Nevada
Great Basin

New Mexico
Carlsbad Caverns

North Carolina
Great Smoky Mountains

North Dakota
Theodore Roosevelt

Oregon
Crater Lake

South Dakota
Badlands
Wind Cave

Texas
Big Bend
Guadalupe Mountains

Tennessee
Great Smoky Mountains

U.S. Virgin Islands
Virgin Islands

Utah
Arches
Bryce Canyon
Canyonlands
Capitol Reef
Zion

Virginia
Shenandoah

Washington
Mount Rainier
North Cascades
Olympic

Wyoming
Grand Teton
Yellowstone

INDEX

Join AAA today and let our travel professionals take the complications out of vacations.

We can help you with:

- Complete travel agency services, including expert travel planning and all travel reservations
- Passport photos and International Driving Permits
- Fee-free American Express® Travelers Cheques
- Discounts on Hertz car rentals
- Hotel reservations
- Rail tickets

- Individual and escorted tours
- Travel insurance
- Tour Operator Default Protection Plan
- TripAssist, including 24-hour emergency access to legal, medical, and travel-related services worldwide
- AND emergency road service is available 24 hours a day, 365 days a year

To join AAA today just call
1-800-222-4357

AAA Membership Application

☐ I'd like to start saving. Send me my AAA membership card.
I am fully protected under the terms of your 30-day money-back guarantee.

☐ Charge my VISA   ☐ Charge my MasterCard   ☐ Bill me

Credit Card Number: _____

Expiration Date: _____   Bank#(MC only) _____

Signature (for charges) _____

☐ Please send me more information about AAA membership.

Name _____

Address _____

(Membership is available only to residents of the United States and Canada. Home address only.)

City _____   State _____   Zip _____

Telephone: Home (____) _____   Office (____) _____

NP-94

Discover the benefits of membership BEFORE you take your next trip.

Complete the postage-paid reply card TODAY.

Box 49
Dept 1740